Charles Lanman, Arinori Mori

**The Japanese in America**

Charles Lanman, Arinori Mori

**The Japanese in America**

ISBN/EAN: 9783742891488

Manufactured in Europe, USA, Canada, Australia, Japa

Cover: Foto ©ninafisch / pixelio.de

Manufactured and distributed by brebook publishing software (www.brebook.com)

Charles Lanman, Arinori Mori

**The Japanese in America**

# THE
# JAPANESE
# IN AMERICA.

EDITED BY

CHARLES LANMAN,

AMERICAN SECRETARY OF JAPANESE LEGATION IN WASHINGTON.

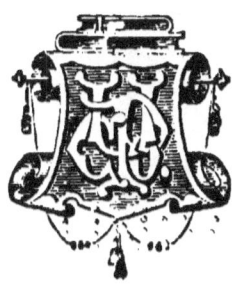

NEW YORK:
UNIVERSITY PUBLISHING COMPANY,
155 AND 157 CROSBY STREET.
1872.

# PREFACE.

The threefold object of this volume is to give an account, from official sources, of the Embassy recently accredited to the United States by the Tenno of Japan; to print a collection of essays written by the Japanese students now residing in this country and illustrating their style of thought and expression; and to republish a little work on America, compiled under the direction of Jugoi Arinori Mori, the Chargé d'Affaires from Japan. An edition of the last-named production was printed under the title of *Life and Resources in America*, and intended for exclusive circulation in Japan, where it is to be translated into the language of that country. It having been suggested to Mr. Mori, by many of his friends, that the American public would be glad to read the volume, he considered the question in a friendly spirit, and consented to its republication in the present form.

# CONTENTS.

## PART I.
|   | PAGE |
|---|---|
| THE JAPANESE EMBASSY.................................. | 7 |

## PART II.
| | | |
|---|---|---|
| THE JAPANESE STUDENTS.... ........................... | | 55 |
| THE PRACTICAL AMERICANS..................... | *Enouye.* | 67 |
| THE CHINESE AMBASSADORS IN FRANCE........ | *Toyama.* | 72 |
| CO-EDUCATION OF BOYS AND GIRLS.............. | *Takato.* | 78 |
| ORIENTAL CIVILIZATION................. ...... | *Hicomaro.* | 81 |
| HISTORY OF JAPAN............................. | *Megata.* | 86 |
| CHRISTIANITY IN JAPAN........................ | *Hyash.* | 91 |
| THE STRENGTH AND WEAKNESS OF REPUBLICS.. | *Enouye.* | 94 |
| JAPANESE COSTUME............................. | *Kanda.* | 100 |
| A FATHER'S LETTER........... ................ | *Neero.* | 103 |
| THE MEMORABLE YEAR.... ..................... | *Enouye.* | 108 |
| GEORGE WASHINGTON............................ | *Kanda.* | 114 |
| PUBLIC AND PRIVATE SCHOOLS.................. | *Enouye.* | 117 |
| CHRISTMAS........................................ | *Kanda.* | 124 |
| JAPANESE POETRY.............................. | *Takaki.* | 127 |

## PART III.

| | PAGE |
|---|---|
| LIFE AND RESOURCES IN AMERICA | 137 |
| INTRODUCTION | 139 |
| OFFICIAL AND POLITICAL LIFE | 143 |
| LIFE AMONG THE FARMERS AND PLANTERS | 159 |
| COMMERCIAL LIFE AND DEVELOPMENTS | 186 |
| LIFE AMONG THE MECHANICS | 203 |
| RELIGIOUS LIFE AND INSTITUTIONS | 215 |
| LIFE IN THE FACTORIES | 246 |
| EDUCATIONAL LIFE AND INSTITUTIONS | 265 |
| LITERARY, ARTISTIC, AND SCIENTIFIC LIFE | 282 |
| LIFE AMONG THE MINERS | 301 |
| LIFE IN THE ARMY AND NAVY | 312 |
| LIFE IN THE LEADING CITIES | 322 |
| FRONTIER LIFE AND DEVELOPMENTS | 337 |
| JUDICIAL LIFE | 344 |
| ADDITIONAL NOTES | 351 |

# PART I.

## THE JAPANESE EMBASSY.

On the 12th day of January, 1872, Jujoi Arinori Mori, the Japanese Chargé d'Affaires in Washington, addressed a letter to the Hon. Hamilton Fish, Secretary of State, from which we extract the following paragraphs: "I have the honor to inform you that I have received dispatches from my Government, communicating the information that a Special Embassy from the Tenno of Japan to the Government of the United States would soon arrive in this country. On what particular day they were to sail I do not know; but I presume they will reach Washington about the close of the present month. . . . The object to be attained by this Embassy will be fully stated on a future occasion; but, in the mean time, I may remark that one of them will be to increase the friendly relations already existing between Japan and the United States."

In November, 1871, his Majesty Montsohito, Emperor of Japan, had, at a dinner given to his nobles at his palace in Tokei, before sending forth the Ambassadors of Japan and Suite, accredited to the Fifteen Foreign Treaty Powers, delivered the following

## ADDRESS:*

"AFTER careful study and observation, I am deeply impressed with the belief that the most powerful and enlightened nations of the world are those who have made diligent effort to cultivate their minds, and sought to develop their country in the fullest and most perfect manner.

"Thus convinced, it becomes my responsible duty, as a Sovereign, to lead our people wisely, in a way to attain for them results equally beneficial; and their duty is to assist diligently and unitedly in all efforts to attain these ends. How, otherwise, can Japan advance and sustain herself upon an independent footing among the nations of the world?

"From you, nobles of this realm, whose dignified position is honored and conspicuous in the eyes of the people at large, I ask and expect conduct well becoming your exalted position—ever calculated to endorse, by your personal example, those goodly precepts to be employed hereafter in elevating the masses of our people.

"I have to-day assembled your honorable body in our presence-chamber that I might first express to you my intentions, and, in foreshadowing my policy, also impress you all with the fact that both this Government and people will expect from you diligence and wisdom, while leading and encouraging those in your several districts, to move forward in paths of progress. Remember, your responsibility to your country is both great and important. Whatever our natural capacity for intellectual development, diligent effort and cultivation is required to attain successful results.

"If we would profit by the useful arts and sciences and conditions of society prevailing among more enlightened nations, we must either study these at home as best we can, or send abroad an expedition of practical observers, to foreign lands, competent to acquire for us those things

*Translated by NORIUKI GAH.

our people lack, which are best calculated to benefit this nation.

"Travel in foreign countries, properly indulged in, will increase your store of useful knowledge; and although some of you may be advanced in age, unfitted for the vigorous study of new ways, all may bring back to our people much valuable information. Great national defects require immediate remedies.

"We lack superior institutions for high female culture. Our women should not be ignorant of those great principles on which the happiness of daily life frequently depends. How important the education of mothers, on whom future generations almost wholly rely for the early cultivation of those intellectual tastes which an enlightened system of training is designed to develop!

"Liberty is therefore granted wives and sisters to accompany their relatives on foreign tours, that they may acquaint themselves with better forms of female education, and, on their return, introduce beneficial improvements in the training of our children.

"With diligent and united efforts, manifested by all classes and conditions of people throughout the empire, we may attain successively the highest degrees of civilization within our reach, and shall experience no serious difficulty in maintaining power, independence, and respect among nations.

"To you, nobles, I look for the endorsement of these views; fulfill my best expectations by carrying out these suggestions, and you will perform faithfully your individual duties to the satisfaction of the people of Japan."

On the morning of January 15th, the steamer *America* arrived at San Francisco, having on board one hundred and seven Japanese passengers, of whom forty-nine constituted the Embassy, while the remainder consisted of five young ladies and fifty-three young gentlemen and servants, who were accompanied by the Hon. Charles E. DeLong,

American Minister to Japan, and his family, and W. S. Rice, Esq., Interpreter of the United States Legation in Japan. The official list of officers composing the Embassy is as follows:

### Ambassador Extraordinary.

NAMES AND RANK.          OFFICIAL POSITION IN JAPAN.

Sionii TOMOMI IWAKURA. .......... Junior Prime Minister.

### Vice-Ambassadors Extraordinary.

Jussammi TAKAYOSSI KIDO......... Council of State.
Jussammi TOSSIMITSI OKUBO........ Minister of Finance.
Jushie HIROBUMI ITO.............. Acting Minister of Public Works.
Jushie MASSOUKA YAMAGUTSI....... Assistant Minister of the Foreign Affairs.

### First Secretaries.

YASKAZOU TANABÉ................. Foreign Department.
NORIUKI GAH..................... Foreign Department.
ATSNOBOU SHIODA................. Foreign Department.
GHEN-ITSIHO FOUKOUTSI........... Treasury Department.

### Second Secretaries.

HIROMOTO WATANABE.............. Foreign Department.
TERMORI COMATZ................. Foreign Department.
TADAS HYASH.................... Foreign Department.
KELJIRO NAGANO................. Foreign Department.

### Third Secretary.

QUANDO KAWAGE.................. Foreign Department.

### Fourth Secretaries.

MASSATSNÉ IKEDA................ Educational Department.
TADATSNÉ ANDO.................. Foreign Department.

### Private Secretary to Chief Ambassador.

KOUNITAKÉ KOUMÉ................ Clerk to the Legislative Code.

### Attache.

YASSI NOMOURA.................. Foreign Department.

## HISTORY OF THE EMBASSY.

### Commissioners connected with the Ambassadors.

| NAMES AND RANK. | OFFICIAL POSITION IN JAPAN. |
|---|---|
| Jushie Takanori Sassaki | Acting Minister of the Judicial Department. |
| Jussammi Mitsitomi Higassikouzé | Chief Chamberlain of the Imperial Court. |
| Jugoi Akiyossi Yamada | Brigadier-General of the Imperial Army. |
| Mits-Aki Tanaka | Commissioner of the Bureau of Census, Treas. Dept. |
| Fouzimar Tanaka | Chief Clerk of the Educational Department. |
| Tameyossi Hida | Commissioner of Dockyards, Public Work Department. |
| Nobouyossi Nakayama | Vice Governor of Hiogo. |
| Yassoukaz Yassouba | Deputy Commiss'r of Revenue. |
| Jushie Yassounaka Itsoutsouzi | Assistant Director of Ceremony, Imperial Court. |
| Tadakats Outsmi | Secretary to the Governor of Kanagawa. |

### Officers attached to the said Commissioners.

| | |
|---|---|
| Yossikazou Wakayama | Treasury Department. |
| Hissom Abé | Treasury Department. |
| Morikata Oki | Treasury Department. |
| Kazounari Souguiyama | Treasury Department. |
| Noriyas Tomita | Treasury Department. |
| Nagamassa Yo Io | Treasury Department. |
| Kasoumitsi Harada | War Department. |
| Noritsougou Nagayo | Educational Department. |
| Nagamoto Nakassima | Educational Department. |
| Massatsna Kondo | Educational Department. |
| Waro Imamoura | Educational Department. |
| Kimihira Outsimoura | Educational Department. |
| Takato O-Sima | Public Works Department. |
| Fourou Ouriu | Public Works Department. |
| Také-Akira Nakano | Judicial Department. |
| Siguetossi Oka-Outsi | Judicial Department. |
| Yossinari Hiraka | Judicial Department. |
| Houmiakira Nagano | Judicial Department. |
| Tsounemits Mourata | Imperial Court. |
| Yossinaga Takatsouzi | Imperial Court. |
| Hiroyas Kagawa | Imperial Court. |

The formal reception of the Embassy took place on the day following their arrival at San Francisco, and the kind wishes of the citizens and the hospitalities of the city were tendered to the distinguished strangers by the Mayor, the Hon. William Alvord. By special request of the Board of Supervisors, the Mayor was also requested to address a letter of welcome to the Embassy, which was accordingly done on the 18th, and in which he remarked as follows: " As the nearest neighbor, on this continent, of the Empire of Japan, the people of San Francisco feel a special pride in welcoming you to our city, the landing-place, in America, of an Embassy whose labors are doubtless destined to be followed by results in the highest degree interesting and important in their bearings upon the progress and enlightenment of all nations, and especially to the commercial prosperity of Japan and the United States. The Board take pleasure in extending to your Excellencies every facility for visiting and examining our public institutions, and cheerfully place at your disposal all means of information, trusting that your stay here will be agreeable, and that the great objects of the Embassy will be achieved by bringing into nearer intimacy the ancient and modern civilizations, cementing still closer our mutual relations of trade and commerce, and strengthening the ties of international friendship." The Press of San Francisco, in a body, paid their respects to the members of the Embassy, and were treated with attention. A committee of citizens also waited upon the dignitaries, and, in reply to an address of welcome from R. B. Swain, President of the Board of Commerce, the Chief Ambassador replied, through an interpreter, as follows:

"GENTLEMEN. Being commissioned by His Imperial Majesty, the Tenno of Japan, to visit all the Treaty Powers, we have reached your city on our way, and have been greatly pleased at receiving so warm a welcome upon the threshold of your Continent. We receive it thankfully, as a distinguished honor paid to our sovereign and our country.

"Commerce, following in the path of our first friendly relation, has been an active agent in drawing our respective countries nearer together, in the strongest bonds of friendship. Our people have, by its means, become acquainted with the civilization of more enlightened nations, and they now seek to advance themselves in a knowledge of the arts, sciences, products, and mechanisms of western nations.

"The true spirit of our mission is to establish peaceful relations more firmly, and to see how greater privileges may be granted in the true interests of a righteous government and a free people.

"Our mission being one of investigation, we shall inspect with pleasure your manufactures and machinery, your colleges and schools, and your system of justice; and as these are to become the guide of our nation in the future, this study will be one tending to promote our national welfare, and, as commerce is reciprocal, may be of future direct interest to your city.

"Your kind offer to share with us your acquired knowledge, and exhibit to us your various industries, we gladly accept, and shall not fail to note them carefully, and aim in the future to establish with you active intercourse and practical results.

"We assure you, that as soon as His Imperial Majesty, the Tenno of Japan, is informed, from our letter, of your generous hospitality, he will undoubtedly testify his eminent satisfaction, and the hearts of the whole people of Japan will feel deeply grateful."

In the evening of the same day, the citizens of San Francisco gathered around the Grand Hotel and gave an admirable serenade, and, on being called out on the balcony, the Chief Ambassador, as before, delivered the following address:

"CITIZENS OF SAN FRANCISCO: It is now a recognized fact in Japan, since the conclusion of the treaty between the United States and our country, that our true prosperity has greatly increased with our new commercial intercourse. Our advancement in the arts and sciences of western nations we now consider a substantial benefit to our nation, and desire that with every increase of national intercourse there shall be an increase of international friendship. (Cheers.)

"With a view of hastening these results, and further facilitating the instruction of our people in the civilization of western nations, His Imperial Majesty, the Tenno, has commissioned us to visit all those countries having treaties with Japan, in the capacity of Ambassadors Plenipotentiary, first visiting your country. The warmth of our reception is unquestionable proof to us of the friendship of Americans, and I assure you it is more than echoed in the hearts of our people. (Cheers.)

"Your expression of feeling, when announced to His Imperial Majesty, will be made known throughout Japan, and assist in cementing a mutual friendship between our countries, which it is the wish of the Japanese people should constantly increase, as by intercourse we get to know each other better." (Cheers.)

On the same day the Chief Ambassador, on behalf of the Embassy, sent a telegram through to Nagasaki, Japan, announcing to his Government their safe arrival in this city, and the cordial reception they had met with. This dispatch went direct to Hongkong, whence it was transmitted by cable to Nagasaki.

He also sent word across the continent to his three sons, who are students in Rutgers College, Brunswick, New Jersey. An answer was received just as he had concluded his first address to the American people. It announced the good health of his sons, and their joy at his safe arrival in this country. The contents and the occasion combined to render him exceedingly happy.

During the whole of their stay in San Francisco the members of the Embassy were treated with marked kindness and cordiality; but the great event of their visit was a superb banquet, which was given to them by the leading citizens, at the Grand Hotel, on the 23d of January. After the preliminary toasts had been disposed of, that of "Our Distinguished Guests" was proposed, when the Chief Ambassador rose, and was greeted with prolonged applause. He spoke in his native tongue. Mr. Tadas Ilyash then read the following remarks in English:

"GENTLEMEN: I earnestly desire to express, on behalf of the other members of this Embassy, and in my own behalf, our warmest thanks for all the kind honors you have shown us. The particulars of our reception, and the princely hospitality of your banquet this evening, will be sources of great gratification to our Emperor and his subjects.

"The relative situation of this port to Japan is such that your prosperity will be the promoter of our civilization, and we hope our progress will contribute to enrich your city. We promise our best exertions to uphold and increase friendly relations between our countries, by which, in future, we will have many mutual interests. The gratitude I feel for your great kindness is beyond my power of expression. Governor Ito, one of our ambassadors, will respond more fully in our behalf."

The Vice-Ambassador Ito, in furtherance of the response, read the following words in a clear voice, so as to be distinctly understood by all present:

"GENTLEMEN: Being honored by your kind generosity, I gladly express to you, and through you to the citizens of San Francisco, our heartfelt gratitude for the friendly reception which has everywhere greeted the Embassy since its arrival in your State, and especially for the marked compliment paid this evening to our nation.

"This is perhaps a fitting opportunity to give a brief and reliable outline of many improvements being introduced into Japan. Few but native Japanese have any correct knowledge of our country's internal condition.

"Friendly intercourse with the Treaty Powers has been maintained (first among which was the United States), and a good understanding on the part of our people has increased commercial relations.

"Our mission, under special instruction from His Majesty, the Emperor, while seeking to protect the rights and interests of our respective nations, will seek to unite them more closely in the future, convinced that we shall appreciate each other more when we know each other better.

"By reading, hearing, and by observation in foreign lands, our people have acquired a general knowledge of constitutions, habits, and manners, as they exist in most foreign countries. Foreign customs are now generally understood throughout Japan.

"To-day it is the earnest wish of both our Government and people to strive for the highest points of civilization enjoyed by more enlightened countries. Looking to this end, we have adopted their military, naval, scientific, and educational institutions, and knowledge has flowed to us freely in the wake of foreign commerce. Although our improvement has been rapid in material civilization, the mental improvement of our people has been far greater. Our wisest men, after careful observation, agree in this opinion.

"While held in absolute obedience by despotic sovereigns through many thousand years, our people knew no freedom or liberty of thought.

"With our material improvement, they learned to understand their rightful privileges, which, for ages, have been denied them. Civil war was but a temporary result.

"Our Daimios magnanimously surrendered their principalities, and their voluntary action was accepted by the General Government. Within a year a feudal system, firmly established many centuries ago, has been completely abolished, without firing a gun or shedding a drop of blood. These wonderful results have been accomplished by the united action of a Government and people, now pressing jointly forward in the peaceful paths of progress. What country in the middle ages broke down its feudal system without war?

"These facts assure us that mental changes in Japan exceed even the material improvements. By educating our women, we hope to insure greater intelligence in future generations. With this end in view, our maidens have already commenced to come to you for their education.

"Japan cannot claim originality as yet, but it will aim to exercise practical wisdom by adopting the advantages, and avoiding the errors, taught her by the history of those enlightened nations whose experience is her teacher.

"Scarcely a year ago, I examined minutely the financial system of the United States, and, while in Washington, received most valuable assistance from distinguished officers of your Treasury Department. Every detail learned was faithfully reported to my Government, and suggestions then made have been adopted, and some of them are now already in practical operation.

"In the Department of Public Works, now under my administration, the progress has been satisfactory. Railroads are being built, both in the eastern and western portions of the Empire. Telegraph wires are stretching over many hundred miles of our territory, and nearly one thousand miles will be completed within a few months. Light-houses now line our coasts, and our ship-yards are active. All these assist our civilization, and we fully acknowledge our indebtedness to you and other foreign nations.

"As Ambassadors and as men, our greatest hope is to return from this mission laden with results—valuable to our beloved country and calculated to advance permanently her material and intellectual condition.

"While in duty bound to protect the rights and privileges of our people, we shall aim to increase our commerce, and, by a corresponding increase of our productions, hope to create a healthy basis for this greater activity.

"As distinguished citizens of a great commercial nation, prepared for business, desirous of participating in the new commercial era now dawning auspiciously upon the Pacific, Japan offers you her hearty co operation.

"Your modern inventions and results of accumulated knowledge, enable you to do more in days than our fathers accomplished in years.

"Time, so condensed with precious opportunities, we can ill afford to waste. Japan is anxious to press forward.

"The red disk in the centre of our national flag shall no longer appear like a wafer over a sealed empire, but henceforth be in fact what it is designed to be, the noble emblem of the rising sun, moving onward and upward amid the enlightened nations of the world."

This response was repeatedly interrupted by applause and cheers, and when he sat down the clapping of hands was deafening.

The next toast, "Our Relations with Japan," was responded to by Hon. C. E. DeLong. His remarks were as follows:

"GENTLEMEN: The toast that I am called upon to respond to is one about which I would most love to speak with freedom, but it is at the same time the one of all other subjects that I, as American Representative to the Empire of Japan, am least at liberty to discuss.

"I will venture a few words, however, in the hope of not transgressing my instructions, and yet, in part, responding to your call.

"What were our relations with that Empire in the past and what are they now? No intelligent Japanese or American can ever hear the name of Commodore Perry mentioned with indifference. His gallantry first bore down the outer walls of seclusion that had walled that Empire in from any but the most limited communication with other powers, for unknown centuries of time. Under his auspices the foothold was gained which is revolutionizing that land.

"To day what do we behold?

"Under the wise administration of His Imperial Majesty, the Tenno, we see thirty odd millions of people marching at a 'double-quick' into full fellowship with foreign states.

"The reign of his Majesty, signalized by its enlightenment, must make its own history forever illustrious. In this noble and unprecedented work of reform it is but proper to add that his Majesty finds most able and effectual support from the counsel of the noble Ministers of the Empire, some of whom it is our good fortune to be able to meet and honor in our land.

"The mighty change, from our relations as they were to our relations as they are, is so sudden, so complete, so very wonderful as to be bewildering.

"Allow me to note a few of the prominent landmarks in this road of reform upon which this nation is travelling. The Japanese Government has been centralized by the abolishment of Daimiates, thus resolving its political condition from one of numberless and comparatively small principalities into a consolidated nation of over thirty millions of people, containing over two millions of men born to the profession of arms,—men whose martial valor none who knows them doubts, and who are rapidly being armed, uniformed, and drilled with the best of arms, under the tuition of the best of foreign military teachers.

"But the other day his Majesty received his fleet of ten steam-vessels of war, including two powerful iron-clads, and in a few days a flying squadron, composed of three of his Majesty's vessels of war, will sail to circumnavigate the globe.

"A railroad completed and in running order, from Yeddo to Yokohama, conveyed these gentlemen, our noble guests, on the commencement of their journey.

"Telegraph lines in working order, operated by Japanese operatives, are already constructed, and more contemplated.

"Light-houses and light-ships have been constructed at all necessary points along the Japanese coast, where well-kept beacons guide and welcome commerce in safety to their ports.

"An Imperial Mint, complete in all of its appointments, has coined millions of dollars of the precious metals, and is still in active operation.

"A dry-dock has been constructed in which, but the other day, one of the largest of our vessels of war, the flagship *Colorado*, was docked with all of her guns in position, and repairs to her bottom most successfully made.

"Hundreds of the young nobility of Japan are being educated in our own country and in Europe. A college, numerously attended, is in full operation in Yeddo, under the jurisdiction of an American gentleman, assisted by European and American subordinates.

"Private schools are numerous throughout the Empire, conducted by foreigners, and with me come five Japanese ladies, seeking foreign culture, and marking by their advent the promise of a most noble reform.

"Thus I might proceed, and enumerate, at a great length, the evidences of this nation's progress, but I feel that more extended allusions are not necessary in the face of the one great fact that meets us here, face to face tonight, in the presence of this noble array of Japanese dignitaries, representing, as they do, not only all departments of that Government, but the dignity of the throne itself—a throne which but yesterday, as it were, was one of the most secluded and mysterious on earth.

"Who of you all, gentlemen, can fail to see in this sight the harbinger of greater events still to follow, that shall place Japan, in a very brief future, in complete alignment with the most advanced nations of the earth? We are proud of the past, proud of the present, and confident of the future. In this spirit I am sure the whole heart of the American nation will leap up to welcome the noble Ambassadors of our sister nation."

The advent of the Embassy on American soil called forth a large number of hearty editorials of welcome in the San Francisco papers, but the most satisfactory one, on account of its authentic facts, appeared in the *Daily Evening Bulletin;* and no apology is needed for introducing a portion of it in this place.

"Japan is to-day, all the circumstances of her previous condition considered, the most progressive nation on the globe. Less than twenty years have elapsed since the first treaty was made by Perry in 1854, for harbors of refuge for shipwrecked seamen and supplies for vessels in distress, and still less since the treaty was made by Minister Harris for purposes of trade. Prior to the period named, the penalty of death was visited upon Japanese who had had intercourse with foreigners, and trade was simply impossible. The government of the empire was in the hands of a number of Princes, or Daimios, who nominally ruled in the name of the Mikado, but practically in their own right. Each Daimio had his armed retainers, who wore the uniforms and marched under the distinctive banners of their chief. The Mikado was termed the spiritual Emperor, and had his own court at Kioto; while the Shogoon, or Tycoon, which title was hereditary in the Tokagawa family, exercised temporal authority at Yeddo, under the Gorogio, or Council of State, composed of some of the Daimios of highest rank. The distinctions of caste were rigorously enforced, and feudalism, in its most ultra form, was prevalent throughout the empire. This state of things prevailed less than twenty years ago, since when more radical changes have taken place than in any other country known.

"Among the principal changes, there has been an entire revolution in the system of government, the Mikado having become the active head of the temporal power. The entire system of feudalism has been swept away, and all the forces of the empire, both on land and sea, have been consolidated, and are fed and clothed in European style, and paid from the national treasury. The Government possesses a large fleet of war and transport steamers, among which are the *Stonewall*, and other iron-clads and rams. It also has constructed a stone dry-dock that will admit steamers of the largest size, with ways for repairing smaller vessels, and foundries, machine-shops, and forges, capable of doing the largest class of work, the machinery used being the best obtainable in France, at a cost of over two million dollars. This establishment gives employment to eighteen hundred men, about a score of them being foreigners and the remainder Japanese. The government is also building a railroad, which, when completed, will extend from Hiogo to Yeddo, a distance of about four hundred miles.

"The government schools at Yeddo contain about sixteen hundred pupils, studying foreign languages, three-fourths of whom are under American teachers, receiving an English education. The principal of this school and some twenty sub-teachers are Americans, while many subjects of other nations are employed in different capacities in other departments. An American fills the highest office that a foreigner can hold under the Japanese Government —that is, Imperial Councillor, whose duty is to frame codes of general laws for the empire. Four Americans compose a scientific commission, to introduce new methods of agriculture, mechanics, mining, roads, etc., while another American has been appointed to revise and organize a system of internal revenue somewhat similar to our own. In addition, during the last four years, nearly one thousand young men of intelligence and ability have been sent abroad to study the languages, laws, habits, manufactures, methods of government, and all other matters appertaining to western civilization, the greater part of which is to be introduced into Japan.

" Japan, to-day, has a population of thirty-five millions, or within a few millions of that of the United States. Unlike the Chinese, its people readily make changes in clothing, food, manufactures, and modes of living, when they see improvement therein. They are, as a race, impulsive, highly intelligent, brave to rashness, cleanly in their habits, have a high sense of personal honor, and are universally polite, from the highest dignitary to the lowest in the land, and withal are kindly disposed toward foreigners, especially Americans. Unlike the Chinese, again, the people of Japan are warmly attached to their country, and will not emigrate on Coolie contracts, the thirst for knowledge being the incentive of those who seek foreign lands. A Japanese who can speak and write foreign languages, the English in particular, is assured of profitable employment under his Government, with favorable prospects of promotion. The law that forbade marriages between the noble and the common classes has been repealed, with the effect to elevate the marriage ties, by improving the moral and social status of woman. The barriers of caste that allowed nobles only to bear arms, or to hold military or civic office, have been modified so that all classes, except the tanners, whose occupation is deemed unclean, are now eligible.

"Another important change made has been the withdrawal of Government assistance to the Buddhist religion, leaving it to continue only through the voluntary support of the people. The priests, having no income, have been advised by the Government to enter the army as soldiers, so that Sintooism, which is only a moral code, is all the religion left for the guidance of the people. This circumstance seems to prepare the way for the introduction of Christianity, for it is now well-known that the repressive measures taken by the Japanese Government against it, were mainly caused by its interference with the temporal authority. The Embassy that is about to visit the United States and Europe, will see for themselves that Christianity does not necessarily interfere with good government, either republican or monarchical; and the young men studying abroad, on their return will take with them additional proof of this, and perhaps themselves be the means of introducing the belief in many places where no foreign missionary could reach. It needs only that patience and forbearance be exercised by foreigners in this matter, so as not to excite undue anxiety in the minds of the opponents of Christianity, to insure for it the same tolerant recognition which is accorded all religions in America.

"The present situation of Japan appeals strongly to all

well-wishers to the race, that no impediments nor difficulty, either social, moral, political, or religious, be placed in the way of her progress. We need only show her people the effects of western civilization, in a kindly and courteous spirit, without needlessly exciting prejudices in so doing. The natural intelligence of the Japanese, which has no superior, will satisfy itself, and work out the problem of what to introduce in their own country, to a conclusion satisfactory to all concerned."

Before leaving the Pacific coast, an incident occurred which must not be omitted in this place. Charles Wolcott Brooks, Esq., the Japanese Consul in San Francisco, was officially informed by the Ministers, that his administration of their affairs had been so faithful, his salary should be increased to the extent of two thousand of Mexican dollars, and that they were anxious to have him accompany them on their mission to Europe,—so that he thus became a member of the Embassy. In view of the fact that the Embassy is accredited to all the Treaty Powers, it might seem strange to some that an American was selected to accompany the mission, but it should be recollected that Mr. Brooks had been eighteen years in the employ of the Japanese Government, six years as commercial agent, and twelve years as Consul.

The very last act performed by the Embassy in San Francisco, was to sign and cause to be published the following card of acknowledgment—which was signed by all the Ambassadors:

"The undersigned, since their arrival in the city of San Francisco, having received from the officials of the State, city, and county alike, and also from all classes of the people with whom they have the honor to come in contact, the most kind attention and generous hospitality, beg leave respectfully to return their most sincere thanks, with their assurances that it will afford them great pleasure to reciprocate the same whenever opportunity offers."

The Embassy left San Francisco by railway on the 31st of January, and their first stopping-place was Sacramento, where they became the guests of the Legislature, and on the evening of February 1st were treated to a banquet, on which occasion Governor Ito delivered the following speech :

"In acknowledging the generous hospitality of your welcome, we feel from the depths of grateful hearts the honor conferred upon us. His Majesty our Emperor having the noble desire to increase our prosperity and extend our commercial relations with friendly powers, has sent us to your country on this important mission. Our people require much that you can furnish us, and we shall look largely to our nearest enlightened neighbors for those supplies of which we stand in need. The object of our mission is to inspect and examine into the various mechanic arts and sciences which have assisted your country in gaining the present high position she occupies before the world. We come to study your strength, that, by adopting wisely your better ways, we may hereafter be stronger ourselves. We shall require your mechanics to teach our people many things, and the more our intercourse increases the more we shall call upon you. We shall labor to place Japan on an equal basis, in the future, with those countries whose modern civilization is now our guide. The friendly intercourse of commerce will necessarily draw us closer together, and the State of California will be among the first to receive such benefits as must necessarily flow from more intimate relations. Notwithstanding the various customs, manners, and institutions of the different nations, we are all members of one large human family, and under control of the same Almighty Being, and we believe it is our common destiny to reach a yet nobler civilization than the world has yet seen. Now, I am sure that you are the advocates of these principles; and these hospitalities, so generously offered, we receive as a compliment to our nation, and as the public expression of these magnanimous sentiments. With thankful hearts, therefore, let us drink to a closer friendship between our countries—one whose benefits shall be mutual and lasting."

The Embassy left Sacramento on the 31st of January; and, on reaching Salt Lake City on the 4th of February, they were blockaded by the snow, and compelled to remain at that place until the 21st of February. During their sojourn there they were comfortably housed, and were treated with great kindness by the authorities and citizens. A banquet was given to the Embassy in that place, and a toast was offered by the Chief Ambassador in the following words: "On this, the first day of the fifth year of the reign of the Emperor, I propose the health of the President of the United States." Of course, in this connection we must allude to the famous Mormon leader, Brigam Young, but this we do in the language of one of the local papers, as follows:

"One of the principal members of the Japanese Embassy was waited upon yesterday by a messenger from the 'Prophet Brigham,' requesting the Oriental Prince to call on the Western Prophet. His Highness remarked that it was not etiquette in Japan for persons of his rank, when among strangers, to make calls, but awaited the calls of people among whom they may be sojourning.

"The Prophet's messenger replied that the Seer and Revelator was very anxious to see the representatives of His Majesty, but was sorry to admit that it was impossible for him to do so immediately. The Royal Ambassador inquired why the Prophet could not call? To this the messenger replied that the Prophet was unwillingly confined to his room in charge of a Federal officer. The Prince saw the point at once, and, with a frown, said: 'We came to the United States to see the President of this great nation; we do not know how he would like for us to call on a man who had broken the laws of his country and was under arrest.'"

Their next stopping-place was Chicago, where they remained less than two days, and were treated with warm hospitality; and that visit they commemorated by presenting to the Mayor the sum of five thousand dollars, for the benefit of the poor of that lately devastated city.

The correspondence on that occasion was as follows:

"SECRETARY'S OFFICE OF THE
    JAPANESE EMBASSY,
"CHICAGO, Feb. 27, 1872.

"*To His Excellency J. Medill, Mayor of the City of Chicago:*

"SIR: Permit us to add a small offering to the relief fund which the benevolent of your nation have donated to alleviate the distress of those of your people who suffered by the late fire. Kindly accept and dispose of it as your best judgment may dictate. With many thanks for your kind civilities, we remain yours respectfully,

"Sionii TOMOMI IWAKURA,
*    Ambassador Extraordinary of Japan.*
Jussammi TAKAYOSSI KIDO,
*    Vice-Ambassador Extraordinary.*
Jussammi TOSSIMITSI OKUBO,
*    Vice-Ambassador Extraordinary.*
Jushie HIROBUMIE ITO,
*    Vice-Ambassador Extraordinary.*
Jushie MASSONKA YAMAGUTSI,
*    Vice-Ambassador Extraordinary.*"

His honor returned the following reply:

"*To Sionii Tomomi Iwakura, Jussammi Takayossi Kido, and others, of the Japanese Embassy:*

"GENTLEMEN : I have the honor to acknowledge the receipt of $5,000 from the Embassy of His Imperial Majesty, of which you are the Chief Envoys, at the hands of Mr. Charles W. Brooks, Consul of Japan at San Francisco, donated to alleviate the distress of our citizens who suffered by the late calamitous conflagration. Permit me, in behalf of the people of Chicago, to tender you their most grateful thanks for this wholly unexpected and munificent gift. They will esteem it as an additional proof that the great nation you represent has enrolled itself among the progressive and civilized powers of the earth, as well as a lively testimonial of the personal sympathy of your Embassy for the misfortune of this portion of your American friends. Respectfully yours,

"JOSEPH MEDILL, *Mayor.*"

They left Chicago on the 27th of February and arrived in Washington on the 29th following.

At this point it becomes necessary for us to pause for a moment, to glance at the action of the Government, in connection with the Embassy. On the 30th of January the Congress of the United States made an appropriation of fifty thousand dollars for the purpose of entertaining the Embassy while in this country, and on the next day Mr. Mori wrote to the Secretary of State as follows: "In view of the action which the Congress of the United States has been pleased to take in regard to the Japanese Embassy, now on its way to the Capital, I deem it my duty, as it is certainly my pleasure, to tender my personal and official acknowledgments. It is not on account of the amount of money appropriated, but the spirit which prompted the measure, which will gratify the Tenno of Japan, and my countrymen generally. I can assure you, sir, that this princely act will be fully appreciated, and will result, I trust, in making perennial the cordial friendship which now exists between the United States and the Empire of Japan."

In a subsequent dispatch which Mr. Mori sent to his Government on the 18th of February, he thus alludes to the action of the American Government, and gives his views as to how the money appropriated by Congress should be spent: "Owing to the 'snow blockade' on the Pacific Railroad, the Embassy has not yet arrived in Washington, and it is impossible to say how long the delay may continue. It affords me pleasure to inform you, however, that the Government here has made every preparation for extending a warm welcome to the Embassy. The President and Secretary of State have both exerted themselves in the matter, and a prominent person, General William Myers, has been selected to carry out the wishes of the Government. . . . With regard to the question as to how the money appropriated by Congress shall be expended, I have intimated to the American Secretary of State, that it should not be used in paying the hotel-bills of the Embassy, but simply for carrying out any plans that may be devised for their entertainment."

The appropriation made by Congress was sanctioned with great unanimity; but before their final action, the honorable Members of the Committees of both Houses, on Foreign Affairs and Appropriations, desired some authentic particulars about the present condition of Japan, when, under Mr. Mori's direction, the following notes were prepared:

The influences which have been disseminated among the nations of the East by the various interests of the western nations, have hitherto been injurious rather than beneficial. The people of Japan, as well as all in the Orient, feel the need of increased light in regard to the more elevated interests of humanity; and this is the chief reason why Mr. Mori cherishes a strong desire to do all he can for the education of his people.

The influences alluded to have also done much to keep back from the people of Japan very much of that true spirit of civilization, so eminently characteristic of America. And the fact seems now to be generally acknowledged that the Japanese people not only desire to follow, as far as possible, in all educational and political affairs, the example of the Americans, but that they look upon them as their best friends, among the nations of the globe. A prominent idea with the educated classes of Japan is, that in the very ship which took Commodore M. C. Perry to Japan in 1852, were the germs of Christianity, civilization, and desire for equality and political freedom, and that the seed then planted has been steadily growing from that to the present time.

At first, the Japanese were, from their ignorance of the outer world, unwilling to open their ports to foreigners, or to receive them in their country; but as they began to see and understand, they gradually yielded up their prejudices. A new spirit animated them, and it was this which brought them to the Revolution from which they have recently emerged.

The first concession made by the Japanese was an acknowledgment of the darkness in which they were, and of the superior character of foreign institutions; and the immediate result was that they desired to cement a closer friendship with foreign governments. They naturally looked upon the United States as occupying the first rank. Then they also wished to consolidate the various internal interests of Japan.

The late Tycoon was favorably disposed, but, not being the legitimate head of the nation, the people were against him, did not support him, and hence he was powerless, and in due time resigned the Tycoonite. He was not the supreme ruler, because that position belonged to the hereditary Emperor.

The great party which opposed the Tycoon consisted of the Daimios—the Feudal or Provincial Princes—and a bitter rivalry existed between them. Both were willing to civilize Japan to some extent, but the Tycoon wished to civilize his followers alone, and the Daimios were anxious to secure the same end for their followers. While thus interfering with each other, both of these parties were, in reality, coming into a new light. They soon saw the necessity of uniting their interests, and the present movements now going on in Japan are the result of the co-operation of these two elements.

To help his cause, the Tycoon sent students abroad to be educated; and the Daimios, with the same object in view, also sent some of their followers abroad. Hence it was that the Japanese were soon found scattered among the colleges and seminaries of the United States and Europe, and representatives of both parties—long since reconciled—are now in Washington. Originally, there were leaders in both parties who looked into the future, and did all they could to secure unity of action, and it was the late Revolution which settled the question of consolidation.

Ever since the Japanese began to throw aside the old restrictions, commerce has been steadily increasing, and the present disposition of the Government is to have the freest possible intercourse with all the world. It was the great ignorance which prevailed among the people of Japan, which prevented the development of commerce. The channel is now open, and all that is wanted is to have the people sail into it with determination.

The great aim is now to educate and elevate the people. The system of caste has already been abolished. The middle classes, which were formerly kept back by hereditary pride, are now turning their attention and energies to industrial pursuits. Among the developments which are now going on in Japan, may be mentioned the building of railroads, the establishment of telegraphs, navy-yards, arsenals, and the building of steamships. By competent scholars, English books, in great numbers, are being translated into the Japanese language; and newspapers—even daily journals—are becoming a necessity. Hospitals managed according to Western ideas have been established; also, institutions for the employment of the poor, and many successful schools. And, by way of showing the zeal of some of the native scholars, it may be stated that there is one man in Yeddo who has educated at his own house not less than two thousand Japanese children, and to-day has a school of three hundred and fifty pupils.

The intelligent people of the Empire are hungering and thirsting after knowledge, and the study of the English language is considered the best means for accomplishing the end which is so strongly desired.

On the 29th of February, the Japanese Embassy arrived in Washington City; and at the railway station, the Governor of the Territory of Columbia, Hon. Henry D. Cooke, with several officials, as well as the Japanese Minister and many Japanese students, were in waiting to receive them; and after the proper arrangements had been made, the Governor delivered the following speech of welcome:

"I take very great pleasure in extending to you and your associates a hearty and sincere welcome to the capital of this country. I trust that your visit here may not only be agreeable to you personally, but that it may result in closer ties and more intimate relations between our two countries. I extend to you, on behalf of the citizens of the District, its cordial hospitalities. I have now the pleasure of introducing to you General Myers, of the army, who has been intrusted with the pleasant duty of providing for your comfort during your visit; and I beg also to present General Chipman, the Representative of this District in the Congress of the United States."

The address was interpreted by Mr. Mori, to which the following response was made by the Chief Ambassador (Mr. Mori interpreting):

"I thank you kindly for your remarks and expressions, and have no doubt but the sentiments expressed will be appreciated and reciprocated. I am very glad at having arrived safe, and having met with no accident. I have been informed by Mr. Mori that you have been here some time awaiting our arrival. I thank you very much for taking this trouble, and feel very much impressed by this reception."

The preliminaries of the reception and formal welcome over, the visitors were escorted to carriages, and proceeded to their headquarters, at the Arlington Hotel. Among the students assembled to greet the ambassadors were three particularly good English scholars, who were in Paris, and two of whom were about to return to Japan, when they were summoned by telegram from San Francisco, to report themselves in Washington, to accompany the Embassy in their going round the world.

On Monday, the 4th day of March, at noon, the Embassy had an audience with the President of the United States, Ulysses S. Grant, which was admirably arranged; and when the proper moment arrived, the Prime Minister read from a Japanese manuscript the following address of their Excellencies, the Ambassadors from Japan:

" His Majesty the Emperor of Japan, our most august sovereign, has sought, since the achievement of our national reconstruction, to attain a more perfect organization in the administrative powers of his Government. He has studied with interest the results attained by Western nations, and having a sincere desire to establish permanent and friendly relations with foreign powers on a still closer footing, has commissioned us his ambassadors extraordinary to all powers having treaty with Japan. Upon the soil of your country we first present our credentials, delivering to you personally the letter of our august sovereign at this public official audience."

Minister Iwakura here presented to the President their credential letter, folded in an envelope some two feet long and six inches wide, and curiously wrought with flowers of gold. The following is the text of the letter

### THE LETTER OF THE EMPEROR.

[Official Translation.]

" Moutsoukito, Emperor of Japan, etc., to the President of the United States of America.

" *Our Good Brother and Faithful Friend, Greeting:*

" Mr. President:—Whereas, since our accession by the blessing of Heaven to the sacred throne on which our ancestors reigned from time immemorial, we have not despatched any embassy to the courts and Governments of friendly countries: We have thought fit to select our trusty and honored Minister Sionii Tomomi Iwakura, the Junior Prime Minister, as Ambassador Extraordinary, and have associated with him Iussammi Takayossi Kido, Member of the Privy Council; Iussammi Tossimitsi Okubo, Minister of Finance; Iushie Hirobumie Ito, Acting Minister of Public Works, and Iushie Massouha Yamugutsi, Assistant Minister for Foreign Affairs, Associate Ambassadors Extraordinary, and invested them with full powers to proceed to the Government of the United States, as well as to other Governments, in order to declare our cordial friendship, and to place the peaceful relations between our respective nations on a firmer and broader basis.

"The period for revising the treaties now existing between ourselves and the United States, is less than one year distant. We expect and intend to reform and improve the same so as to stand upon a similar footing with the most enlightened nations, and to attain the full development of public right and interest. The civilization and institutions of Japan are so different from those of other countries, that we cannot expect to reach the desired end at once.

"It is our purpose to select from the various institutions prevailing among enlightened nations such as are best suited to our present condition, and adopt them, in gradual reforms and improvements of our policy and customs, so as to be upon an equality with them.

"With this object, we desire to fully disclose to the United States Government the condition of affairs in our Empire, and to consult upon the means of giving greater efficiency to our institutions, at present and in the future; and as soon as the said Embassy returns home we will consider about the revision of the treaties, and accomplish what we have expected and intended.

"The Ministers who compose this Embassy have our confidence and esteem. We request you to favor them with full credence and due regard; and we earnestly pray for your continued health and happiness, and for the peace and prosperity of your great Republic.

"In witness whereof we have hereunto set our hand and the great seal of our Empire, at our palace, in the city of Tokio, this 4th of eleventh month of fourth year of Meiji.

"Your affectionate brother and friend,

"Moutsoukito.

"Juichii Sanetonii Sanjo,
"*Prime Minister.*"

After this ceremony, the Minister resumed, and concluded his address as follows:

"The objects of the mission with which we are charged by our Government are somewhat set forth in this letter. We are authorized to consult with your Government on all international questions, directing our efforts to promote and develop wider commercial relations and draw into closer bonds the strong friendship already existing between our respective peoples. Thus we hope to gain fresh impulse in the paths of progress, gaining good from every form of civilization. This we shall aim to do while in the exercise of strict integrity to our own national interests, so trustingly confided by a generous sovereign, and shall earnestly hope to receive your kind co-operation in facilitating the task assigned us by our Government. We gladly avail ourselves of this happy meeting to convey personally to your Excellency our sincere wishes for your continued prosperity and happiness, and, as national representatives, we extend the same wish to all the people of the United States."

With the last words of the above he bowed very low, and with great dignity stepped back a single pace.

The President of the United States then read to the Ambassadors the following reply:—

"GENTLEMEN: I am gratified that this country and that my administration will be distinguished in history as the first which has received an Embassy from the nation with which the United States was the first to establish diplomatic and commercial intercourse. The objects which you say have given rise to your mission do honor to the intelligence and wisdom of your sovereign, and reflect credit on you in having been chosen as the instruments for carrying them into effect. The time must be regarded as gone, never to return, when any nation can keep apart from all others, and expect to enjoy the prosperity and happiness which depend more or less upon the mutual adoption of improvements, not only in the science of government, but in those other sciences and arts which contribute to the dignity of mankind, and national wealth and power. Though Japan is one of the most ancient of organized communities and the United States rank among the most recent, we flatter ourselves that we have made some improvements upon the political institutions of the nations from which we are descended. Our experience leads us to believe that the wealth, the power, and the happiness of a people are advanced by the encouragement of trade and commercial intercourse with other powers, by the elevation and dignity of labor, by the practical adaptation of science to the manufactures and the arts, by increased facilities of frequent and rapid communication between different parts of the country, by the encouragement of immigration, which brings with it the varied habits and diverse genius and industry of other lands, by a free press, by freedom of thought and of conscience, and a liberal toleration in matters of religion, not only to citizens, but to all foreigners resident among us. It will be a pleasure to us to enter upon that consultation upon international questions in which you say you are authorized to engage. The improvement of the commercial relations between our respective countries is important and desirable, and cannot fail to strengthen the bonds which unite us. I will heartily co-operate in so desirable an object. Your kind wishes for me personally, gentlemen, are cordially reciprocated. I trust that your abode with us may be agreeable to you, and may contribute to a more intimate acquaintance and intercourse between our respective peoples."

The President next introduced each member of his Cabinet by name to the Ambassadors. The officers of the various Departments were then called forward, commencing with the Department of State.

After these introductions were over, the President offered his arm to Prime Minister Iwakura, and, with the Embassy, the Cabinet officers, and a few others, proceeded to the Blue Room.

Here were stationed several ladies.

After formal introductions had been made to the ladies, Mrs. Grant, Mr. Mori acting as interpreter, held a very pleasant conversation with Mr. Iwakura and other members of the Embassy. They all remained in the Blue Room for half an hour, and then withdrew, bowing very low to the ladies, and not averting their faces until they were in the main corridor of the Executive Mansion.

They repaired at once to the Arlington, to prepare for a splendid social entertainment afforded them in the evening at the residence of Hon. James Brooks. This dinner was given by Mr. Brooks as a recognition of the handsome courtesies extended to him during his visit in Japan, and was one of the most elegant entertainments ever given in Washington.

On Wednesday, the 6th of March, the Congress of the United States, by special invitation, gave the Japanese Embassy a formal reception. Long before the appointed hour the galleries of the House of Representatives were filled to their utmost capacity; and when, at eleven o'clock, the Embassy arrived at the Capitol, the Chief Ambassador was escorted by the Hon. Nathaniel P. Banks, Chairman of the Committee of Foreign Affairs, and the other Ambassadors by the remaining members of the same. Committee. As they entered the hall, the members and clerks rose and received them standing, and the visitors were escorted to the semicircle in front of the Speaker's desk, the chief Ambassadors taking positions nearest the desk, and the *attachés* in the rear of them. Amid profound silence, General Banks then introduced the distinguished visitors, and as each name was mentioned the person designated bowed low. A moment afterward, the Hon. James G. Blaine, Speaker of the House of Representatives, addressed the Embassy as follows:

"YOUR EXCELLENCIES: On behalf of the House of Representatives I welcome your Imperial Embassy to this hall. The reception which is thus extended to you so unanimously and so cordially by the members of this body is significant of the interest which our whole people feel in the rapidly developing relations between the Japanese Empire and the American Republic

"The course of migration for the human race has for many centuries been steadily westward—a course always marked by conquest, and too often by rapine. Reaching the boundary of our continent, we encountered a returning tide from your country setting eastward, seeking, not the trophies of war, but the more shining victories of peace; and these two currents of population appropriately meet and mingle on the shores of the great Pacific Sea. It will be my pleasure to present to you personally the representatives of the people; and I beg to assure you, for them and for myself, that during your stay at our capital you will be at all times welcome to the privileges and courtesies of this floor."

At the close of the Speaker's address the Chief Ambassador was introduced, and deliberately unrolling a parchment, he proceeded to read an address in his native tongue.

At the conclusion of this address, which was delivered in a clear and distinct, though not powerful, voice, and with a peculiar and somewhat monotonous intonation, which made the strange scene the more striking, General Banks, at the request of the Prince, read the following translation of the Chief Ambassador's address, which he requested might be spread upon the journal of the House.

"*Mr. Speaker, and Honorable Members of the House of Representatives of the United States:*

"On behalf of the Ambassadors of Japan, our sovereign, and the people whom we represent, we tender to you our sincere thanks and warmest friendship. We fully appreciate the distinguished honor which places us, face to face, in presence of that mighty power which rules the great American Republic.

'Governments are strong when built upon the hearts of an enlightened people. We came for enlightenment, and gladly find it here. Journeying eastward from the empire of sunrise toward the sun-rising, we behold a new sunrise beyond the one we before enjoyed.

"New knowledge rises daily before us, and when a completed trip shall shall have passed in review, an encircled globe shall gather together our treasures of knowledge; remembering that however we have advanced toward the sources of light, each onward move has revealed a further step beyond. The Government of Japan already appreciates the value of an enlightened policy toward itself and all nations; but our mutual assurances on our return will confirm to the people at large the friendliness of feeling so frequently expressed heretofore, and now so generously exhibited to this Embassy.

"In the future an extended commerce will unite our national interests in a thousand forms, as drops of water will commingle, flowing from our several rivers to that common ocean that divides our countries.

"Let us express the hope that our national friendship may be as difficult to sunder or estrange as to divide the once blended drops composing our common Pacific Ocean."

This concluded, the Embassy faced the body of the Representatives, and the latter filed past and were severally introduced. The Hon. Schuyler Colfax, Vice-President of the United States and President of the Senate, honored the occasion with his presence, and was the first dignitary presented to the Embassy; and the Hon. Henry L. Dawes, on behalf of the Representatives, took occasion to say that they had all listened with great pleasure to the speech delivered by the Ambassador; after which the entire body paid an informal visit to the Chamber of the United States Senate, then in session, and were next shown about the Capitol building generally. During the remainder of their stay in Washington, the members of the Embassy were constantly engaged in attending to their business with the Government or in accepting hospitalities, and they were to leave the Metropolis only to enjoy a continuous series of welcoming entertainments in the cities of the North, to which they were invited by many delegations of distinguished gentlemen.

Having now seen that the Japanese Embassy is in the hands of the American Government, and that they are visiting the institutions of the nation, under official escort, and that they are being hospitably entertained by corporate bodies in all the leading cities on the Atlantic coast, we proceed to give a few particulars of a personal character.

And first, as to the Chief Ambassador, Tomomi Iwakura. He was born in 1825, and is a man of superior abilities. He does not speak English, but has manifested his regard for education by sending three of his sons to be educated in this country. He is the Left-hand President of His Japanese Imperial Majesty's Ministry—Sandeo being the Right-hand President—and is, in fact, the principal working executive officer of the Japanese Government. His visit confers the same degree of honor from Japan, as the visit in person of the Premier of Great Britain would confer from that power. He was an inveterate opponent of the Tycoon in the late war, and was for several years held as a prisoner by the Tycoon's Government. To him, more than any other man, is due the late revolution and its wonderful results, and he now wields a corresponding influence in the Japanese Ministry.

His first public audience at Court was in December, 1858. He was appointed to the Privy Council in December, 1863, soon after the formation of the present Government. He was elected Vice-President of the Ministry (Cabinet) January 9, 1868. The title of "Sionii," the second honorary grade of the imperial order, was conferred upon him, February, 1869. This is the first title below the imperial title. On the 26th day of September, 1869, the Emperor issued the following decree:

"TOMOMI,—Being zealous in strengthening the Imperial authority throughout our Empire, you have at length succeeded in establishing our Government in its present form, and have taken upon yourself this great task of administration.

"You have, indeed, labored industriously, vigorously, and nobly at this difficult task, and your plans and suggestions have always been suited to the requirements of our Empire. You are the founder of our present style of Government, and the indispensable member of my councils. As I am heartily gratified with your distinguished merit, it is my pleasure to bestow upon you the augmental salary perpetually, without chance of discontinuation.

"In future I expect to rely upon your assistance as much as I have in the past."

He was appointed Minister of Foreign Affairs, July, 1871, and raised to the rank of Junior Prime Minister, October, 1871, and is now Ambassador Extraordinary, charged with the most important mission that has ever left the shores of Japan, and one more important than any which ever reached our shores from any Eastern nation.

During his visit to San Francisco, Consul Brooks had two imperial photographs taken of His Excellency, one of them in his official Japanese costume, and one in the prevailing American dress. When copies of these portraits were presented to Mr. Mori in Washington, he had them put into one frame, side by side, and hung up in the guest-chamber of the Legation; and, in view of the great changes now going on in the East, had them labelled with these words in Japanese characters—*Ancient and Modern Japan.*

With regard to the four associate Ambassadors, we are only able at present to give the following particulars:

Takayossi Kido is of the clan Choshieu, which holds the lower end of the Island of Nipon, commanding the Straits of Simonoseky. This was one of the first clans to raise the standard of revolt against the Tycoon, and Kido was one of the chief emissaries under Iwakura for the organizing of the army, uniting the other clans in the cause. Since the revolution he has been made a member of the Privy Council. He is thirty-nine years of age, was a leading man before the revolution, but since that event has been held in greater esteem. He does not speak English, and has never before been out of Japan. Tossimitsi Okubo is forty-three years old, and belongs to the warlike clan of Satsma, which holds the Loo Choo group and the south end of Kanchin. He is now Chief Minister of Finance. His knowledge of English is very limited, and he has never before been out of Japan.

It is said of him that upon news of a defeat in the first battle of the revolution (which was the outgrowth of 600 years, so slow do great movements ripen in Japan) some one asked in the General Council what they should do with themselves and the Mikado. Okubo replied, "Let us expect no more than to die here; but while a Satsma lives, the usurpation of the Tycoon will be resisted." It was Okubo's soldiers that at last turned the battle and defeated the Tycoon.

Hirobumi Ito is said to be thirty-two years of age, speaks English fluently, is a close observer of men and things, visited England about ten years ago, and took part in negotiating the Treaty which called for the payment of $3,000,000 to the four Powers, and his present visit is the second he has made to this country. He was formerly Governor of Hiogo and Kobe; put in operation the present system of revenue in Japan; and, as Acting Minister of Public Works, he has been intrusted with authority to purchase or order to be built and put in operation a great variety of things having reference to the material prosperity of his country. His friendship for America and American institutions is conspicuous, and during his former visit to Washington he made many warm personal friends.

Massouka Yamagutsi is the fifth Ambassador; he is the Assistant Minister of Foreign Affairs, and about thirty-four years old; has some knowledge of international law; and is recognized as a man of ability. He does not speak English, and has never been out of Japan before.

The honorable Commissioners, who form a part of the Embassy, are all men of high rank in the Army and Civil List of Japan, and their business is to inquire into whatever may be of advantage, in the special departments of the Government to which they are attached.

It is now our duty, and most certainly our pleasure, to make a special allusion to Jugoi Arinori Mori, *Chargé d'Affaires* from Japan in Washington, to whom was assigned the task of receiving and providing for the comfort of his diplomatic associates during their sojourn in America. He was born in the southern part of Japan, and is not yet twenty-five years old. He was among the first Japanese students sent to England to be educated, and, after remaining in London two years, he returned to Japan. He took a leading part in the Home Parliament after the late revolution, and was afterward, on account of his talents and Western education, appointed Minister to this country—having been the first to receive a diplomatic mission from his Government.

He is greatly interested in the progress of knowledge, earnest and desirous of promoting the advancement of his country in all good things. By his intercourse with our official representatives, and by his visits to different parts of the country, he has gained the confidence and esteem of very many distinguished Americans.

While occupying a seat in the National Legislature of his country, Mr. Mori introduced a proposition to abolish the ancient custom of wearing two swords, by one of the great privileged classes; for a time the measure met with determined hostility, but was subsequently successful; and the following letter connected with this subject, addressed to the Hon. Wm. W. Belknap, Secretary of War, by Mr. Mori, will be read with interest:

"I have the honor to ask your acceptance of the accompanying Japanese sword, to be deposited in the Military Museum attached to your Department. It has hitherto been worn by one of the provincial officials of Japan, who is now travelling in this country. He brought it with him, because of his former devotion to the ancient custom of wearing that weapon in duplicate; but having, since his arrival here, been convinced of the uselessness of that custom, he thought proper to present the weapon to me. And if you will pardon me, I may add that the significance of this act on the part of my friend (Mr. Kondo) is enhanced by the fact that the original proposition for abolishing the wearing of two swords was submitted in the Japanese Parliament by myself, and that Mr. Kondo was one of those who, at that time, deprecated my proposition. It may be well enough for me to add that the blade of this sword was manufactured more than three hundred years ago, and that the metal is considered far more valuable than that employed in modern times."

Some time ago, when Professor Joseph Henry, of the Smithsonian Institution, was informed that the Japanese Government had been compelled to pay to the United States an indemnity of about seven hundred and fifty thousand dollars, on the strength of what many think an unjust claim, and that this money was held by the Department of State, and not deposited in the Treasury, he inaugurated a plan for the restoration of the money. He consulted with Mr. Mori, and when that gentleman earnestly expressed the hope that the money, if returned, should be devoted exclusively to educational purposes, the Professor at once addressed a letter to the Joint Committee on the Library of Congress, setting forth his views at considerable length; and as that letter is both interesting and valuable, we are glad to print it, as follows:

"SMITHSONIAN INSTITUTION,
WASHINGTON, *Jan.* 10*th*, 1872.

*To the Joint Committee on the Library of Congress, Capitol:*

"GENTLEMEN: The Smithsonian Institution, in its mission for the 'increase and diffusion of knowledge among men,' has entered into friendly relations with the authorities of Japan for the exchange of specimens of natural history and ethnology, and for the establishment of meteorological, magnetic, and other physical observations. In relation to these matters, I have had frequent intercourse with Mr. A. Mori, the Japanese Minister, and have been informed as to his various plans for elevating the intellectual condition of his people. One of the most important of these is the establishment of a National Institution in the city of Jeddo for educational purposes, to be furnished with a Library in which shall be represented the science and literature of Western Europe and the United States, with specimens, apparatus, and models, to fully illustrate all the principles of abstract science, as well as their application to the practical uses of life.

"This Institution is designed to be a great central university, and to serve as a normal school, in which teachers may finish their education as rapidly as a knowledge of the English language is disseminated throughout the country.

"In view of the intimate relations existing between the United States and Japan, and the manner in which the money known as the Indemnity Fund has been obtained, it has been suggested that this might with propriety be appropriated by Congress, for the benefit of the proposed Institution; and it is the object of this letter to respectfully present this suggestion to you for your consideration, and through you, should it meet your approbation, to the Congress of the United States.

"I may be allowed to say, in favor of the suggestion, that its adoption would indicate a proper appreciation of the sentiments entertained by the Japanese people with regard to the character and institutions of our country, and be a manifestation of a desire on our part to encourage and aid them in the remarkable efforts they are now making to become imbued with the principles and habits of modern civilization. Furthermore, it would tend, beyond anything else, to show that in our intercourse with them we are actuated by other and higher motives than those which pertain to commercial benefits merely, and strengthen the unreserved confidence with which they are now receiving our advice and adopting our instruction.

"I have the honor to be, very respectfully,
"Your obedient servant,
(Signed) "JOSEPH HENRY, *Sect. S. Inst.*"

The gentlemen of that Committee were favorably impressed with the proposition, but referred it to the Committee on Foreign Affairs, which was equally favorable; it also met with the hearty co-operation of the President and Secretary of State; and either that or another kindred proposition, founded upon the opening of the ports of Japan, would seem to be in a fair way of being accomplished. As it is quite likely that Congress will be influenced by Mr. Mori's opinions and wishes on this important subject, we may state them in outline as follows: He would take about one-third of the amount, and erect in Japan a number of appropriate buildings in the leading cities, and furnish them with all the necessaries, including libraries and scientific apparatus, for a complete course of education; he would have them supplied with professors and subordinate teachers, taken from the United States; and would then have the balance of five hundred thousand dollars invested in United States securities, and kept in Washington, the interest of which should be used to support the institutions in Japan. The idea is indeed a splendid one, and in strict keeping with the many and unwearied efforts of Mr. Mori to elevate and promote the permanent prosperity and happiness of his people.

One of the most remarkable and interesting features connected with the advent of the Embassy in this country, was the fact that it was accompanied by a party of young Japanese girls, who were brought hither for the purpose of being educated; and we feel certain that, in concluding this account, a few words about them will be acceptable to the public.

In 1871, a Japanese gentleman, named R. Kuroda, passed through the United States on his way from England to Japan. He subsequently returned to America, and in his official capacity as Commissioner of the Island of Yesso, concluded arrangements which resulted in securing the services of General Horace Capron for the benefit of Japan. During his two brief visits to this country, he became so deeply impressed with the happy condition of the American woman, that he began to inquire into the cause of such a state of things, and was told that it was because the women of the country were educated, treated with the highest consideration, and are regarded equal to men in all the higher qualities of humanity. With his friend, Mr. Arinori Mori, he held several long discussions on the subject, took the advanced ground that the Japanese ought to intermarry with the people of the more enlightened foreign nations, and, in his zeal, went so far as to insist that Mr. Mori should marry an American lady without delay. To this the youthful minister replied, that he considered himself a true patriot, and would like to oblige his friend, but did not think it necessary for him to go into the marrying business quite so suddenly. From that time, however, Mr. Kuroda thought and talked unceasingly about the importance of educating the women of his native land. The letter which he wrote to his Government on this subject deserves to be printed in gold. A copy of it was brought to this country by the Embassy, and delivered to Mr. Mori. After commenting upon the importance of colonizing the wilder parts of Japan, the writer goes on to speak of the importance of education. To send ignorant men into the new regions would be quite useless, and, therefore, the first thing to be done was to educate the women of the Empire, so that the coming generation might be enlightened. While children under ten years of age were wholly under the influence of their mothers, it was, of course, of the utmost importance that they should be educated. As a little leaven leavens the whole lump, so would the education of women elevate the people of Japan. The Government had sent its young men to America and Europe to be educated, and was already reaping a valuable return; and now was the time for Japan to begin to educate its women; and hence he would have a delegation of girls sent to America without delay, and he knew that a great many others would follow in this pathway of enlightenment. What was new with Mr. Kuroda, however, was an old story with Mr. Mori, who, if a little less enthusiastic, was quite as deeply interested as the commissioner. On his return to Japan, he broached the idea to his Government of sending a number of young girls to America to be educated; reported the fact that he was fully indorsed by Mr. Mori, and, having obtained the hearty co-operation of Tomomi Iwakura, the Junior Prime Minister of Japan, an arrangement was made by which five Japanese girls were permitted to accompany the great Embassy to Washington. As the American Minister, Mr. Charles E. DeLong, was

about to visit the United States on private business, he joined the Embassy; and, as he was accompanied by his wife, she took charge of the Japanese girls during their long journey from Yeddo to Washington; and treated them with great kindness and attention, and received their gratitude in return. Before leaving home they were summoned to Yeddo, and in testimony of the good-will of the Mikado, and according to an ancient custom, they were each presented, by the attendants of the Court, with beautiful specimens of crimson crape, and an order was issued that their expenses while in America should be paid by the Government.

The names of this delegation of Japanese girls are as follows: Lio Yoshimas, aged 15; Tei Wooyeda, aged about 15; Stematz Yamagawa, aged 12; Shinge Nagai, aged 10, and Ume Tsuda, aged 8 years. They represent in their persons five distinct families, and while they are not immediately connected with the imperial family of Japan, they do belong to that particular class, which would, in this country, be called the aristocracy of intellect and wealth combined. How these particular girls happened to be selected is not important; and, although their fathers or friends were abundantly able to send them abroad, they have in reality come to this country as the wards of the Japanese Government. Their fathers are all connected with the present Government, and rank as follows: Yoshimas, retainer of a prince of Tokzyawa; Wooyeda, Second Secretary of the Department of State; Yamagawa, First Chamberlain to the Prince of Adzu; Nagai was formerly a retainer of the Tycoon, but now holds allegiance to the ruling power, and has a public position; Tsuda is one of the Secretaries of Agriculture, as well as a Geologist and Civil Engineer. They were consigned to the care of the Japanese Minister, Mr. Mori, in Washington; and, in view of very numerous applications that were made by educational institutions throughout the country, to take them in charge, and while debating what was best to do with the girls, Mr. Mori resolved to keep them for a few months under his immediate protection, and obtained comfortable and cheerful homes for them in Georgetown, under the general supervision of the Editor of this volume.

With regard to the kind of education which the Government of Japan would have bestowed upon these girls, that is a question which will probably be decided by Mr. Mori, and his personal views have been freely expressed in Washington society. He would, in the first place, have them made fully acquainted with the blessings of *home life* in the United States; and, in the second place, he would have their minds fully stored with all those kinds of information which will make them true ladies.

The glitter and folly of fashionable life may do for those who have no love or respect for what is called true culture; but that is not the arena in which he would place the bright-eyed daughters of his native land. That the Tenno of Japan is in hearty sympathy with the educational movement now under consideration is proven by one of his recent declarations, in which, to the astonishment of the world, he has uttered the following sentiment:

"My country is now undergoing a complete change from old to new ideas, which I sincerely desire, and therefore call upon all the wise and strong-minded to appear, and become good guides to the Government. During youth time, it is positively necessary to view foreign countries, so as to become enlightened as to the ideas of the world; and boys as well as girls, who will themselves soon become men and women, should be allowed to go abroad, and my country will benefit by the knowledge thus acquired. Females heretofore have had no position socially, because it was considered they were without understanding; but if educated and intelligent, they should have due respect."

We are pleased to know that since their arrival in the District, they have appeared very happy, and have expressed themselves well pleased with the temporary arrangement which Mr. Mori has made for them. They are all eager to learn the English language, and they have already become acquainted with many common words and their uses. The most interesting feature among them is probably the fact that the youngest was sent by her mother, who voluntarily makes the sacrifice of her own happiness for the benefit of her child. Her father is a good English scholar, and has already taught the little one many words; and among her valuables, carefully packed away by them for her, is an illustrated cyclopædia, in two large Japanese volumes, in which is written, "My dear daughter Ume, from father; Yeddo, Dec. 19, 1871," and a good supply of letter-paper, pencils, and India-ink, which she seems to appreciate. She is very bright, and quickly learns what she is taught. They have all been more pleased with a selection of American primers than anything they have been shown. Their time seems to be most cheerfully and satisfactorily employed, which is devoted to the spelling of words, expressing the common articles in daily use on the table and about the house, and the oldest assists in the duties of the household, at her own request. They all know the English alphabet, and are apt at forming words therefrom.

They have brought with them several handsome dresses, which are of elegant materials, and embroidered in gold and colored silks, mostly upon a fabric of Canton crape.

The youngest has brought from her home pictures of her father's house, with the family on the porch or balcony in front; in one scene the house looks upon a rice-field; in another, upon a beautiful lake, and another gives a glimpse of river scenery, with the banks lined with cherry-trees. Her mother is seated, with her little sister in her lap, her father by her side, and her mother, a very old person, beside him. There is also another picture of the mother with her little Ume's hand in hers, and this seems to be a pleasant picture to the little wanderer. She does not seem to be at all homesick, and her companions say that she has never been unhappy since she left Japan. The two older ones are graceful, sprightly, and attractive, although not beautiful, and are very neat in their habits and persons. The other two are full of mischief and glee, making the house ring with their merry laughter. They are anxious to assume the American garb, and are impatient to have their wardrobes completed at once. They do not use any paint or powder, as has been asserted, and have abandoned their pomatums, hoping thereby to be better enabled to arrange their luxuriant hair in the American bushy style. They are all exceedingly polite and gentle in their manners.

It having been intimated to these girls, on their arrival in San Francisco, that they ought to be, or might be, supplied with jewelry, the older ones declined any such arrangement. They said that their Government had been very kind in sending them here to be educated, that the expenses attending their education would be great, and that they would be perfectly willing to dress in the most humble manner until their return to Japan. And these are the people whom some of the fools of America would treat with ridicule!

It may be mentioned that, although the majority of the Japanese in this country seem anxious to see the women educated, there is to be found an occasional dissenter, one of whom happens to be at school in Norwich, Connecticut, and is the brother of one of these young girls; and, on hearing that his sister was coming with the Embassy, he wrote to Mr. Mori that he was opposed to the educational system for women, and hoped that he would not send his sister anywhere in his vicinity, but would keep her under his own eye. It should be added, however, that he subsequently discussed the matter with Mr. Mori in person, and was at once converted to the more enlightened doctrine, and is now very glad that his sister is in this country.

It is generally supposed, as we learn from a Japanese, that the nations of Asia pay little respect to ladies, and it is true, in many cases. This degradation of woman unfortunately arose from mistaken views, inculcated in the philosophy of China, for Chinese classics found their way into Japan much as those of Greece and Rome did among scholars of western nations. He also says that "from the earliest dawn of *our* recorded history, women have enjoyed equal rights with men, and, although abuses may have crept in among our lower classes, womanhood has never been degraded in Japan. Whatever customs have been introduced in among the lower classes, through the pernicious teachings of Chinese literature, they have been constantly resisted by our better classes. Never original to Japan, our efforts have been to eradicate them as fast as possible. In proof of these assertions, I refer to our ancient history, showing that out of one hundred and twenty-four sovereigns, rulers of Japan, eight empresses are included in the list. These ladies ruled long and wisely. Under the rule of an empress, Japan attacked and conquered Corea, after a brilliant campaign, which country she held as a dependency for over six hundred years, when, finding it had become more care than value, we voluntarily relinquished it. Under the rule of an empress, Japan attained high literary culture, religion was inculcated and respected, and facilities for general education were greatly improved. China never had an empress. Throughout most of the countries of Europe and Asia, lines of hereditary descent have been wholly male; but I am happy to say, Japan has prospered under eight such reigns. Finding our ancient practice confirmed by the experience of western nations, Japan need not hesitate now to enforce among all classes that respect and consideration for woman which has never been wanting about her Court, and among her better families. Thus may Japan hope to insure the *stability* of her civilization, and regain her early chivalry, and, by enlisting the assistance of educated mothers and daughters, secure a noble future."

While the women of Japan are not treated with very great respect by the male inhabitants, there is an old law which has existed for hundreds of years, and which is yet, in spirit and letter, rigidly enforced, by which a mother, in Japan, is held responsible for her children. If they are good, she receives all the credit; if they are bad, she is punished. Their young minds are singularly free from all evil tendencies, and it is something almost unseen or unheard of, to find unruly children. They are singularly obedient, and are taught habits of courtesy, and an abiding faith in a mother's influence. The only exceptions to this rule are those naturally depraved persons, who are to be found wherever the sun shines. In the main, however, the Japanese race are polite, attractive, charitable, and noble. One of the earliest faiths instilled into the mind of the young of both sexes, is that which forms so important a part of their religious belief, and this faith is inculcated in them when they are but prattling babes, learning to lisp their own language.

The story is that of one of the earlier princesses, who, thousands of years ago, was a ruling power in the Great Land of the Rising Sun. Her virtue, her honesty, and her integrity, are discoursed upon at length, and the children are taught that they must emulate her illustrious example. In order that they may do so there have been placed in different parts of the islands temples to the Goddess Issa. In each of these temples are to be found a precious stone, large, pure, and polished, a mirror, and a sharp sword.

The application is as follows: They must ever preserve their honor and their virtue as a precious jewel. In deciding upon important questions, or in the lesser affairs of life, should there be any doubt as to the proper course to pursue, or should they imagine they are not acting as prompted by the heart, they look in this mirror and examine their own eye. The eye being the index of the soul, the gazer can the more easily determine the honesty of his intentions. Then, satisfied that he is right, the seeker after knowledge takes the sword and defends his faith to the death.

In Japan there are but two classes or grades of society, those who are of the nobility, and those who are not. They never intermingle, and it is only the latter that are ever seen on the streets or in public.

The wives of common people will walk abroad; but a lady never goes except in a close carriage.

The prevalent pagan sentiment of inferiority creates this disadvantage. They are completely subject to their husband's orders, and even should he be willing for his wife to go abroad, the inexorable law of caste would interpose objections. They are, in fact, in unwholesome restraint.

The present experiment of sending females to America to be educated will doubtless prove a successful one, and the selection made would seem to insure a happy result for Japan.

# PART II.

## THE JAPANESE STUDENTS.

The total number of Japanese students who have visited America is estimated at five hundred, but the number now studying in this country is about two hundred. They are chiefly congregated in the New England States, and New York, New Jersey, Pennsylvania, and Maryland. Nearly the whole of them are supported by their Government, a few by their rich relatives, and perhaps half a dozen by themselves. Their annual expenses average about one thousand dollars, and all the money is received by the students through their Minister in Washington. The institutions which they attend are various in character, and have been selected, in each instance, so as to meet the peculiar desires of each student, in view of his future profession or position under the Government; and the official reports which are regularly sent to Washington, prove conclusively that the sons of Japan are quite equal to those of America in their intellectual progress, their morals, and general good conduct. One distinguished teacher in New England remarked that if all the Japanese resembled his scholars, he would like to move his school to the Empire of Japan. Another gentleman, who had closely studied the manners and habits of the students in his charge, on being questioned as to his intention of going to Japan, quietly remarked that he hoped so, because he wished to *improve his own education* in some important particulars. Professor J. D. Butler of Illinois, who had the privilege of travelling in the West, by railway, with a party of twenty-nine newly-arrived students, furnishes us with this testimony:—" I have never seen a more promising set of students. Each has two swords—his badge of nobility—but these were almost all packed up in the baggage, and instead of such vanities, most had books, each on his seat or table; not merely guide-books and maps of the route, but lexicons, grammars, and polyglot phrase-books. When weary of gazing at corn-oceans, and the grain in harvested wheat-fields, each would be busy with his books or writing.

"There was no drinking, no cards, nor any game. I should have thought myself in a school, but for the pipes, with bowls not half as big as thimbles, which appeared in homœopathic smokes." Commodore John L. Worden, of the Naval Academy at Annapolis, on being questioned by the Secretary of the Navy as to the conduct of the Japanese students in that institution, gave a full account of their studies, and paid them this compliment:

"The conduct of the Japanese students has been, as I have stated, excellent, and so far from their interfering in any way with the discipline of the academy, the example they have set of amiability and strict regard for regulations, has been worthy of all praise. They have been and are now subject in all respects to the same rules and routine as the cadet midshipmen of the academy, even to attending morning prayers and divine service on the Sabbath. In the latter regard, their seeming interest and respectful deportment is not at all behind that of their Christian fellow-students. They add nothing to the expenses of the academy, as all charges are paid by their own Government. From the character of the young Japanese who have been admitted to the academy, the interest they take in their studies, and their seeming susceptibility to the influences by which they are surrounded, I do not think I am wrong in auguring the best results to American interests in Japan, as well as to the common cause of Christian civilization, from the wise provision of Congress by which a limited number of her young men are permitted to be educated at this institution."

Looking upon Mr. Mori as their protector in this country, the more advanced students have naturally fallen into the habit of sending to him some of the results of their school education, and the papers which follow have been selected from the hap-hazard collection thus made. The opinions they entertain are as various as their characters, and we happen to know that on several occasions Mr. Mori has thought it his duty to censure these students for uttering their sarcastic remarks, for it is his chief desire that the kindest feelings should be cherished between the Americans and Japanese. Some of the essays are written by very young men, and many of their apparently severe assertions were uttered more from a love of fun than from unkindness. If some of them are rather severe upon certain discreditable phases of American life, it is because the writers have a quick eye to discover the truth, and the honesty to tell us what they really believe. So far as our observations have gone, they enjoy going to the American churches, and what they sometimes say of religion does not prove that they have no proper respect for sacred things, but that they cannot overlook the fact, that mere profession of Christianity is a delusion and a mockery. Nor can they be indifferent to the fact, that some of the most deplorable calamities and internal troubles in their native land have grown directly out of the conduct of the Roman Catholics, in trying to usurp their government; and the more cultivated of the people, as well as the masses, cannot see any great difference in the designs or general deportment of the different Christian sects. This is, of course, unfortunate, but not strange, and the Americans who come in contact with the Japanese are in duty bound, by their upright example, to eradicate, as time progresses, the prejudices against true religion which prevail among the Orientals.

That the Japanese are very close observers of character and of the ways of fashionable society, is pre-eminently true, and on this point a single illustration occurs to us which is worth mentioning. On questioning a resident of Washington as to his reasons for not going to parties, he replied as follows: "Because I am not a man, but only a boy; I am over twenty-one years old, but mentally only a boy. A jacket becomes me better than a swallow-tail. After I have studied five or six years longer, I may be fitted for parties, for drinking, and smoking, and dancing, but not yet. When I have become a full man, I may possibly indulge in such elegancies. I do not think these are the accomplishments in which my country is anxious to have me successful." Now this very student is one of those whose hostility to sham churches cannot be overcome, and yet the plain, frugal, and unselfish manner of his daily life is simply heroic and Spartan-like.

When we come to consider their intellectual characteristics, it will not be easy to estimate them too highly. If we may judge of the gallant two hundred, now in this country, by the few specimens whose productions are printed in this volume, they are abundantly able to compete with students of any other nationality. In their native language they are all liberally educated; and when it is remembered that, with one or two exceptions, none of them have been studying English for more than five years, and a large proportion not more than one or two years, their ability to read, speak, and write good Anglo-Saxon is most amazing. There is one young man, not yet twenty years of age, a taste of whose quality will be found in this volume, whose style of writing is clear, correct, and pointed, and would serve as a model for many professional American writers, and yet he has been studying the English language less than four years; and the thoughts of this writer are quite equal to his style. Another youth, who has been in this country only fifteen months, furnishes a paper which would not be out of place in Addison's *Spectator*. Among our contributors is one, a little older than the preceding, whose sarcasm, analytical style, and comprehensive views, must surely make him a power among the rising statesmen of Japan. If that empire is to be favored with leaders made out of such materials as we have just mentioned, she may well anticipate a career of intellectual greatness. Several of the shorter essays that we publish were written by a mere boy, not over fifteen years of age. The ready adaptation to western forms of expression which all these essays exhibit, forcibly illustrate the fidelity with which the Japanese assume our Anglo-Saxon characteristics.

While these Oriental students generally present rather a demure appearance, they are fond of fun, and when opportunities occur, enter into harmless frolics with great zest. One of them, in a private note which he sent us, makes this allusion to the advent of the Japanese girls: "I tender my sincere thanks to you on behalf of my sisters, who are expected from Japan; but, I pray you, do not initiate them into that western custom among ladies, of henpecking their husbands. Beyond the broad Pacific such an awful thing must not be practised." The same young man, who had gone to Boston to study law, wrote the following: "I succeeded in securing a private teacher for *each* of my three new friends, and also their boarding-houses; but I can't get any place for myself. Thoroughly disgusted with this state of affairs, I instructed my solicitors, Demosthenes, Cicero & Co., Elysium, to purchase for my benefit an elegant residence on Beacon-street. As I was getting ready to leave this noisy hotel, and establish myself in my new residence, a most astounding answer to my *positive* order arrested further proceedings on my part. Substance of this was—Almighty Dollar did not see fit to trust me."

Another youth, from whose room in a boarding-house a favorite book had been taken away by one of the literary boarders, wrote a letter to his landlady to the following effect: "Is it the custom of this country to convey away one's property without asking? I thought my room was my castle. I should be very much obliged if you would acquaint me with any custom of which I am ignorant."

With regard to the habits and physical characteristics of the Japanese students, a passing word may be acceptable. They dress handsomely, but without ostentation; they enjoy our American food, and are generally very temperate in their eating and drinking; and a large proportion of their spare cash is expended for books, and such things as are calculated to elevate the mind. Their sense of honor is exceedingly acute; their confiding dispositions and liberality are proverbial, and hence they are frequently imposed upon by unworthy men; while they are by no means clannish in their feelings, they treat each other with the greatest kindness and consideration,—often excusing an erring brother, rather than reprimanding him; and in their deportment among themselves or strangers, never forget that they are gentlemen. With very few exceptions, they are all quite young,—more of them less than over twenty years of age,—and, although oftentimes delicately developed in their persons, yet they enjoy more than an average degree of good health. Of all who have visited this country, we believe that only three have died here; and this remark carries our mind, with most touching reflections, to a little spot of ground in New Brunswick, New Jersey, where these children lie buried, and where others of their race, in future years, may join them in their dreamless sleep, far, far from their native land. It is pleasant to know, however, that the footsteps of the departed, under the skies of America, are lovingly remembered by many who knew them when they were living, and saw them consigned to the little spot which is the common property of the Japanese brotherhood in this country.

But now, as good examples are more convincing than generalities, we propose to exhibit the pluck and enterprise and wisdom of the Japanese young men generally, by sketching the career of one of their number. To give his name would afford us the greatest pleasure, but we have made a promise not to do so, and, from the excessive modesty of our friend, we expect to be scolded for even making this allusion to him. But his career has been so remarkable, we cannot refrain from giving the leading particulars of his life,—carefully avoiding the mention of certain proper names.

He was born in Yedo, in 1844, and after acquiring a little learning in a native school, studied navigation, and became the secretary of a local prince, who had purchased an American ship, and was trying to do business in that line. On one occasion, when this vessel was about to sail for Hakodado, our young hero volunteered to go as an assistant of the native captain, whose knowledge of sea-navigation was limited, and in that port he remained a number of months, supporting himself by teaching a priest of the Greek Church the Japanese language. He there became acquainted with an English clerk in a commercial house, and with his help acquired a little knowledge of the English language. To that friend he spoke in confidence, and told him that he believed the Almighty intended him to be of some use to his fellow-men, but that he could do nothing in Japan, and was resolved to leave the country. In due time, with the help of his friend, he found a ship in port, which was commanded by an American, and bound to China; he sold his Japanese clothes, and with the money he had earned by teaching, secured a passage on the vessel, going on board in the evening, and hiding himself in the cabin until she was fairly out to sea on the following day. When the captain found his passenger a mere boy of twenty, and well-nigh destitute of means, he arranged to let him work his passage over the Yellow Sea. In China he remained about nine months, wandering from one port to another, now acquiring a knowledge of the Dutch and English languages, and then teaching a merchant's clerk the Japanese language, or working as a cabin-boy, and sometimes as a sailor, on board the coasting vessels. At Shanghai, he became acquainted with the captain of an American ship, to whom he expressed a desire to go to America. The captain took an interest in the Japanese waif, and arranged to take him on board as a passenger—the passage to be paid for by mending and washing the captain's clothes, keeping his books and the cabin in order, and instructing the American in the secrets of the Dutch language; and in this manner he made a full payment for his passage to America. He arrived in Boston, and was employed for about ten weeks as a watchman on the wharf where his ship was lying. The captain had become attached to him, and introduced him to his employer. That good man asked the youth what he wanted to do, and the reply was, "I wish to obtain an education." Arrangements were made, and he was immediately sent to an appropriate school; and between an academy and a still higher institution, he has spent the intervening six and a half years, to the present time.

From the hour that this young man first began to study he has been animated with the single thought of becoming a preacher of the Bible in his native land. In the early part of his career as a student he went to work and translated into Japanese the greater part of the Gospel of St. John. When he came to the sixteenth verse of the third chapter, it riveted his attention and a new light began to dawn upon his mind. He felt that he had never before been a true Christian, but now it was as if a great load was lifted from his back, and all doubts and fears were at once, and forever, cleared away, and the world was full of sunshine. He subsequently always spoke of that passage in the Bible as *his verse*, and he has never ceased to wonder at the goodness of God in protecting and keeping him in a happy state of mind.

Very soon after Mr. Mori's arrival in this country he became acquainted with the history and position of our nameless student, and reported the same to the Home Government, requesting that he might at once be made an official student. The request was promptly granted, the offer made by Mr. Mori, and was very gratefully but decidedly *declined*. The reasons assigned by the student were, that he wished to be free and independent, to pursue his long-cherished idea of becoming a missionary in Japan. He fully appreciated the summons which had been sent to him by his Government, declared himself as truly loyal to the Tenno of Japan, but felt that he could be a more useful friend of his race by pursuing the course he had marked out for himself,—and what was more—his highest allegiance was due to that Great Being who had thus far been his best friend.

When the Japanese Embassy arrived in Washington, the student in question was summoned to Washington by Mr. Mori, who renewed his former proposition, which was again declined. His services were needed in connection with certain proposed plans connected with education; and on the ground that he should be treated as an hired servant and not as a Government student, he went to work for Mr. Mori, and acquitted himself with marked ability and faithfulness; and he was also assigned to the pleasant duty, by the Embassy, of accompanying the Japanese Commission of Education on an exploring tour among the educational institutions of the country.

With regard to his future course as a missionary and a teacher, he is yet undecided. He hopes, however, to leave the United States in about one year from this time. Should he then find that the laws in Japan against missionaries have not been relaxed, he will go and become a simple school-teacher among his people, waiting patiently for the time when he can become a teacher of the Bible. In Japan, as well as here, he will be free from all government patronage, and he has an abiding faith that, when in want of funds, he can always obtain an abundant supply from the good people of the United States.

One more incident, illustrative of another phase of our friend's character, and we will close this notice. Leading, as he has now done, for nearly seven years, the life of a hard-working student, he has, of course, required some relaxation. This he has obtained by visiting the sea-shore or the mountains.

In the former case, his favorite resort has been the home, on Cape Cod, of the good old captain who brought him to this country from China, and where, until the old sailor died, about a year ago, he was always treated as one of the family. And of his mountain-tours, we can only say that one of them was performed on foot to the White Mountains, accompanied by two friends, when he was absent for nearly six weeks and only spent thirty dollars—three of which were paid out for photographic pictures. The pedestrians started with a tent, but it turned into an "elephant," and so, after tramping about twenty-five miles per day with knapsack and staff, and obtaining their meals at farm-houses or from the berry-fields, they usually slept *in clover*, in the barns which were at hand as the sun went down, and to which they were always kindly admitted. This whole expedition was one of great interest, and a minute account of it would make an interesting volume.

We are sorry to say that a promised essay from this student on the importance of making Christianity the foundation of all intellectual culture in Japan, was not received in time to be printed in this volume.

# STUDENTS' ESSAYS.

## THE PRACTICAL AMERICANS.

### By E. R. Enouye.

Is it a disgrace to the Americans that they are a practical people?

Before entering into the discussion which the theme demands, let me define the position from which I am obliged to look at this delicate question. Japan, before the late revolution, was undoubtedly the most aristocratic nation in the world. As is usually the case under such circumstances, the down-trodden mass of the people strikingly manifest that characteristic which is the subject of my present essay—namely, an acquaintance only with those ways of life which relate to the supply of the actual wants and necessities of mankind. This is because, the greater portion of the nation's wealth being in the hands of the ruling class, the lower classes have to make the most of everything within their reach. I, like any other thoughtless born-aristocrat, despised this tendency of the commons. I acknowledge now that this was very unjust, but still something of this spirit will no doubt influence me in the decision of the great question now before us, and I request my kind readers constantly to bear in mind this circumstance.

When Columbus revealed to the astonished inhabitants of the Old World this continent, with its boundless resources, unappreciated by its simple natives, the terrors of the yet unexplored Atlantic were not sufficient to keep back the bands of adventurers who soon flocked from all quarters to this newly-discovered land. Disregarding the rights of the original owners, they appropriated to their use whatever they could obtain, and it was not long before bitter quarrels among themselves began. Mexico had its Cortez, Peru its Pizarro; but that portion of the new continent now the United States of America was contended for by the English, the French, and the Dutch. They settled in various localities of the country, and by their conglomeration was formed the United States of the present day.

The Americans, who unmistakably inherited the virtues as well as the vices of their ancestors, are a nervously energetic, enterprising people. When they threw off the British yoke, what remained was to develop the hidden resources of the country; and how well they have performed this the present prosperity of the country sufficiently attests. In the course of this stupendous undertaking they were being continually brought into contact with new difficulties, and they have always proved themselves equal to any emergency.

The world is indebted to the Americans for the steamboat, telegraph, and many other very useful inventions. It may be broadly asserted that whatever had a practical application was studied and improved by them. A glance at its educational system enables one to form some idea of the people. The cities have their business colleges, while agricultural colleges dot the face of the country. Then there are schools of engineering, architecture, medicine, and other departments of the useful arts, and these are faithfully attended to, while the general education of the youths is designed to make practical men. The fine arts, which refine, ennoble, and delight mankind, are sadly neglected. The fact is, an American does not want to be a painter, sculptor, poet, or rhetorician, but a rich man. Wealth is the sole object of ambition of the people at large. I must say now that I am entering on very serious grounds. I am not so presumptuous as to attempt to trespass on theology, but I must confess I shall go very near the frontiers of it. The Americans who point the fingers of scorn against the rest of Christendom as lukewarm in the cause of religion, and freely condemn without fair trial the rest of mankind as ignorant of the duties of man, seem to think that money-making is the most important business of life; and, taking this as a standard, I shall finish the rest of my essay accordingly. It is not possible that the Americans should be such enthusiastic champions of Christianity, and yet reject its teachings in their ordinary life.

But Christianity teaches them that their souls live after their bodies, and therefore they must better the condition of their minds by the cultivation of virtues in this world. The money-loving Americans are doing just the opposite of this. So-called business men, who constitute a large portion of "the life and the blood" of American society, seemingly have no souls, for they are exposed for sale, if not already exchanged, for hard cash. When their souls are disposed of they receive the millions of money they desire; but what is to be done with it?

Without sympathy, without frankness and generosity of feeling, despising human nature, they have no more use for their riches than the Peruvians had for theirs before the

Spaniards came to rob them. Some men find delight in the fine arts, in philosophy, in science, in the exercise of the benevolent and social affections; but they have no relish for these. They can no more detect beauties in them than a savage can appreciate all the intricate combinations of harmony in music. As to religion, they consent to pay their pew-tax, and to be bored by an occasional sermon on Sunday, for appearance sake; but their real churches are their counting-houses, their real bible their ledger, and last of all, their real god is not Almighty God, but "the almighty dollar."

If money-making is the source of enjoyment to them, as drunkenness and gluttony are to some men, I have only to say that their taste is a corrupted one. It is but just to say that the riches of these men are gained by hard, patient labor; hence they are more to be pitied than condemned, for the question again returns, "What is to be done with these riches, and what have they made themselves by the operation?"

Another set of men, thinking this a rather unprofitable way of making money, adopt a system which combines both theft and perjury, and insures to those men a life of misery, which they richly deserve. I refer to those who seek fortune by a lucky marriage—an excellent mode of self-selling! A man who is so degraded as to go through a formal loving of an innocent, confiding woman for the sake of her money, shows a disposition which, if an opportunity presented, would sell country, religion, anything and everything which mankind so sacredly prizes. All these things arise from that intense love of money which is so deeply ingrafted in the hearts of the Americans. If they should pay more attention to philosophy and the fine arts, they would be far more intellectual as a people; but as long as they are admirers of wealth, no matter how gained, they are merely practical and inconsistent people. Inconsistent, because priding themselves on their republican simplicity, they are the most willing slaves of fashion; or pretending to be true republicans, they are never so happy as when they have an opportunity of paying respect to a prince or a duke. Where is the trouble? The answer is plain. They are too practical.

When Franklin, than whom there cannot be a more practical American, with all the simplicity of Cincinnatus presented himself before the court of Versailles, even the ultra-royalists could not withhold the veneration due the man for true dignity, and he commanded the respect of even the bitterest enemies. Compared with this glorious spectacle, the idea of the Americans of the present day, with much money, trying to imitate the manners of other countries whose teachers they might well become, and making bad blunders, is really disgraceful. In their eagerness to educate all the young persons to be practical, they almost neglect their moral training. Man is both an intellectual and moral being. He must be so educated as to develop both these capacities. If his intellect is trained more than his moral nature, he will be a dangerous man, for his power for evil is increased beyond measure.

In this connection I may again observe a strange inconsistency of the Americans. Though they thus neglect their moral training at home, they send missionaries to teach the wretched heathen to be good, and at the same time send a company of practical men who show their practicability by extracting the riches in every way, and when they could, by cheating those men whom their fellow-countrymen undertake to teach—to be what?—to be good!

So I might go on, but I think I have said enough to make you acknowledge, at least to yourself, that it is a disgrace to the Americans that they are a practical people.

---

### THE CHINESE AMBASSADOR IN FRANCE.
#### By M. Toyama.

The dwarf of yesterday is the giant of to-day. He who appears a dwarf before a giant, appears a giant before a dwarf. He who behaves politely, even timidly, before a greater one than himself, behaves haughtily and confidently before a weaker one than himself. A cat is to a mouse as a dog to a cat. M. Thiers is to the Chinese Ambassador as Bismarck to Thiers.

In the recent interview between Tchong Hoan, Ambassador of the Great Empire of Tsing, and M. Thiers, the illustrious President of the great French Nation, the heathen Ambassador was taught by the Christian President how in Christendom the weaker is to be kicked by the stronger. If the speech by the Ambassador sounds very funny, with so many pompous adjectives, and so much servility, the reply of the President sounds so haughty and commanding that there is no doubt he has already thoroughly learned the Bismarckian style of addressing a weaker one, from the frequent practices exercised upon himself. But Bismarck makes a consistent speech, while Thiers makes an inconsistent one.

Let me see how he goes on. He says: "The French

nation is too humane to take pleasure in the shedding of blood." But if there has been any nation since the creation which has taken pleasure in the shedding of blood, it is this very French nation. Again, he says: "It demands only that severity which is necessary to restrain the wicked." Well, if it is so, the relations of the victims of the recent barbarous executions in France, in cold blood, would have been more fortunate, and a grand funeral procession would never have taken place in New York on Sunday, the 17th of December, 1871. Again, he says: "Your Government is too enlightened not to appreciate the merits of those missionaries—men of great worth—who expatriate themselves in order to spread abroad throughout the world principles of civilization, against whom evil-disposed persons have not feared recently to excite the popular hatred."

What is meant by these merits? Are they serviceable for France or the Pope? And what is their worth? These missionaries might perhaps be worth a good thrashing, for expatriating themselves in order to spread abroad throughout the world superstition and sectarian fanaticism instead of the principles of civilization, which are directly against their interest, and to meddle with politics, disturb the authorities, and cheat the people under cover of the sacred name of religion. A great many good authorities are witnesses to how much mischief has been brought upon the world, instead of good, through the work of those French and Spanish missionaries. It would be a pity if the Chinese Government is too enlightened to appreciate the merits of these missionaries. Suppose that they are the real ministers of the Gospel. In that case they had better stay at home, because their hard labor would be more necessary there than anywhere else. If Paris does not require as many missionaries as the whole number among the heathen Chinese, Sodom must have been a pretty holy place. Well, this is really a conceited world!

Again, Thiers says: "The people will respect the foreigners when they shall see their own magistrates treating them with respect." If this is true, M. Thiers is accusing himself. How can he excuse himself from so many hard complaints of outrages committed upon the Prussians by the French, because this is not done by the French people, but by the French magistrates? If such is the case, no compassion would be felt toward the magistrates for the troubles arising from this direction, but they ought to be effectually punished. Thiers might say that the French have a great deal of prejudice against the Prussians; so the Chinamen have many prejudices against the foreigners, especially against those nominal Christians who might be called the Shylockian Pecksniffs. It does not always follow that the magistrates do not respect foreigners when the people do not respect them. Is there any Government which treats foreigners as respectfully as that of the United States? Yet look at the oft-repeated outrages committed upon the Chinamen by the people of the United States. Does M. Thiers think that this is because of the lack of respect for foreigners by the magistrates of the United States? If even the people of the more cosmopolitan United States, whose motto is universal intercourse among nations, have such prejudices against some foreigners, how much more could it not be expected from the ignorant people of conservative heathen China? The hatred of foreigners occurs in two cases; when the people have mere prejudice against them, and when they have real cause of hatred on account of their haughty or impudent conduct, their disrespect to the natives, their disregard of the laws of the land, and, most of all, their violation and ridicule of their most sacred customs, which drive sometimes even the more civilized people into madness.

But in most cases these two causes are joined; this is at least the case with the hatred of foreigners in the eastern countries. How can foreigners expect to be respected by the natives when they do not respect the natives? They are not to expect from the heathen Chinamen that they should let them smite their other cheek when they have smitten their right cheek. This is indeed too much for the heathen. Here is the merit of which Thiers spoke. When they have converted the nations to perfect Christians according to their mould, and insinuated their passive doctrines into their innocent minds completely, then is the time when foreigners may smite both cheeks of the natives, disinter the dead bodies, kidnap their children, without incurring any hatred, nay, be still beloved by them all the more. Such is the invaluable merit of those Roman Catholic missionaries. Then there would be no need of those silver-headed heavy canes for coercing the will of the natives summarily. The conduct of foreigners, excepting some of the better class of the missionaries and a few laymen, is a very shame to the name of Christianity and civilization, and retards the progress of both. They do not pay the prices of things they buy, and even the boat-fares required of them; but no sooner do they observe a shadow of discontent in the face of the person who demands it, than the heavy cane is over his head. At home such behavior would be properly chastised by indictment for assault and battery, but in the eastern countries the European tyrants are under the protection of guns and powder; moreover, of that sacred cross of St. George, or the Tricolor. So that, whenever they treat a native outrageously, if he do not lose his senses he would keep his anger to himself, because, if he resent it, the fate of his darling country would be endangered even by the loss of a single hair of theirs.

There is no mystery in the fact that Christianity has not made any considerable progress beyond Europe, when we know that those Christians who go out to foreign countries behave themselves worse than the heathen, or, at least, no better than they. First of all they are the slaves of Mammon, go to houses of ill-repute, swear without almost any cause, insult the natives, kick and beat them, and behave as haughtily as Julius Cæsar. Moreover, these things take place on Sunday more than any other day of the week, because on other days they have things of more material interest to attend to.

It is in vain that some really good Christians try to persuade the natives that Christianity is the true religion of God, while they are beset on all sides by these splendid specimens of nominal Christians; and when they look back at their conduct they would not find any reason why they should feel particularly ashamed before Christians. A traitor is worse than an enemy. Yet these nominal Christians are such. How can one be blamed when he cannot find out the right way, when he has no guide? But how could one be excused when he goes a wrong way by his own perverseness and wicked intention, when he has a sure, infallible guide? The eastern nations could not help being heathen, because they had no good guide to take them to the right path. But among the western nations was there not an infallible guide who sacrificed himself for their sake? Those who call themselves Christians, yet behave quite unlike them, are far worse than the pure heathen; while, if there were no such mock Christians, Christianity would have made its progress smoothly. It loses credit through their conduct among the ignorant heathen, and its progress is thus obstructed. Woe to the betrayers of the Master! If He should appear in this world at this time, He could scarcely recognize his own people. Oh! Has He shed his blood in vain! May we hope that God will forbid that! We can get over any difficulty when we are in earnest. Our way is always open when we are willing. Lack not your will, that is the only passport to pass the gate! Let those true Christians who are going to enter the gate, and wish to take with them as many fellow-creatures as they can, pay more attention to their followers, purify their camp first, then go out to the expedition. A rotten root can never bear a good fruit.

But I have digressed too much. To return to the foreigners talked about by M. Thiers. I think that before the Frenchmen can teach the Chinamen how to respect foreigners, they should first learn how to do so themselves, because it was for their want of such respect that they were lately caught by the Prussians. Perhaps Thiers has learned the evil consequences of this want of respect for foreigners, by his recent experience, and may have spoken with a true kindness, lest China might meet with the same misfortune. But I am afraid that although the President has learned to respect the stronger, he has yet little respect for the weaker, as I do not find much respect for the foreigner in his late speech addressed to the Chinese Ambassador. Even the Indian Commissioner here in the United States addresses the Indians in more respectful words.

Thiers also says: "It is again the province of the Chinese Government to show by its attitude and by its proceedings, with respect to diplomatic and consular agents, the extent of the special consideration which is due to their public character, by virtue of the rules universally received among all nations."

There is nothing to be said if this is reciprocal. Why, is there not likewise a proper conduct for diplomatic and consular agents universally received among all nations? They, as the more civilized people, should first set an example as to the decorum to be observed.

But, in the eastern countries, many Catacazys would go with impunity.

## CO-EDUCATION OF BOYS AND GIRLS.

### By Shioji Takato.

In music, there are a thousand instruments, each differing from the other in its pitch and sound. The object, however, is not to separate them, but to unite and harmonize them, so as to produce an enchanting melody, which can never be obtained from any single sound. So the object of God in creating all things and beings, and giving them forms and characters differing one from another, is, no doubt, to unite them and produce a temperate and accomplished whole. The burning wind of the tropics uniting with the freezing blasts from the poles, causes the mild and temperate clime, where spring-flowers smile and spontaneous products grow. God has given the man a character bold and strong; the woman, one mild and gentle, differing one from the other as the piercing sound of the flute from the soft tones of the harp. His object is evident in itself, and requires no solution. Look at the nations who are treating woman as a slave or as instrument of their sport, they are very low in their civilization, and, like wild beasts, are constantly biting and fighting.

From the law of God, and the instances furnished by those nations, I see then, clearly, that the characters of the sexes must blend and help each other; or otherwise great discord in the music of nature will be the result. Female colleges and academies are excellent and important institutions; but they have nothing to do in the matter of tempering the characters of the sexes. Only in co-education of the sexes can we secure both ends at once: the cultivation of their intellects and the harmonizing of their characters. In thus co-educating, we teach them in the same school, by the same professors, and with the same books; therefore, during the entire session, from day to day, and from month to month, the opinions and purposes of the sexes will gradually and naturally harmonize; the saucy mischievousness of the boys will be tempered by the gentle politeness of the girls, and the vain fancy and timid weakness of the girls will take on the primitive simplicity and determined steadiness of the boys; and, at last, a moderate, accomplished, and unblemished virtue and culture will be attained by both the sexes. Some say, the wives of officers have nothing to do in the offices, and the wives of merchants do not interfere with the business; consequently, for woman there is no need of such an education as that required for man. The opinion is worthy of the farmer in the old story, who, thinking that the trees, and not the ground, bore the fruits, scattered his fertilizers over the leaves and boughs of the trees, and left the ground unenriched and uncultivated. But, ere his boast of the new economical invention spread to his neighbors, all his trees had died. If we are able to make the world fruitful by cultivating man only, leaving woman a desert, the trees of the farmer should have borne the fruit.

When a tree is young it easily bends; a pin for a post and a thread for a rope are enough to twist it into any shape. A small rivulet can be stopped or led in any direction without difficulty, even by a single hoe in the hand of a child. But after the tree has grown into a towering trunk, with its boughs mingling with clouds; or after the rivulet has become a mighty river with billows on its surface, and carrying down millions of tons of soil every year, nothing in the world can either stop the one or bend the other. It is plain, then, that if we teach men from their youth, the effort will be successful, and we have no doubt of success in the attempt to harmonize the sexes by co-educating them from their youth. The great disadvantage of co-education, as urged by many, is that it will make young gentlemen and ladies too intimate, and occasion objectionable associations.

But what is the province of the school, and what are the subsequent relations of the sexes? The school is not the place in which reading and ciphering alone are to be taught, and the subsequent relations of the sexes is not to be that of opposition and isolation. It seems then, to me, very foolish, that men should attempt to prevent the occurrence of injuries by keeping their children separated closely one sex from the other. Two country people once caught two young foxes and brought them home to domesticate; A put his fox into a yard with domestic fowls; while B kept his closely hidden away from the sight of fowls, fearing that the fox would catch them. But to the surprise of B, A's fox did no harm to the fowls, but played with them, and slept with them, though it grew big and strong. So B, following the example of A, let his fox loose and free among the fowls that had been kept away from its eyes. But again, to his surprise, his fox caught one of the fowls and fled away with it. If we co-educate the sexes from their youth, as A did his young fox and fowls, I am certain that they will agree and dwell in concord, and no trouble will occur, provided the rules in the school are perfect and carefully observed. But if we should follow the policy of B, I am afraid, or rather sure, that at the time when the sexes reach their full age and are set free, the pic-nic and the party will become a scene of wrong and a field of shame, as when B's fox ran at large among the fowls of the yard.

## ORIENTAL CIVILIZATION.

### By Yashida Hicomaro

[A Dissertation delivered at the Annual Exhibition at Monson Academy. This student is probably better read in Latin and Greek than any other of the Japanese. On account of his impaired health he was obliged to visit Europe, and has since returned to Japan.]

Since the time when the world was proved to be spherical in form, by its circumnavigation by Magellan, the terms oriental and occidental have not been used with strictly scientific accuracy; for the United States of America are east of Japan, and yet Japan is called an oriental nation, though in fact it is occidental in relation to them.

Notwithstanding this geographical absurdity in their application, still these terms have, in history and literature, a signification which is well enough understood, since the term oriental designates those countries and whatever belongs to them, which are south and east of the Black Sea, while all Europe and the American Continent are spoken of as occidental.

It is an evident and remarkable fact, that, throughout the East, a striking uniformity exists as to the type of civilization called oriental, relating to ideas, customs, habits, and manners, though it includes many different races, nationalities, and religions. So there is in the general character of western or occidental civilization a general uniformity which is very evident.

Why there is that marked distinction in the character of a people, which is expressed by these general terms of locality, I cannot understand. The difference in the local condition and character of mankind are infinite, and cannot be determined definitely.

We know what changes are produced by the vicissitudes of time; but, notwithstanding the infinite diversity in the condition of mankind, we know that human nature is the same everywhere and always; that there is unity in the consciousness of mankind in all places alike; and all are animated with love and hatred, with grief and fits of passion.

Men in every land have conscience, or the power to judge what is right or wrong in acts. Integrity is as highly valued in Japan as in the western nations. In the great cities of the West, such as London, Paris, and New York, the degraded classes are not unlike those who live in the great emporiums of the East, such as Calcutta and Yeddo.

Persons not conscious or reflective, are apt to treat unfairly and unjustly, with conceited biases and prejudices, such facts as these. Bound as I am by so much love and sympathy for the oriental country to which I belong, I may carry philosophy too far, and flatter too much the civilization of the East; and yet I cannot but regard the East as being the cradle of civilization, and as the earliest source of light of every kind which relates to the arts and philosophy.

The eastern nations mirrored forth their intellectual life before Greece and Rome began to exist, and long before other European nations, whether Teutonic or Celtic, were anything but strictly barbarous, being buried in utter darkness and ignorance. Long before the ages of improvement in the West, the faculties of the mind, endowed by the Creator, were not undervalued in the East. The metaphysical speculations of India, and the theologico-philosophical doctrines of the Vedas, were not surpassed by the Greek or Roman writers. The uninspired wisdom of Confucius made the nearest approach to the divine morality of the gospel. The rationalistic discourses of Loo reached a climax of excellence. The pantheistic theory of the philosopher Hagel was understood in the East very early.

It is certain that very long ago in the East there were many theories, systems of philosophy battling each other with various forms and principles, just as we now see these conflicts going on to-day in the western world.

By this I infer that the theories of social life, and ideas or opinions concerning philosophy, metaphysics, morality, and theology must continue to battle each other as they always have, from the earliest times; that opinions and systems will conquer and be conquered, will rise and fall again and again, as the history of the human mind and human nature shows in all ages and countries, East and West.

We trust and earnestly hope that, by and by, this process of struggles will bring all thinking minds into a certain equilibrium as to the matters of belief and right action, though that end we have come far short of, as yet.

If we turn now and ask for reasons why Asia, long the seat of so much mental activity and conflict, and the source of so many systems of philosophy, should now be sunk into such utter darkness, why the progress in philosophy made in ancient time should now be checked, and why social life in all its forms and institutions should now be confined, as it were, by mechanical rules, there are many reasons, of course, to account for this; such as despotic government, the organization of caste, the vain formalities of social etiquette, which are each and all especially paralyzing in their influence, and so preventing the progress of civilization. But the greatest, the most specific and essential obstacle of all which retards and holds us back, is the total absence of freedom in the spirit and in the mind of the people. This lack of freedom has tended to the result which in turn has become a great hindrance to progress, that is, a want of that flexible and versatile character of mind which once so distinguished the Greeks, and is not wanting among modern occidental nations. If this want of flexibility and versatility must remain as the fault of the eastern nations, then they must decay continually. Social stagnation and utter decline is the great danger of our people, unless they are shaken out of this lethargic condition by some vehement convulsion.

We look to the western nations for this hoped-for wakening power. The steamship, railway, and telegraph, are pushing their mighty forces further and further into the profundities of oriental life. The quickening effects of western activity and enterprise are felt everywhere, and are causing rapid and more surprising changes in many respects. As to the final result, western influence on the national character and civilization of the East no doubt will work counter changes, and have great reactive power. History has shown us that changes in civilization have been intensely slow in their beginning, and often very rapid in the latter stage of assimilation.

I firmly hope that the people of my native land will soon incorporate many of the noble ideas and principles of the western world into our own institutions; especially that we, as a nation, may be able to penetrate and understand the eternal truth of God and his great providential scheme. Then, I trust, our ancient civilization will become more noble than ever before, and especially, so I trust, that the great empires of the East will cherish and maintain a magnanimous spirit, so that they may forget and forgive every injustice long practised by some of the western nations; and also remember, with amity and good-will, the kindness of those nations, especially the people of the United States of America, who desire to do them good.

## HISTORY OF JAPAN.

### By T. Megata.

[The subjoined was delivered as a Lecture before the Lyceum of West Newton, Massachusetts. Tanetarow Megata is about twenty years of age, and has been in this country only since October, 1870. He speaks English very fluently, and writes a neat, bold hand. He has here given the first lecture ever spoken by a Japanese in this or any other land. His subject was "Japan, its History, Recent Reforms, and Present Social and Religious Condition."]

The great crusading army that, with the power of all Europe, planted its cross in the East, brought back no news from the extremest East. Marco Polo, the great traveller in the thirteenth century, first mentioned the existence of the islands lying in groups east of China, by the name of Zipango. He says, in his great story, that the country is fertile and abounds in gold, silver, and other valuable metals. This was the first time that the existence of the islands came to the knowledge of the world. Though in a later time the Portuguese and Dutch came to the islands for trade, yet there was no intercourse with other nations until about nineteen years ago, when the doors that kept the nation without being known to others were knocked at by the hands of Commodore Perry, who was sent from this country to make a treaty of commerce with us. The name of Japan, by which it is now known, arose from some mistake among foreigners. The whole islands are known among the natives by the name of Niphon, which is given by foreigners to the largest island of the group. The real history of the country goes as far back as 600 B.C., when there reigned an emperor who, coming from the western part of the country, subjected it entirely to his dominion, and became the founder of the present dynasty of the Mikado. Some time previous to this emperor there was another by the long name of Ten-show Dai-jin, which means "the great spirit of the celestial splendors." This emperor is believed to be the true founder of the present dynasty of the Mikado, as well as of the religion of Sinto. But his history being old and obscure, we take the former for the first era of the history of Japan. From this emperor, who reigned as far back as 600 B.C., our present Mikado is descended. The present Mikado is the 127th monarch of this noble family. This is the singularity of our imperial family, and causes us to respect it with utmost love. As for the religion of the country, there are several sects. First, Sinto; second, Buddhism: third, Confucianism; the latter of which can hardly be called a religion, as it does not teach about the worship of any god. Of the religion of Sinto, its founder was, as I said above, the Emperor Ten-show Dai-jin. This old religion teaches about the worship of One Supreme Being. Though it admits the worship of other deities, yet it never makes idols. This religion has a great resemblance to the Grecian mythology. Divine honors are paid to meritorious emperors and other personages. Those who taught this religion lived in the same way as the common people did. They had their houses near the divine temple and attended its worship. But they are now abolished. Their temples are left in ruin; their estates have been confiscated. Second is the Buddhist religion, which was introduced from Corea during 439 A.D. It had once a great power in the country. This religion is divided into eight different sects, each differing in doctrine more or less, but believing in the same faith.

The lecturer then gave a concise history of Japan from the most remote periods to the recent revolution and the changes introduced by the intercourse with foreigners. He then continued: Since the revolution the institutions of our Government have undergone a complete change, and now resemble those of America or the other countries of Europe. The Government is divided into eleven different departments. The Prime Minister and privy councils constitute the Cabinet of the Mikado. The House of Representatives is an important part of the Government. It is similar to the Congress at Washington. Each province of the Empire sends its delegates to the capital, as each State in this country sends its delegates to Washington. Like India, or some other country of Asia, the people of Japan were divided into a certain number of castes. They were divided into four different classes, viz.: First, military class; second, husbandmen or farmers; third, mechanics and artists; fourth, merchants. Among these castes there existed great distinctions of customs and feeling. Their occupations were hereditary. The son followed the occupation of his father. The military class used to enjoy more privileges than the rest, and were supported by revenues paid by their tenants. The class of husbandman or farmer ranked higher than the other two. Different from other countries, in Japan the resources of the Government and the people were obtained from the taxes laid on the products raised by the husbandman more than those on other articles of merchandise. From these circumstances they ranked higher than the other two classes. These distinctions of caste are most disadvantageous in a nation. They create a different feeling among them. During the last few years, however, these things have been rapidly changing. The costume of our people was rather peculiar. We wore long and loose robes. The climate of the country being mild, our clothes were rather for covering than protecting our bodies. So it was a common thing for us to go out bareheaded. There were few distinctions between the clothes of men and women. The ceremony of marriage and death bore rather different characters from those of other nations. In marriage the most important thing is to get the consent of the parents, or, in some cases, that of other relatives, without which the law would not protect them. Before the marriage both the bride and bridegroom choose a gentleman and lady as the proposers of the marriage. Then a present of a dry fish and some flax are exchanged between the parties. This custom shows the simplicity in which our forefathers lived, and warns both to live in harmony and frugality. At the appointed day the bride is taken to the house of the bridegroom. The proposers of the parties preside on the occasion. The chief ceremony is then performed, viz.: the bridegroom takes a glass with drops of wine and offers it to the bride, which is returned to him again. After the ceremony a banquet is given, which is followed by music and dancing. The ceremony of the burial of the dead is rather similar to that of other countries. The late political revolution has produced an entire change in social affairs. The whole country has, since that time, undergone a complete change. That strong feudalism that had its sway over the country during the eight centuries, was abolished in a single year without shedding of blood. At the same time the power of the Mikado, which was absolute before, became very much limited. The reformation of education was made. Our Government stimulates education by a sort of compulsory system, and sends out its students to foreign countries to bring back the acquirements of others. At present there are about 400 or 800 students abroad pursuing their course of studies. The building of railroads and telegraphs is encouraged. The object of Europeanizing or Americanizing the country is executed with rapid success. The changes which had taken place during the last nineteen years, since the opening of the country to foreign intercourse, are entirely new to the eyes of the people who were born some thirty or forty years ago. When we knew not others, we felt ourselves proud and superior; but when we know them, we feel our inferiority, and struggle to take the same step with them. We owe much to the United States. The United States was the country that entered first into a treaty with us; or, I say, that the United States was the country that awakened us from our sleep. We are like a man who, waking late from his sleep in the morning, goes to work hastily. We have slept too much. But we have now waked up from our long sleep. We are struggling to trace the same road of civilization wherein you have advanced. Happy will be Japan, when she attains her desire to teach the highest degree of civilization for which she aims.

## CHRISTIANITY IN JAPAN.

### By Tozabro Hyash.

[The writer of the following account of the Christian religion in Japan acquired his knowledge of the English language in America as well as Europe, and after his return to Japan, was employed as a clerk and interpreter at the American Legation, in Yeddo. The facts communicated by him were drawn forth by a request made by the American Minister, and by him transmitted to the Department of State in Washington, in 1871.]

In reply to your request for me to state to you in brief what I know about the history of Christianity in Japan, and the present condition of native Christian converts, I beg leave to state: That about the sixteenth century Christianity was propagated with so much success in the country, that the Tycoon, Nobunagaya himself, is said to have confessed his belief in the faith. A certain essential part of a castle is always built in imitation of the steeple of a Christian church, which the chief of the castle at times used as a place of worship. This part, which is called "Tenshu," (meaning, dedicated to the Heavenly Lord,) continued to be built long after the prohibition of Christianity in this empire, thus proving that this religion was still, for some time, tolerated among natives.

The Christian missionaries, seeing their growing influence over the consciences of the people, commenced to meddle with the politics of the state, whereupon the Dutch warned our people of the danger from this. Acting upon this suggestion, the Government prohibited its propagation, and compelled all foreigners, except the Dutch, to leave the country.

At the siege, and subsequent fall of Osaca, the final victory of the ancestors of the Tokungawa family was gained, and many leading officers who were in the city escaped to

Shimabarra, near Nagasaki, where the people generally professed Christianity, and excited them to open insurrection, by deluding them into the belief that the Government intended to prohibit Christian worship. Those people, laboring under this delusion, rebelled against the Government, and maintained their position for over two years; and soon after they were overcome they still continued to be rebellious and fanatical, mixing their religious belief with party spirit. This caused the Government to take steps to prohibit this worship entirely throughout the empire; therefore, on this account, and not on account of the belief itself, it was prohibited. This is further proved to have been the motive by the fact that Buddhism was not also prohibited, which is not the faith of the Mikado, he being Sintoo in his faith. These things occurred about the year 1630.

At the time Commodore Perry entered Yeddo, the Tycoon made the treaty with him in opposition to the sentiments of the several of the great daimios, who, having long been jealous of the Tokungawa clan (of which the Tycoon was a member), took advantage of the anti-foreign sentiment of the people, then prevailing, and pretending also to make war to uphold the religion of the Mikado, rebelled against and overthrew the Tycoon, and put his majesty, the Mikado, on the throne in his stead. In fact, they made use of the Mikado as a puppet, to execute their desires in his name, and seemingly by his authority.

The present Government, owing to its declarations, was necessarily severe against any who followed any foreign religion. Against those who professed Buddhism—which being generally professed in the Empire—they took measures only against the priests, who were deprived of many privileges hitherto granted to them.

Whatever promises may have been made by it relative to the mild treatment accorded to native converts, their punishment continues to be severe and cruel.

Under the late Government the punishment was the crucifixion of the convert, but by the law of this Government the punishment extends over eight families, to wit: parents, grandparents, elder and younger brothers and sisters, uncles, aunts, sons, daughters, grandchildren, and male and female cousins of the convert, and is death. It certainly has done away with the punishment by crucifixion, but simply doing this can hardly be called mild treatment.

Those converts who were imprisoned year before last would have been killed according to this law, but for the remonstrances of the foreign representatives. They are yet kept in close confinement.

\* \* \* \* \* \* \* \*

In reply to your request for me to give you the definition of the term "Meidi," I have to say: The Emperor of Japan gives a certain title to the year when he ascends the throne, and thus counts the years of his reign as first, second, third, fourth, etc., of such title. Formerly, if there occurred during the course of his reign any great calamities, such as great earthquakes, famines, tempests, etc., he would change the title, and commence to count the years anew from that time, thinking the title unfortunate and productive of bad results. This superstition was originally introduced here from China about one thousand two hundred years ago. The usage has been so long in force here that the people have become accustomed to it. "Meidi" is the title given to the year by the present Emperor at his succession to the throne, which was four years ago, this being the fourth year of "Meidi."

By the present law of this empire, our Emperor is not allowed to name the year but once during his reign; therefore the present title "Meidi," which means "peace," after enlightened manners, will continue until the present Emperor dies.

## THE STRENGTH AND THE WEAKNESS OF REPUBLICS.
### By E. R. Enouye.

The republican form of government is now generally conceded to be "theoretically the best," but its claim to be also the strongest is still disputed, or at least not yet firmly established. The Declaration of Independence by the American Colonies, the French Revolution, and various important subsequent events, until the present time, all unite in proclaiming to the nations of the world the right of a people to govern itself, and by so doing demonstrated clearly the absurdity of the divine rights of the kings to rule.

The whole political heaven is, as it were, being charged with republican electricity. The explosion will come sooner or later. Meanwhile, the diffusion of intelligence among the people makes them more enlightened and more jealous of their rights than ever before; despots tremble on their thrones, and as they make concessions most reluctantly, most readily do the people call for more. Judging from such circumstances, it would appear that all the nations of the world, as if by common consent, are converging rapidly toward that point where Republicanism reigns supreme.

It is then a matter of the utmost importance to us to endeavor to discover in what lie the strength and the weakness of republics.

Nothing is more plain than the theory of a republican government.

There is a body politic composed of so many citizens. It is an impossibility for the members of a State to assemble in a body to make their laws; hence they elect a certain number of the citizens as their representatives, who transact business for the whole people.

In a republic, every citizen is interested in any measure before the government, and it would be safe to set this down as one of the great elements of strength.

The government is influenced, to a great extent, not by the opinions of a king, or, what is worse, those of a few ambitious politicians, but by the mighty voice of an almost infallible people. It is evident that the government thus situated will be more faithful in the execution of its duties than in monarchical countries, where the character of the government depends a good deal on the disposition of the sovereign. Another strong point in a republic, is the bicameral feature of its government. One body acts as a check on another, and, if their characters are different, for instance, the first radical, and the second conservative, the course of legislation will be neither too progressive, with which the people cannot keep pace, nor so conservative as to interfere with the enterprises of the country. The right to struggle for fame, for learning, and wealth, is the grandest heritage of humanity, and this right is most scrupulously respected in almost all the republican countries of the present day; hence, the poorest and humblest can have fair play to become superior in position to any other.

This state of things keeps the people ever in activity.

We can hardly think it otherwise. In whatever direction an individual may go, his energies for the advancement of his position in life, his actions, are fettered by no arbitrary laws, but, on the other hand, every encouragement is given to him for the success of his enterprise. If, thus favorably situated, men are poor, it is no fault of the government, but their own. What, perhaps, exerts a most powerful influence in the affairs of the republic is undoubtedly a spirit of competition. The highest honors of the State are within reach of the meanest citizen. Men love honor, and we are sorry to add, they love wealth and power just as much as honor, if not more; hence the perpetual struggle for the offices of the country. As a very few succeed, they will be qualified for their posts, at least intellectually, if not morally. We said perhaps not morally, because, in the tortuous way which a politician takes to the object of his ambition, he too often treads on the grounds which are clearly forbidden by his conscience. The government composed of such materials cannot fail to be strong. If the government of the Jacobins was guilty of the most atrocious deeds, it was beyond all question the most energetic body which France, perhaps the world, ever saw. In order to appreciate the enormous amount of work which that body accomplished, we must hastily glance at the position of France at that time.

The whole circuit of France was begirt with enemies. Disunion within and difficulties without did not stop here. Her commerce was destroyed by the invincible navy of

Great Britain. The provisions were scarce. Never was a country in such an appalling condition. How they encountered and overcame these difficulties we shall not discuss. If we go back a few years in the history of the world, we shall find the true strength of republicanism displayed in the American war. We do not purpose to look at that memorable contest in all its bearings, but will content ourselves with an observation illustrating one of the secrets of the success of the Americans. Every historian has dwelt with enthusiasm on the retreat of Washington through New Jersey with a few thousand of the barefooted and famishing soldiers. Was it the devotion to their illustrious commander which enabled those brave men to encounter so cheerfully the manifold dangers of that disastrous campaign?

No, noble Washington did much, but the real strength of the army lay in the fact, that every soldier was also a citizen, imbued with a hatred of the tyrant, and conscious of fighting in the cause of freedom and humanity.

When we see so much dignity in common soldiers, we shall not be dazzled by the sublime spectacle of the Revolutionary Congress defying the power of the strongest nation in the world, often fleeing before the victorious foe, yet firm and unyielding, and, at last, after a long struggle, giving the country a glorious peace, and placing her by the side of the proudest nations of the world!

Thus far, we have looked at the strong sides of the republic. Now we shall investigate some of the causes of its weakness. "When you assemble a number of men to have the advantage of their joint wisdom, you inevitably assemble with those men all their prejudices, their passions, their errors of opinion, their local interests and selfish views."

The history of every republic too clearly illustrates the above remarks of Franklin. Grant that all the legislators chosen are conscientious men; they determine to be true to their sacred trust. But alas! they do not, nay, cannot, agree as to the best method of promoting the interests of their constituents, for nothing is dearer to a man than his theory; and especially is this true of such upright men as we suppose them to be. And then, a particular member, in pleading the cause of his constituents, may badly interfere with carrying out of a measure which will be beneficial to the whole people as a nation. It may be contended that the majority will rule; but, if our supposed member happen to be also an influential man, he may so exert his powers as to cause the very majority to enter into his views.

Now, for the working of the machinery of the government by such persons. A good deal of valuable time is consumed in making a law for, not saying of the various forms being attended to; the members advance their respective opinions, some of which are at direct variance with one another. It may be all right in a time of profound peace, but there are times when the destinies of a state depend on the passing moments. To deliberate under such circumstances will not only be foolish, but ruinous. To remedy this evil, the ancient Romans found it necessary to create the office of dictator. We have hastily glanced at the bright side of the republican institution, and, as regards its strength, we are not very well satisfied with our observation.

This is the case when we supposed that all the legislators are honest and sagacious men. Throwing this Utopian vision aside, let us look at the stern realities.

In the first place, it will be admitted that the officers of a republic are not always the best and ablest men of the land, but that they sometimes are the most cunning, perhaps the most unprincipled.

By the most unprincipled, we refer to that class of politicians called demagogues. These persons rarely succeed in securing the confidence of the respectable portion of the people, and when they do so, they cannot retain it long.

To the mere outsiders, they would seem to be wholly incapable of doing any serious injury to the state. But when we study the effect of their proceedings, we shall be very likely to change our opinion. Too often have the glories of the state been tarnished by the disgraceful conduct of these men, too often their impudence, vulgarity, and recklessness have so prevented an enlightened statesman from carrying out his plans, that they deserve to be set down as at once worse than traitors.

At the head of this class of men stands Alcibiades, the name closely connected with the events which resulted in the ruin of the Athenian greatness. Lavishly endowed by nature with the qualities of a great soldier and statesman, the darling of the Athenian democracy, graceful and beautiful, in fact, with all the means of being the first man and the greatest benefactor of his country, he proved himself its meanest trickster, its most mischievous citizen. In a republic, a constant change of officers exerts a very baneful influence, and is the cause of bitter political and party strife. Thus there can be no stability in the government. And the stability, it must be remembered, is an important element of the strength.

Beholding a republic with her weakness and strength

before us, and a monarchy with hers in the same position, we shall fear the latter as our enemy, for she is strong, but the former we shall love as we love the truth; we shall encourage as we would an inexperienced youth, for her strength is not yet as fully developed as that of her elder sister, monarchy!

## JAPANESE COSTUME.
### By N. Kanda.

It is not uncommon for both nobility and peasantry in Japan to walk in the street without wearing anything on their heads, while the Europeans wear hats or caps out of doors. But, in the summer, when the sun is very hot, only the men wear large rounded hats about a foot and a half in diameter, to protect their faces from being burnt by the sun. And the women carry parasols which are always made of paper, and often men carry them too. They have two kinds of umbrellas, one for protecting them from the hot sun in the summer, and the other for the rainy weather, called an "amagasa," which is also made of paper, and afterwards spread over with a certain oil, and dried. In the cold winter days, the men and women wear almost the same kind of covering over their heads. They are sometimes made of soft crape and sometimes of camlet, and are made in different styles. But one of them I will explain. This is made in the shape of a Shaker-bonnet, only not so stiff, and it has a little longer cape. Now, I will describe how the men dress their hair as well as I can. It is a good deal longer and coarser than that of the European.

They keep it long, for they want to arrange it, and coarse, because they shave their fine hair in childhood.

The hair of the men is generally arranged by a barber once in two days, with a quantity of hair-oil, and so they don't comb their hair every morning. It is almost of equal length, and is tied or arranged in an indescribable manner, and it is commonly shaved off the width of two inches from the forehead to the top of the head, which is generally done at the age of fifteen. The hair of the women is gathered, and tied in bunches, smaller than those of the Europeans. And they tie around it beautifully dyed crapes and red corals, and stick through it, from one end to the other, the long four-cornered tortoise-shell pin, made by putting a number of them together, and warming and pressing them, till the whole appears like one pin of shell, and it is then polished. I have now written all about their heads, and I will next speak of their bodies.

There is not much difference in the shape of the common dresses of the ladies and gentlemen. But there is a difference in the noble ladies' dresses, which have trails like those of the European ladies. But, of course, there is a difference in the materials, almost as much as there is in the Europeans'.

The dresses are made very long, which are about as long as the length of the vest and pants, and are twice as wide as the common European coat. The sleeves are like large flowing sleeves, only sewed about half-way up to the arms, forming a pocket. The dresses are made of different materials, according to the different ranks. The dress of the nobility is sometimes made of silk, and sometimes of crape, while the people of the lower class wear dresses of calico, or something of the kind. Both nobility and peasantry wear belts of different material around their waists, as the former and latter wear different dresses. It is a kind of sash, being about four yards long, and about four inches wide. It is doubled and stiffened.

Japanese did not wear such tight-sleeved under-shirt as is now generally worn. However, it was their own custom to wear a kind of drawers under their robes in the winter. It was generally made of silk or a cheaper material, and was dyed dark-purple, or gray, or some other colors, but never white, nor red, nor any light color. They wear socks of cotton, which are generally fastened to feet by means of strings or clasp. The women always wear white socks, and the men wear very dark purple-colored ones. It is made so that big toe is separated from the rest of the toes, in order to hold between them a thong, by which the shoes are fastened to feet. There are many kinds of shoes, almost as many as there are in America. The general name for articles worn on their feet is "haki-mono." Under the head of "haki-mono," there are "ama-geta," which means rainy shoes, and are worn in rainy weather only. They are only made little higher than those which are worn in clear weather; and "hiyori-geta," which are worn in clear weather, and "koma-geta," which are also worn in clear weather. "Koma-geta" is like those mentioned before, made of wood, but of one piece of wood, and cut into the shape of the shoes mentioned before. They are both made without anything on, and with mats of ratan made for the purpose. "Zori," which are made of straw only, are always worn in dry weather, and are worn generally by attendants when they go along with their masters. "Setta," which are worn by both nobility and peasantry, are made better than "zori," though it is also made of straw, and have leather of some animal under them.

---

## A FATHER'S LETTER.

### By G. Neero.

[Giobu Neero is the name of a gentleman who resides in the Province of Satsuma Japan, and who was formerly a Cabinet Minister under the Prince of that famous province. He belongs to a noted family, and was one of the first men in that Empire who advocated a change in the policy of the nation, from a state of semi-barbarism to one of civilization. He took no part in the late Japanese Revolution, and has never been anxious to be connected with the general government. In 1865, on account of his high character and rare abilities, he was commissioned by his Government to take charge of sixteen young Japanese boys, with whom he visited Europe, and whom he located at various institutions of learning. One of those boys is the present chargé d'affaires from Japan, Mr. Arinori Mori. On his return to Japan, Giobu Neero immediately arranged to send his son to France to be educated, and the following letter, written in the latter part of 1871, was sent to that son by his devoted and noble-minded father. It was originally written in the character-as well as letter-language of Japan, and the present is a literal translation.]

I have received your letter dated February 19, 1871. I am greatly pleased to learn of your progress in educational matters and health. It was unlike the former letter. It seems that you have come to know that I do not like to receive from you presents and the like, and this accords with my views precisely. You have said nothing about the great war. This shows that you are earnest in your studies, and it is my sincere hope that you should so continue. It is now five years since I have seen you. As you have reached your sixteenth year, it is proper for me, at this epoch of your life, when you are entering upon the more important objects of your career, to address you with kindest feeling. First, it is a parental duty that a man should sacrifice his beloved son for the sake of his country. Regretting that we have no proper educational system in Japan, I have had fears that my son might grow up without education. It was quite unexpected that I should have been appointed to go abroad in the Spring of 1865. During the voyage I witnessed an incident at Singapore, which I will relate. There were among the passengers a husband and wife, with three children under seven years of age; they had embarked in our mail-steamer, and when it was announced as ready to depart this husband and wife were in utter distress, with sad faces and many tears. The wife remained on the steamer with the children, while the husband had to return to the shore, in a sorrowful state of mind. At the sight of this, two hundred and fifty passengers were struck with grief. There was a perfect silence, as all on board knew the circumstances; but our Japanese, although strangers among foreigners, and having no knowledge of the language, were influenced to sympathize with the party, and we also shed tears. I asked one of the passengers as to the particulars, and he told me that this family were Dutch; they had been staying a long time in Singapore, and their children were born in that place. The parents having determined that their children should receive a good education in their native land of Holland, and knowing that Singapore was not the proper place for them, their object was to educate their children so that they might love them more, and so they had sacrificed all their affections and comfort and pleasure for them. This struck me with great force. Even a small nation like Holland was so anxious to have her children educated, and Holland knows her children would do great things. This influence induced the husband to be satisfied with parting from his wife and sacrificing his happiness. Thus, I came to appreciate those great western nations, like England

and France, where civilization has attained the highest point, and where there is no lack of education; and it was then I determined to send my son to those countries. I arrived in London after a voyage of more than two months, and I employed the time, when not engaged in official business, in the cause of education, and I learned the real condition of it, which was all wonderful to me. I solved the whole problem in regard to the education of my son. As I thought England and France were like two hands, left and right, both essential to civilization, I thought I would send my two sons, one to each of these countries. But, during my stay in London, the sad news reached me that your brother had died, and my grief was great. My mind was then wholly set upon yourself alone. It was my great anxiety to find a teacher for you. I met a French gentleman, Mr. Montblanc, and I told him my views, and that I desired you should be acquainted with political economy chiefly. He understood me well, and assured me he would do his best for you. The above is a brief history of my anxiety and efforts in your behalf.

You were not sent abroad to come back soon, certainly not before the accomplishment of your education. I desire, after you have finished your studies, that you should visit different countries and places in enlightened Europe. You should also visit Pekin, in China, when you return. I am not satisfied with your knowledge of the French alone, but you should also become acquainted with the English language. All these particulars Mr. M. understood and agreed to fulfill.

Second. When I returned home from Europe I begged my parents to send you abroad, and it was gratifying to me that they were so deeply interested, and granted their consent at once. It was not only a blessing to you alone, but to me also. You were then only eleven years old, and you had no knowledge of my earnest desire. There was a strong effort made to stop the movement by friends and relatives, because of your age, and also because of the recent loss of my second son. But I succeeded with great difficulty in appeasing their anxiety. It was indeed the blessing of heaven that you could leave home and could go over the sea ten thousand miles away for such a purpose. This should be borne in your mind deeply.

Third. The principal object of education is to do our most for the benefit of one's country. We use Chinese characters in our country to a great extent, and the letters we have are also derived from the Chinese. As those Japanese you meet abroad will use Japanese or Chinese, and it will be inconvenient for you not to understand them, it was my great fear that you might be induced to think you should learn those languages in order to become acquainted with Japanese affairs. This is a most important time for you. You should be aware of the great object of the future, and not to be occupied in trifling. You should have your whole mind on western education. It will not be too late for you to learn Japanese and Chinese after your return home. It is of the utmost importance that you should not be confused on this subject.

Fourth. For the few communications I have made to you there is some reason. It is from my deep love for you. It is quite natural for one who is still young to think of home when he is in a distant land, but communications from home do more harm than good, because they are apt to excite the feelings, and hence disturb your studies. You parted with your mother when you were not quite three years old, and have been brought up since in my bosom alone. How could my love for you, under such circumstances, be less intense? You should not mistake me for so rarely communicating with you.

Fifth. Your cousin in London felt lonesome and wished to have another Japanese for a companion. This, to me, was a great mistake, and I will avoid it in your case. You should carefully remember that you have gone abroad for a great purpose. You are expected to have, therefore, the highest aims in regard to the future. It impressed me deeply when I learned that Napoleon Bonaparte, when very young, was asked by his mother about his object in life, and said, " that he would like to have all the historical parts of the world in his mind, and to go from one end of the world to the other with a single sword." His age was not then more than yours. I think this is a very good thing for you to consider.

Sixth. I have heard that you told Mr. Mayeda you intended soon to return to Japan. What was your reason for this? The object for which I sent you abroad is already stated fully. I shall only be delighted to hear of your return after you have fully finished your education; there could be no greater satisfaction to me. I fear that what you said was the result of truant thoughts of home. You have to direct your whole attention to hasten the accomplishment of your education. This is the only thing you need. Your last letter to me informs me how you advance, and it is my greatest expectation to see the full development of your capacities. You will try to bear this important idea in your mind. I have read your letter over and over, and I felt as if you were talking to me face to face; and I hope this letter will be the same to you, and that my deep-felt and sole desire for your education will be remembered forever.

## THE MEMORABLE YEAR.

### By E. R. ENOUYE.

The sun of 1871 is fast sinking below the horizon. Before we lose sight of it entirely, let us review the important events with which this year is so closely united.

We are not yet recovered from the shock which we at first experienced in witnessing the utter humiliation of one of the most haughty of the great powers of Europe, or surprise at the glorious triumph of her hereditary foe; or the sudden brightening up of the sky where we saw, in the direction of England, nothing but the dark clouds of war; or, still later, the horror which seized us all at the cry of despair from the west in our own country. We begin our remarks with the closing scene in the Franco-Prussian war. Notwithstanding the assurances of fiery Gambetta, France has finally lost all hope in the prosecution of a successful struggle. As to Trochu in Paris, he is entirely powerless, and all that he is trying to do seems to be the postponement of the inevitable surrender. The cry of despair rises from all quarters. Something must be done or all will be lost. At this juncture Bourbaki makes the last effort for France, but fails signally before Belfort, and his shattered army saves itself from annihilation by taking refuge in peaceful Switzerland. Almost simultaneously with this event, the army of the North, in spite of the strenuous exertion of its brave commander, Faiderbe, is utterly defeated; while the army of the Loire, beaten in detail, has no prospect of offering any resistance to the foe. To complete the catastrophe, Paris falls with a tremendous crash. On the other hand, the Germans, triumphant even beyond their expectation, proceed to reconstruct the fabric of their ancient empire. It lasted one thousand years from its foundation, and having been overthrown by the genius of the great Napoleon, it was thus eventually restored to more than its former greatness by the incapacity of his nephew. King William was crowned the Emperor of Germany in the palace of Versailles.

But where is the sovereign whose dream it was to march to Berlin, dictate peace, return with a large portion of territory secured by triumph over a fallen foe, and as a reward for this service to France was to ask her to tolerate his son on the throne which he usurped? The answer is a sad but conclusive one. He is a lone exile in a foreign land. When, in October, 1870, Prince Gortschakoff issued his notes on the Treaty of Paris, it almost amounted to the declaration of war. It recites the successive violations of European treaties, among them that of 1857. Russia wished to increase her defensive power, especially in the Black Sea, hence she disavowed her obligation to the limited enjoyment of the empire, and invited the Sultan to enjoy equal rights with her. England would have gone to war, but, not to speak of her own decline in power, her trusted ally was utterly prostrated. As to her other ally in the Crimean war, the King of Italy, he had enough to do at home.

Nothing could be expected from either terrified Turkey or

incapable Austria. At this state of affairs, it was agreed that a conference between the great powers of Europe should decide all the differences. This congress, which assembled in London, in the early part of this year, gratified every wish of Russia. She has already turned this to account in the furthering of her own interests. She has built many ships of war, and the work is still going on with great energy.

Sebastopol, Odessa, and other principal ports of the Black Sea are being fortified with great care. We know what all this means, namely, the capture of Constantinople ultimately, and the absolute supremacy of Russia in the councils of European nations afterward. Among the events which have taken place in England, the most important has been the abolition of the purchase-system in the army. Taught by the example of France, and fearing a collision with Germany, she proceeded to put her forces in good condition, which was impossible as long as that absurd custom existed. This was not accomplished without opposition. It almost resulted in the fall of the ministry of Mr. Gladstone. Next, we turn to Italy. Rome is taken by the Italian army, and the temporal power of the Pope is forever gone. All in good time Rome is made the national capital, and that dream of illustrious Cavour, the unification of Italy, is now complete.

Anarchical Spain next claims our attention. In the Duke of Aosta she found her king, but scarcely does he find himself on the shore of Spain ere Marshal Prim, the soldier to whom he owed his throne, falls by the hands of assassins. Ministry after ministry is formed, all to no purpose. Much may be said of her condition, but we will leave young Amadeus to struggle alone with his destiny, and turn our attention again to Paris.

Paris, fighting against whole France, presented us with the spectacle of a ship frozen amid the ice of the polar sea, and its crew, without the means of wintering there, engaged in a desperate contest with nature itself. Such a state of things cannot long continue. Although the provisional government was obliged to temporize at the beginning of this mad revolt, as soon as it rallied its forces it acted with firmness, and punished the insurgents to their hearts' content. The last hours of the Commune of Paris were disgraced by their wanton destruction of those great works of art of which Paris was so justly proud. Well might Madame Roland exclaim, "Oh, Liberty, how many crimes are committed in thy name!" By the fall of France, the republican government is firmly established in France, *for the time being.* We dare not speculate on her future. Who is her president? M. Thiers, the ex-minister of Louis Philippe! This is not an encouraging prospect for France.

Besides, are there not the Bourbonists, the Orleanists, and the Bonapartists, madly engaged in their selfish intrigues? Her destiny depends a great deal on her president. It will be a real blessing to her if M. Thiers proves himself a Washington to France, but we have reason to fear he will be another Talleyrand, who treated his enemies as if they might be his friends in future, and *vice versa.* In America the San Domingo question is agitating the public mind. The president, although he has often declared that he has no policy opposed to the will of the people, seems determined on annexing the island to the United

States, but he is not supported by the people at large. The excitement was becoming greater and greater, when the Administration yielded the point, and the subject was dropped, for the time being; because the West Indies, by their situation, are unmistakably destined at no distant day to form the outposts of this grand republic. The San Domingo question lost much of its importance on account of the Alabama claims, which sought the attention of the nation. This difficulty, together with the so-called fishery question, was the cause of much feeling between the United States and Great Britain. It threatened a war between the two nations; but, after protracted preliminary negotiations, in which the recriminations, evasions, and "assurances of the distinguished considerations" were curiously intermixed, it was agreed that the Joint High Commission should settle all the differences. The result of their labors was the Treaty of Washington, which is justly considered one of the triumphs of modern civilization. By its provisions the Tribunal of Arbitration is shortly to assemble in Geneva, Switzerland. This august court is composed of the members appointed respectively by the United States, Great Britain, Brazil, Italy, and Switzerland. We have every reason to believe that the difficulty will be satisfactorily settled.

An event which called forth expressions of sympathy from every quarter is the great fire at Chicago, which almost destroyed that empire city of the West. We all know how the conflagration was caused by an accident, how the strong wind rendered futile the efforts of its gallant firemen, how the thousands of people were made homeless, how the world poured its beautiful charity into the devastated city. A circumstance which is particularly deserving of notice is that its inhabitants, nothing daunted by the magnitude of their calamity, set themselves at once to the work of reconstruction. Speaking of the Chicago fire, we should not overlook that great fire which raged in the forests of some of the western States.

The completion of the Mont Cenis tunnel is one of the greatest triumphs of scientific engineering, and an event which well-nigh reconciles us to this year, which has been so full of calamities to mankind. The honor of this great achievement belongs unitedly to Louis Napoleon, Emperor of France, and Count Cavour, the Prime Minister of Victor Emanuel. Cavour's immediate object was to establish perfect means of intercourse between two divisions of the kingdom over which his sovereign then ruled; but its importance to Europe, especially France, was so manifest, that the French government agreed to pay half the expense, which is about thirty million dollars. It was commenced in 1857, and completed in September of this memorable year. Its length is seven and one-half miles. It was well France shared the expense, for, by the Treaty of Villa Franca, Napoleon III. wrested from Sardinia the rich province of Savoy, which is one of the divisions previously referred to, as a compensation for the aid to her in the Austrian war. At the advent, this year was enveloped in the thick clouds of war. One by one they have disappeared. Now, sinking beneath the western horizon, she sends us her farewell light in the forms of many scientific improvements and higher civilization; but alas! a cloud still obscures a spot on the earth's surface, over which are written the words, "*The Eastern Question.*"

## GEORGE WASHINGTON.

### By N. Kanda.

George Washington, who was a great patriot, and the first President of the United States, was born in Westmoreland, in the eastern part of the State of Virginia, on the 22d of February, 1732. His father was a rich man, but Washington received only the usual education which any one could receive in this country at that time. He might have been sent to Europe to receive a further education if he had wanted to. Washington knew the French language, which he learned after he became a general, for the purpose of talking with the French soldiers who were sent here to unite with the Army of Independence. Washington was a very good surveyor. When he was but sixteen years of age, he was employed in surveying the great wilderness near the Alleghany mountains, belonging to his relation, Lord Fairfax. Before he was twenty years old, he was made one of the important officers in the army, called Adjutant-General. When he was about twenty-two years old he became an important general in the war of English and French, in America, of 1754, which war lasted for six years, from 1754 until 1760. When the war closed, the Americans hoped that there would be better times, as a new king had ascended the throne, whose name was George the Third. Because, at those times, the governors of the colonies were sent from England, and they oppressed them very much with strict laws. But instead of better times came more troublous times, as follows: During the war just ended the king spent all the money he had, and he asked his advisers how he might get more. Then his advisers said, "Tax the Americans, for they are rich and will not mind it." And men were sent from England to collect taxes. But the people murmured about paying taxes, and disliked them. James Otis, a great patriot of Massachusetts, advised the people not to pay a penny. So the king could not get much money. Therefore the king and his advisers made another law to take the money from the Americans, called "The Stamp Act." But this failed also, by the advice to the people by a great patriot, named Patrick Henry. And again the king and his advisers tried another way to get money, which was to make Americans pay taxes on any tea, paper, glass, painters' colors, etc., brought in ships from England. And, knowing that the Americans would not like to pay, they sent soldiers to compel the people to pay. And this made the Americans very angry. The people in many colonies drove their governors away, and said to the king and his advisers, "We are all ready to fight for freedom; send your soldiers as much as you please." So the Americans now began to strive for freedom.

The first battle for independence was fought in Lexington, near the city of Boston, Massachusetts, on the 19th of April, 1775. They appointed George Washington to be Commander-in-Chief, and several other great patriots as his assistants. Washington first took the command of the army under the elm-tree, still standing, in Cambridge, near Boston, on the 3d of July, 1775. The army was made up of all kinds of people. Their dresses were not uniform, nor were their weapons alike, but some had pitchforks, and some poles, etc. Washington soon changed their dresses and weapons, and made them soldiers.

On the 4th day of July, 1776, the "Declaration of Independence" was agreed in the State House, Philadelphia. So every year on that day, the bells are rung in the morning and at night, and guns are fired. Boys fire crackers from morning till night. After the independence was declared, hard wars continued for eight years in many different places, from 1775 till 1782.

George Washington was Commander-in-Chief of the army all through the war, and gained a great many victories over the British, in many places. He was a great general, and a very brave soldier. When the Americans became independent they thought they must have somebody to govern them, so they chose Washington to be their Chief Ruler or President; and John Adams was chosen Vice-President.

Washington was inaugurated the first President of the United States on the 30th of April, 1789.

After faithfully governing the people for eight years, he retired from his office on the 4th of March, 1797, and went to his home on Mount Vernon, and lived there quietly until the 14th of December, 1799, and he died. His tomb is in Mount Vernon, near his old house, which is yet standing.

## PUBLIC AND PRIVATE SCHOOLS.
### By E. R. Enouye.

It may be universally affirmed that, in every country, public schools were established long after the people were fairly started on their road to civilization. Prior to this period, such learning as was known to the country was chiefly in the hands of priests. At last, a long series of bloody wars has ceased; what had been mere clusters of tents and rude huts are now replaced by more substantial villages and cities; men leave the implements of war for those of agriculture and other useful industries: in fact, all is peace throughout the country. Education of the young no longer consists in mere physical culture, and in the art of war; but some attention begins to be paid to the cultivation of their mental faculties. Now, for the first time, we shall find private schools established, mainly under the auspices of priests, where children of the wealthy are educated. The time intervening between this period and the appearance of public schools, of course varies with different countries, but in all cases are full of most important events in the history of the mind of man.

It would be a very interesting task to investigate these stages of progress, but, as the object of our present essay is merely to discuss the merits of public and private schools, an elaborate history of their origin will not be attempted. Suffice it, then, to say that, by degrees, the diffusion of intelligence among the people demands better facilities for education than that hitherto afforded by private schools; hence the establishment of public institutions of learning. The design of private schools is to secure to the young a thorough learning in every needed department of science, when such opportunities would not be secured by public institutions.

At the present day, most private schools are founded on the principles of home discipline.

When a child enters a private school, he is, to a certain extent, severed from his own home, and home authority is, in this case, transferred to the school. Henceforth, he is to be treated as one of the children of the principal.

As he who can afford to send his child to a private school must be a man of some property, the child in question will find himself in comparatively limited, and at the same time quite a select, company. By a select company, I do not mean the individuals composing it will be by nature more morally disposed than the same number elsewhere are likely to be, but that characterized by the absence of common vulgarity, which is invariably found in most public schools. Though the company is thus small, yet it is sufficiently large to enable one to form some idea of the duties and trials of life to come.

A member of such a school as I have tried to describe above, is peculiarly subject to temptations of learning more serious vices than those he may have to encounter in a public school.

Thrown upon his own responsibility, and daily mingling with a limited number of associates, he soon learns numerous little things, in which the bad far outnumber the good.

And then, like a capricious coquette, he will have his likes and dislikes, to whom he usually gives such elegant designations as "good fellows" and "nasty fellows." Thus, he takes his first lessons in unduly extolling or in hating his fellow-beings. But, as he himself is one of the "nasty fellows," he will be compelled to drink the first draught of this world's bitterness.

In this way, definitions of such words as hate, meanness, jealousy, and false honor, and various others of this class, are indelibly stamped on his wild and inexperienced imagination. But all this falls into insignificance when we contemplate the effect on his morals and after-life of those innumerable little conspiracies which too often constitute one of his chief amusements.

It may be contended that these are nothing more than mere practical jokes, and wholly harmless in their consequence. But when such a view is advanced, we must remember that the disrespect of the child at the fireside has but a step to go to disobedience of the civil and divine law.

Amid all these faults of private schools, as institutions of learning, two advantages secured here are at once so manifestly great as to cause the defects above mentioned to be usually overlooked by their patrons. First, it is only in private schools that a variety of study can be pursued; and, secondly, instruction given is far more thorough there than that is likely to be in public schools. This circumstance is easily explained.

A limited number of pupils being always under the eyes of their teachers, who are generally greater in number in proportion to their pupils than are afforded in public institutions, therefore their scholars receive better attention than in public schools.

Besides this, as the private schools stand only by their reputation, everything is done to obtain this desired object.

Public schools are designed for the general education of the people. The system employed differs in every country, but their fundamental principle is the same, which, briefly told, is as follows: They are founded and maintained at the expense of the people. The necessary amount of money is raised in the form of taxation, and their administrations are in the hands of officers appointed by the government for that purpose.

Such being the case, every citizen has a right to send his child to a public school in his district.

I have said that, in a private school, the company is select; but here the table is turned. In a public school every grade of society, intelligence, and refinement, has its representatives, and usually in such numbers as to overcrowd recitation rooms.

Such being the state of things, we shall not be surprised to find that each pupil does not receive as much attention as might be wished. This, no doubt, is a strong disadvantage of public education, and consequently loudly decried by the advocates of private schools.

Admitting their accusation to be well founded, there is another thing in public schools which almost redeems this defect.

Everything is done so openly and impartially here that scholars soon feel that in order to obtain the honors of the school, they must first distinguish themselves in their studies.

This circumstance fosters laudable ambition among them, especially that strong incentive to faithful labor, emulation. Nobody will question that this state of things will have a most beneficial effect upon their character.

Another charge brought against public schools is, that the course of study is not sufficiently extended for the various requirements of its members.

Those who say this, are thinking only of the interest of a small portion of the community, and not that of the whole, sovereign community.

The mass of people want a simple course of education, which is exactly what public schools purpose to give to their scholars. There is but one road to the field of knowledge, and those who think there are several, will never reach that glorious goal. In a public school, students must pursue such a course of study as may be prescribed; in a private school, studies are, to some extent, at the option of its pupils.

The pupil of a public school, when told what he has to do, in nine cases out of ten concentrates all his energy on the work before him, and comes out of the severe ordeal with something substantial, with which he may begin the arduous duties of life with some hope of success.

In a private school, the case is far different. In the first place, a young gentleman is not sure what studies he will undertake. When at last the important question is settled, he is not pleased with the stern realities of the work. Let us take a case: A young gentleman, besides the regular studies, to which he does not do justice, begins the French, for instance, because it is fashionable, or because he remembers, with chagrin, an occasion when he was laughed at, for writing in a friend's autograph-book "*votre amie*," which elegant phrase was, to his astonishment, translated, Your female friend. By the time he can say "*Comment vous portez vous?"* without reference, he has had enough of the French language, and turns his weary eye to the German, or Latin, in which he will fare no better.

If the critical history of a private school be written, it will be found that it has sent out by far the greater portion of its students to swell the ranks of that class of persons who know a little of a good many things, but nothing in particular to any extent. I think, however, that the chief merit of public schools lies in the fact that the child is not sent away from home at a tender age, the time when his character, still all chaos, so to speak, is just forming itself into some shape, and with whose completion his destiny is to be fixed.

How critical a period this is for him, no sensible man will question.

It is true, that as he goes to school daily, he sees all sorts of juvenile vices, but he does not associate with their possessors to such an extent as to be influenced to a great extent; and even if he is affected a little, there is on hand a good remedy in the love of his parents. The reason why public schools are not fully appreciated, is because there are so many in the country.

Whatever is abundant is very apt to be slighted. Thus, a man once observed, after profound consideration, that the rays of the moon are more precious than those of the sun, because the former we get in the night, which would otherwise be dark, while the latter comes to us in the daytime, when we do not want any light at all. In order to appreciate fully the importance of public schools, imagine them all destroyed. In the course of time the people would be utterly degraded, and only a small minority of the people have an opportunity of education, and also that of exercising a most galling tyranny over the ignorant mass of people.

As men in this state are actually dead to the intellectual world, we cannot measure the loss to humanity of those great minds which, though containing all the power of shining as star of the first magnitude, go out of existence as quietly and as little developed as those of the lower orders of creation. To illustrate this, let us refer to the life of the late Professor Mahan of West Point. We need not here speak of his long, steady, and glorious career. We need not speak of his melancholy death, but let us ask how his great mind was developed. His parents were poor, and, in all probability, could not have given to their son a good education; but the brightness of the boy so attracted the attention of Hon. Willoughby Newton, in whose congressional district he was born, that he became a warm patron of the boy, and sent him to the Military Academy at West Point, thus snatching as it were from the hands of fate, one of the greatest scientific soldiers of modern times. The relation which private schools sustain to public schools is very similar to that between cavalry and infantry in the army. Cavalry can be employed only on the plains. Infantry can be employed under every possible circumstance. It is true, cavalry does great service, but the fact that it cannot act independently, brings it at once to a secondary rank. The same may be said of private schools.

That an army may, if necessary, dispense with the service of cavalry, is evident when we study the campaigns of Napoleon in Egypt.

The battle of the Pyramids, for instance, was gained only

by the bayonets of the French soldiers, against the array which the best cavalry then in the world charged in vain.

In the same manner, public schools can educate the people without any help from private schools. From what has been said, it will be evident that private schools, with all their excellencies as institutions of learning, are but so many squadrons of cavalry, in the army of education; hence we come to the conclusion that the system of the private schools is a strong auxiliary force to that of public schools, but that they ought never to supersede wholly the latter.

## CHRISTMAS.
### By N. Kanda.

Every nation in the world, where the people receive Christianity, observes the 25th of December as a holiday, because it is the birthday of Jesus Christ, the Son of God, who was born in Bethlehem of Judea, a part of Palestine in the western part of Asia, on the shore of the Mediterranean Sea. The mother of Jesus was Mary, the wife of Joseph.

Jesus Christ was sent from God. "For God so loved the world that he gave his only-begotten Son, that whosoever believeth in him should not perish, but have everlasting life." He was on the earth for thirty-two years, preaching the Gospel, and doing a great many miracles; and great multitudes of people believed in him. He had twelve apostles, who always followed him from place to place, as he went preaching the Gospel and doing miracles. There were a great many who did not believe that he was sent from God, and they tried to find some fault in him, that they might put him to death; but they found none, and at last, on a Friday, the chief priests, scribes, and elders held counsel with each other, and bound Jesus, and took him to Pilate, a Roman Governor, who was then ruling over them. And Pilate sought to release him many times, saying, 'Why, what evil hath he done?" because he found no fault in him; but they cried out, "Crucify him," and so Pilate, though unwilling to put Christ to death, but willing to content the people, delivered Jesus Christ to be crucified. And they dressed him with purple robes, and put a crown of thorns on his head, and worshipped him, and struck his head with a staff, and spit on his face. And afterward they took the robes, and put his own dress on, and led him to be crucified. About nine o'clock in the morning he was crucified, and the following superscription was written over his head, "The King of the Jews." And there were crucified two thieves with him, one on his right-hand side, and the other on the left. And that night the Jews who believed on him came, and asked for his body; and they gave the body to Joseph of Arimathea, and he wrapped him in linen, and put him in a sepulchre, and laid a large stone at the mouth of it.

There was a great earthquake very early on the first day of the week, and the angel of God descended from heaven, and rolled back the stone which was at the opening of the sepulchre. "His countenance was like lightning, and his raiment white as snow. And for fear of him keepers did shake, and became as dead men!" And when the women came they found the stone rolled away, but did not find Jesus in the tomb, but an angel, dressed in white, sitting at the entrance. And he spoke to them, "Be not affrighted

Jesus, whom they crucified, is risen, and go to Galilee, and you will see him there." So they and Jesus' apostles went there and saw him. He was on the earth for forty days after he had risen from the dead, and he appeared to his apostles and disciples many times, and on the fortieth day he ascended to heaven, being carried by a cloud, and all his apostles and disciples looked up to heaven steadfastly till he went out of their sight.

Christmas-day, the birthday of Jesus Christ, who came to this world to save sinners, is celebrated as a holiday. In the evening, in some houses is placed an evergreen-tree lit with a great many candles, and on it are hung many round glass balls which reflect the light from the candles, and make the tree look more beautiful. And on it are hung many presents, which are given to each one in the family. The room is shut until everything is ready, and they open the room where the tree is lighted with a great many candles and balls, and the presents are growing on the tree like fruit. And some one cuts the fruit off from the tree, and gives to the person to whom it is addressed.

# JAPANESE POETRY.

The collection of oriental books which forms a leading feature of the Japanese Legation in Washington, has among its treasures a compilation of ancient Japanese Poetry. The work is called *Man-yo-Shiu*, is in three volumes, each one about three inches long, and less than half an inch in thickness, and beautifully printed on gossamer paper. There is also embodied in these volumes a Poetical Anthology entitled *Shi-ku-Shiu*. Some editions of this work are in large type and copiously illustrated. The poems, so called, were written between the years A.D. 905 and 1201, nor are they, by any means, the earliest poems extant. They are numerous, and while some of the more ancient specimens fill several pages, with accompanying notes, the majority do not occupy more than half a page, and others only a single line of Chinese and Japanese characters combined. They purport to have been written by emperors and princes, court minstrels or poets-laureate, by priests and common men; and they touch upon the various themes of love and war, the feelings of joy and sorrow, upon birds, insects, flowers, trees, and all the wonders of nature. Many authors composed all their poetry in couplets, which were executed with skill, and no subjects were too formidable for them to grapple. Some of them are addressed to friends, in the form of letters, and occasionally different parts of a poem are written by different men. For example, if a fortress is reduced, the emperor relates the cause of the war, and the successful and defeated generals give their respective experiences, and thus complete the story. Owing to the mixed characters in which the poems are written—a kind of oriental black-letter—some of them cannot possibly be translated, and those most easily understood lose their peculiar beauty in the English tongue. The collection in question has passed through many editions, and been printed in various styles, but the miniature copy now before the writer was published in Miako, the cradle of Japanese literature, in 1717, and the binding consists of thin paper covered with blue silk.

Before submitting to the public a few literal translations from the little volumes referred to (made chiefly by Mr. Samro Takaki of the Japanese Legation, and formerly a student in New Brunswick), it may gratify the reader to look at a synopsis of the Introduction. These poems, as the compiler informs us, are founded on the human heart. The thousands of words which compose them convey a similar number of thoughts, which are the result of seeing and hearing. As the birds chirp among the flowers, the frogs croak in the still waters, and all animated beings have a voice to be heard, so is it with those who compose songs. They echo the spirit of the universe, and move to pity the hearts of the gods and demi-gods, who are not seen with human eyes, and who have power to prevent famine among the people, cure diseases, and abate the most terrible storms. They strengthen the affections between men and women, soften the passions of ferocious warriors, and have existed from the beginning of the world.

It has come down to the present race in tradition, that the art of poetry originated in heaven, and is perpetuated upon earth by the wise. By direction of one of the early emperors, the poems to be thereafter written were limited to thirty-one syllables, whereas before that time the number was unlimited. But few of those more ancient poems, however, are now in existence. As the art of poetry progressed, it increased the expression of human feelings for nature, until there was found a deep meaning, even in dewdrops, and birds, and flowers. Among all the poems written in the olden times, and in as many as six different styles, there were two which were greater than all the rest, and equal in ability, and these should always be learned by beginners. Some of the ancient emperors, in the " beautiful mornings of flowery Spring, and the moonlight nights of Autumn," were wont to call the members of their courts together, to compose poems on the works of nature, and in that manner they became acquainted with what was in the hearts of their people. And it was in this manner also that many celebrated poems came into existence, which are still cherished and repeated in the domestic circles of Japan.

Accompanying many of the verses under consideration are elaborate notes, connecting them with important historical events and personages. It is related of one of the emperors, for example, that he always composed his poetry by the side of a favorite waterfall; and of a certain prince, that he had been sheltered in a monastery on a stormy night, and having written a poem on the subject, presented it to the institution, whereby it obtained a fortune. Among the most ancient and distinguished women who wrote poetry was one of the Empresses of Japan, named *Soo-tood-hime*, but much of it is said to be "like the complainings of a beautiful girl in her sickness." Among the poetesses who is thought never to have been excelled, was *Onono-Komatch*, and she is remembered to this day with religious veneration. She was originally attached to one of the Imperial Courts of Japan, and her style or power of playing with words, which cannot be illustrated in English, was considered the perfection of art. But on account of the coldness and indifference with which she received the homage of her many admirers, she became reduced to beggary, and as a lonely and friendless minstrel she spent the greater part of her life. For many years she wandered, barefooted, from village to village, selling her treasures of thought and sentiment to any who would purchase them, and teaching the little children who gathered around her, how to recite her poetry on the beauties and sublimities of creation. Very many of the poems in the collection before us have become popular as songs, and as these are more easily translated than the longer poems, the subjoined specimens are exclusively of that character.

These productions are undoubtedly more nearly allied to the lyric than to any other form of composition, although many of them are merely poetic aphorisms; and yet, so far as they are pervaded by one leading idea, they might, barring their length, resemble the sonnet more closely. To the casual reader they may occasionally appear somewhat trivial, but they certainly give us many glimpses into the Japanese mind;—but when we consider their origin and great antiquity, they cannot but be read with interest and pleasure.

Some of the longer poems in the collection are founded

upon the customs, as well as the traditions, of the Empire, and we submit a single specimen, in which the beautiful and the sorrowful are happily combined. Among the numerous holidays which the Japanese formerly celebrated with great care, there were three of them which they devoted to the Festival of Departed Spirits. It occurred in July, between the 13th and 16th of the month. On the first day a fire was built in front of every house in the Empire, which was a signal or invitation for all the departed members of the house to revisit their old homes. A suitable place in each house was arranged, where food of various kinds was kept constantly in view, for the use of the spirits. On the third day another fire was made, and the spirits were supposed to take their departure with the setting of the sun. On that night, as was believed, the fires of hell were opened, and kept open until the dawn; and during the nocturnal period, ceremonies were performed, and effigies exhibited in honor of Satan. With these preliminary remarks, and avoiding everything like a display of learning in regard to Japanese authors and their productions, we submit the following translations.

### Nature.
Among the things in nature which will never tarry for the pleasure of man, are running rivers, fading flowers, and passing time.

### The Cherry-Trees.
We feel not the cold under the cherry-trees, when the blossoms are falling, and there are snow-showers which do not come from the skies.

### The Moon.
There are many ways of climbing a mountain, but all who reach the summit are sure to look upon the same moon.

### Love.
My love is like a rock in the depths of the ocean, which never gets dry and the secret which I cherish is unknown to all the world.

### Illusions of the Snow.

When the snow lies so deep upon the mountains that we cannot see the winding roads, then it is that the villages are brought nearer to their summits, for the valleys are all filled up, and the pathway, as we look upon it, is distinct and clear.

### Parting from Friends.

When compelled to say farewell to a friend, the parting is like a rock which divides a mountain-stream, the waters of which are sure to meet again.

### The Plum-Tree.

Send me your fragrance upon the eastern winds, O flowers of the plum-tree, and do not forget the Spring, because of the absence of the sun! But the sweetness I enjoy only makes me anxious for more, and so I am tempted to go forth and break down your branches, that I may press you in my hands.

### The New Year.

The year is new, and the singing-voice of the night-bird is unchanged, but the plum-tree may blossom in the snow before the coming of Spring.

### Story of the Smoke.

I climbed the mountain (said an emperor, when his countrymen were suffering from poverty), and, looking down, I saw the smoke rising from unnumbered dwellings, and so I was glad to believe that my people were in comfort, for I love them as a mother does her children.

### The Dewdrop.

Having the pure heart of the lotus, why does the dewdrop, reposing on the leaves, attempt to deceive us by pretending to be a gem?

### The Fat Widow.

I am so large, that you could not encircle me in your arms, yet you must remember that a willow-tree is never anything but a willow-tree; and, whether sitting or lying down, I find that my musquito-netting is larger than I need.

### The Rejected Lover.

I wish to tell you (says the lover), that even the smoke on the sea-coast where the salt-makers are at work, is carried off against its will, and thus may it be with you; and (replies the maiden), I might have obeyed your will, but it would have been at the hazard of my good name.

### The Duties of Life.

As I hope, in the future, to be permitted to study and wander among the stars, I must not forget, during my present life, to respect the gods treat my fellow-men with justice, and keep my heart pure.

### The Deer.

As I walked (said an emperor) in a pensive mood, along the woodland-paths, I heard a doe moaning for her lost mate, which had been killed by a hunter, and so I resolved to issue a decree that nevermore should the deer be used by my people as an article of food.

### The Faithful Lover.

If my beloved doubt me, and would know the extent of my affection, she must go and count the waves along the rocky coast of Tago-no-woora.

### Future Life.

As the fisherman, with rudder lost, floats helpless on the waves of Yura, so uncertain will be my future life.

### The Neglected Wife.

You chide me because I went to sleep, but I waited, wakeful and desolate, for your return, until the morning light came up above the eastern sea.

### The Thinking Lover.

To think, when we are entirely alone, is sometimes painful; yet, without doing this, how can the mind of my beloved be brought to enjoy my thoughts of happiness?

### Treacherous Waves.

When the moon is shining, the receding waves of ocean collect its light, and picture it in its fullness upon their bosoms, but soon they dash it upon the rocky shore, shattering it into unnumbered fragments.

### Love for the Unknown.

I do not know when my heart first began to love, but I do know that it is now yearning towards one, of whom I have heard, but have never seen.

### Autumnal Winds.

Mournful, to my heart, are the sounds of Autumn, as I hear them at the twilight hour, passing over the thatched roof of my house, and the rice-fields growing near

### Wayward Lovers.

I am now in the autumn of life, which I had no desire soon to see, and the hearts of the men who once talked pleasantly to me, have wandered after many things besides love.

### Clean Houses

When the houses of a people are kept clean, you may always be certain that their government is respected and will endure.

### Unlimited Love.

Although I have not told it, my unlimited love is well-known to one who is above the skies.

### The Water on the Grave.

I pray, O water, that I have placed upon the grave of my aged mother, you may never freeze under the influence of the winter's cold!

### The Doubting Wife.

I will not blame you, should your absence be long-continued, but you must not gather the unknown flowers that you may see upon the winding roads.

### The Returned Letter.

By sending back my letter you have filled my eyes with tears, and I now see that your love is like a broken foot-bridge across a mountain-stream.

### A Question.

Why? O why? is not the one I love as faithful in keeping her promise as is the beautiful moon in passing across the heavens?

### Perseverance.

Although the walk of a cow is slow, she can, by perseverance, reach the distance of a thousand miles.

### Sadness.

When I am sad my feelings are like the closing year, and looking at the autumnal moon only increases my sorrow.

### Home.

I call that place my home where I happen to be in all the world.

### The Lover's Unkind Message.

I know that you did not send me that branch of the maple-tree as a token of remembrance, but to show that, like its leaves at the close of autumn, you are tired of the life of love.

### The Returned Wanderer.

Long a wanderer from my early home, I returned only to find that my old friends did not remember me; but I remembered, with rare pleasure, the fragrance of the Spring-flowers.

### Unfading Love.

I promised that my love would not fail until the waves of the sea had swallowed up the mountain of Suye, and is it not true that the clouds are still playing around its lofty summit?

### A Robber going into Banishment.

I ask you, O fishermen, who toil upon the sea, to tell the people of my native village that you have seen me in a frail vessel sailing in banishment to the island of Yassoshima!

### The Dancing-Girl.

As I look upon the dancing-girl, I am reminded of the goddess Otone, as she appears in the sky when the clouds are fleeing before the stormy wind.

### The Snow-Shower.

To please the one I love, I went into the mountains to gather the wakana plant for her enjoyment, and I was caught in a shower of Spring snow.

### A Sleepless Night.

During the long night have I heard the chirping of the grasshopper, and while the hoar-frost was covering all the ground I have in vain tried to obtain repose.

### Running from Troubles.

I did not wish to hear about the troubles of life, and so I fled far away to the distant hills, but even there I heard the painful cry of the wounded deer.

### The Cuckoo.

I heard at night the cry of the cuckoo-bird, and when I went forth to see it, I only saw the morning-moon.

The foregoing poems, with few exceptions, are taken

from the collection to which we have alluded. By way of showing to what extent the art of poetry has been patronized in Japan, we submit the following list of the principal books which have been published in the native language, viz.:

*Chok-sen-shiu,* a Collection of Selections made at the command of the Emperor.

*Go-sen-shiu,* Collection of after Selections.

*Jiu-i-shiu,* Collection of Additional Poems.

*Kin-yo-shiu,* a Collection of Golden Leaves.

*Ko-kin-shiu,* Collection of Ancient and Modern Poems, and

*Shi-ka-shiu,* a poetical Anthology.

JUGOI ARINORI MORI.

# PART III.

## LIFE

AND

## RESOURCES IN AMERICA.

### PRELIMINARY NOTE.

The knowledge furnished by all the better qualified minds of the world is a powerful element, rendering great service in the cause of humanity. It is often the case that enmity and bloodshed are the consequence of storing up prejudices, resulting from the want of mutual knowledge of the parties engaged. The object of this publication is not only to aid in removing those prejudices, but also to invite all the lovers of their race, in Japan, to join in the noble march of progress and human happiness.

In view of the fact that many dates are mentioned in this volume, it has been found necessary, for the sake of convenience, to adopt the western calendar altogether, and it is hoped that this course will not lead to any embarrassment in the mind of the reader.

Arinori Mori.

Washington City, U. S., September, 1871.
   Or, according to the Japanese Calendar, the
      *Seventh month of the Fourth year of Meidi.*

# INTRODUCTION.

By the term America, which appears on the title-page of this book, we mean the United States of America. As we are writing for the information of a class of readers who have never visited this country, we propose to speak in as simple and concise a manner as possible. Whatever statements of fact we may make, shall be founded upon the public and other authentic records; and in submitting any general observations, we shall endeavor to steer a middle course, and give only such opinions as are held in common by the people of the country. Before proceeding to the main object of this volume, however, we think it necessary to take a brief survey of the area and population of the United States, as follows: The total area of the Republic, which extends from the Atlantic Ocean to the Pacific Ocean, and, excepting Alaska, lies wholly in the temperate zone, is about 3,830,000 square miles—an extent of surface larger than the whole of Europe; it has a coast-line, including shores of bays, sounds, and lakes, of 30,000 miles, of which 2,800 are on the Atlantic, 1,800 on the Pacific, and 2,000 on the Gulf of Mexico; it is traversed from north to south by two great ranges of mountains, called the Alleghany and Rocky Mountains; its rivers are numerous, and among the largest in the world; its lakes contain more than one-half of the fresh water on the globe; and its population, according to the census of 1870, is not far from 39,000,000, which is a considerable advance upon the population hitherto claimed for the Empire of Japan. In the last 70 years, the increase has been about 33,000,000. Of these inhabitants, it has been estimated that more than two-fifths of them are immigrants, or the descendants of immigrants, from foreign countries. Great Britain and Ireland have contributed most largely to this immigration, and the other countries which have helped to swell the population are as follows, and we mention them in the order of their contribution, viz.: Germany, France, Prussia, China, West Indies, Switzerland, Norway and Sweden, Holland, Mexico, Spain, Italy, Belgium, South America, Denmark, Azores, Portugal, Sardinia, Poland, and Russia, whose contribution was less than 2,000. Of this great mass of immigrants, it has been ascertained that a very large proportion have changed their circumstances for the better. With regard to the black race, who prior to the year 1860 were in a state of bondage, but are now free, they number nearly 4,900,000; the half-civilized Indian tribes, about 26,000, and the wild Indians have been estimated at 300,000. In 1870 there were of Chinese 63,254, with whom were included 53 Japanese, but since then the latter have reached about 250 in number.* The public lands of the United States are so abundant, that every man who settles in the country can afford, with careful management, to have a small farm for his exclusive benefit, as the price of land is generally so reasonable that

---

*It must not be understood that all these foreigners have been naturalized.

it scarcely exceeds, and seldom equals, the rent payable in England. There is no description of produce, European or tropical, which may not be raised in the United States; and aside from its many other advantages, there is no other country which offers so many inducements to people in search of permanent and comfortable homes; and it is the present condition of the people who enjoy this inheritance, with their manners and customs, that we propose to describe in the following pages of this volume.

But, before concluding this introduction, it is important that two subjects should be mentioned for the special consideration of the Japanese people. While we entertain an exalted opinion of what is called a Republican form of government, we confess that it is not without its disadvantages and dangers. For any foreign nation fully to understand them, must require time and much careful study. The Japanese people have been somewhat fascinated by what they have seen of the American government and institutions, and it is of the utmost importance that they should well consider the subject in all its bearings, before adopting any of its features into their own form of government. The evils resulting from the misuse of freedom in America, are among the most difficult to correct or reform, and ought to be carefully avoided. Another fact that should not be forgotten has reference to the educational qualifications necessary to secure success in a Republican form of government. It is undoubtedly true that the best thinkers in America deplore the fact that the machinations of the politicians have resulted in placing the United States in an unfortunate condition in this respect. It has been so profitable with designing and selfish men to increase the number of voters, that they have secured the passage of laws which allow all men to vote, in view of the single idea of personal freedom. This is undoubtedly all wrong, and the evil effects of this state of things are being manifested every day. A prosperous, happy, and permanent Republican government can only be secured, when the people who live under it are virtuous and well educated.

# OFFICIAL AND POLITICAL LIFE.

As preliminary to this chapter, it would seem to be necessary that we should give an outline of the machinery of the American Government. It is twofold in its character: first, *Federal*, because it is made up of States, and second, *National*, because it acts directly from the people. According to the Constitution, it is divided into three branches, viz., Executive, Legislative, and Judicial. The head of the Executive branch, or governor of the nation, is called the President, who is elected by the votes of the people for the term of four years, and is sometimes re-elected for an additional term of four years. He is also the Commander-in-Chief of the United States Navy and Army. The average cost of each election, in money, has been estimated at two millions of dollars, and these expenses are incurred in part by the Government and people. His office is styled the Executive Mansion, and is identical with his official residence, the White House. He is obliged to be a native and citizen of the country, and thirty-five years of age; and his annual compensation is twenty-five thousand dollars. The second officer of the Government is called the Vice-President, whose business is to preside over the Senate. He is elected in the same manner as the President, and his salary is eight thousand dollars per annum. The Executive departments of the Government are seven in number, viz., the departments of State or Foreign Affairs, Treasury, Interior, Post-Office, War, Navy, and of Justice. The heads of these are called Secretaries, and they form the Cabinet of the President. They each receive a salary of eight thousand dollars, and their jurisdiction, under the President, extends to all the subordinate officers of the Government, whether located in Washington or in the several States of the Union. The Judiciary of the country is vested in a Supreme Court, District Courts, and the Court of Claims; the salaries of the Judges ranging from sixty-five hundred down to thirty-five hundred dollars per annum. The Legislative branch of the Government consists of a Senate and House of Representatives,—the Senators, numbering seventy-four, elected for six years, and the Representatives, two hundred and forty-three, elected for two years,—and their compensation is five thousand dollars per annum. The number of States which form the Union is thirty-seven, with ten Territories or incipient States, and their form of government is precisely similar to that of the nation at large; the leading officers of each State or Territory bearing the titles of Governor and Lieutenant-Governor. To the above may be added the municipal form of government for cities and towns, where the local authority is allied to that generally recognized in Europe, where the chief officers consist of Mayors and Aldermen and their subordinates, although bearing different names in different countries. With these particulars before him, the reader will be able to comprehend the following observations. Although the real and official residence of the President is in Washington, the fashionable season, so called, begins and ends with the sittings of Congress, beginning in December and lasting from three to six months. The position occupied by officials, under the Constitution, gives them necessarily a certain rank, according to the importance and nature of the office, the length of time, and the age, required by law, of the incumbent. The house in which the President resides is the property of the Government; and, to a great extent, his household expenses are paid by public appropriations. The title by which he is addressed in conversation is that of *Mr. President*, and every citizen of the Republic, no matter how humble his position, has a right to visit the Executive in person. During the winter he holds public receptions as often as once a week, and on the Fourth of July, which is a National Holiday, and the First of January, he receives, as a special mark of respect, the Diplomatic Corps and the officers of the Army and the Navy in full uniform, himself always appearing without any uniform. He accepts no invitations to dinners, and makes no calls or visits of ceremony; but is at liberty to visit without ceremony at his pleasure. State-dinners are given by him quite frequently, and persons invited commit a breach of etiquette when they decline invitations. The rules of social intercourse which govern the Cabinet Ministers are similar to those recognized by the President. As their tenure of office is limited, they have, in spite of themselves, a very busy time during their whole term of service: spending their days in dealing out patronage, and their nights in giving or attending parties. Their families take the lead in fashion, and all American citizens have an undisputed right to attend their receptions, and, after that public manner, to be fashionable; and as exclusiveness in

7

the President or his Ministers would be considered undemocratic, and therefore would not be tolerated, there is no end to the so-called enjoyments of life. If a Minister is rich and liberal, he becomes, for the time being, the biggest man of the hour, in spite of his politics; if poor, and dependent only upon his salary, the fact of his having to occupy a large house, and to entertain the people, invariably sends him into retirement a poorer man than he was before. With the Judges of the Supreme Court these matters are somewhat different. They are the only dignitaries who hold office for life, and they can afford to do as they please, and generally please to lead the quiet lives of cultivated gentlemen. They go into society when the spirit moves them, are not disinclined to partake of good dinners with their friends, a Foreign Envoy, or a Cabinet Minister; and perhaps the greatest of their blessings is, that they are not compelled to curry favor with the multitude.

The next layer of Washington society to which we would allude, is made up of the Heads of Bureaus and the Officers of the Army and Navy, their pay ranging from ten to two thousand dollars per annum. They are the men who more immediately manage the machinery of the Government, and upon whom, to a great extent, depends the success of all the public measures enacted by Congress. Though generally well paid, many of them cannot afford to display much style, although they live comfortably, and generally in their own houses, although many officials reside in boarding-houses or hotels. The civil officers are but seldom appointed on their merits, but usually through political influence; and the party which happens to be in power commonly claims all the patronage, and the most worthy and competent men are often dismissed from office without a moment's warning. With the Military and Naval officers the case is somewhat different, for though they may get into office through political influence, they are usually appointed for life, and are not removed without cause. After the above come the Clerks or employés of the Government, which number several thousand in Washington alone. They are, in reality, the hardest working population of the Metropolis. Among them may be found men from every State in the Union, and from many foreign countries; men of no particular mark, who have lost fortunes; ripe scholars, who have been rudely buffeted by the world; men of capacity, who can teach their superiors in office; rare penmen and common-place accountants; and a sisterhood, composed chiefly of respectable widows and orphans who have fled to the Government for support. The custom of employing women as clerks originated out of the disasters which followed the late war, and the number now employed by the Government has already reached several thousand, and they have been found to be quite as useful as men-clerks. Their compensation ranges from nine hundred to twenty-five hundred dollars per annum, and while it is true that many receive more than they earn, because of their idle or inattentive habits, others find it difficult to secure a comfortable support. Occasionally a man may be found who has grown gray in the public service, and is an oracle; but the great majority are, in reality, a floating population. The comparative ease with which these clerks earn their money tends to make them improvident; many instances might be mentioned, however, where clerks have left the government service, and become as distinguished as merchants, or in some of the professions. For a totally different phase of Washington life, and the most influential for evil or for good, we must turn to the brotherhood of Congressmen. Coming as they do from all parts of the country, and representing every variety of population, it is quite as impossible to speak of them collectively as of their individual characteristics. Among them are to be found honest and able statesmen, but that a large proportion of them are mere time-serving politicians is a fact that cannot be questioned. It is frequently the case that after a Congressman has ended his career as a legislator, he turns office-seeker, and many of them, without a knowledge of any language but their own, are sent abroad as diplomatic Ministers. Of these Congressmen, there have been not less than five thousand of them elected since the foundation of the Government; and the several political parties to which they have belonged may be summed up as Federalists, Democrats, Whigs, Locofocos, Freesoilers, Abolitionists, Fire-eaters, Republicans, Copperheads, Native Americans, Secessionists, and Radicals, forming in the aggregate a conglomeration of political ideas quite in keeping with the energetic and free spirit of the American people. Prior to the late civil war, colored men were not admitted to seats in Congress, but at the present time a few of them hold positions in both Houses of Congress,—there being now no distinction recognized on account of color, so far as political rights are concerned. With regard to the permanent population of Washington, little can be said of special interest. Occupying, as this city does, a position on the River Potomac, at the head of navigation, about midway between the Atlantic Ocean and the Alleghany Mountains, it was calculated to become a place of commercial importance. But this idea was not realized, and it became a metropolitan city, chiefly dependent for its support upon the General Government. The local trade is measured by the wants of the population, and there is nothing exported excepting a limited amount of flour, and a considerable quantity of bituminous coal. The only particular, perhaps, in which the inhabitants differ from those of other American cities, is in their free and easy manners, growing out of their intercourse and familiarity with people from all quarters of the globe, drawn hither by business or pleasure. With them, the dignitaries of the land, as well as ambassadors from abroad, are appreciated at their real value; and a man who towers as a giant in the rural districts, is very sure to be measured accurately in the metropolis. But the most peculiar feature of Washington society at the present time (1871), is the position to which the colored or negro population has attained. Before the late civil war, these unhappy people were in a state of bondage, and only enough of them were congregated in the metropolis to supply the demand for household servants. While the war was progressing, which resulted in their emancipation, large numbers fled to this city, as to a place of refuge, and here a large proportion of them have continued to remain to the present time. They have been admitted to all the rights and privileges of citizenship; but, while the more intelligent have profited by their advantages, large numbers of them are content to idle away their time, or depend upon the authorities for support, and they constitute about one-third of the present population. They have not as yet been sufficiently educated to be received in society on the same footing with the white race, and the repugnance to receiving them at the same table, or to intermarrying with them, is as strong as in other times, quite universal, and will probably so continue.

In the further prosecution of our plan, we must direct attention to that large mass of the community engaged in carrying on the business of the nation in the diverse regions of the United States. We begin with the Postmasters, one of whom is located in every city, town, and village throughout the land, and the aggregate number of whom is about twenty-six thousand, exclusive of their numerous assistants. Their duties are, to receive and deliver all letters sent to their several offices, and to look after the prompt dispatch of the mails, by ships and railroads, by coaches and wagons, and on horseback, and their compensation ranges from six thousand dollars to a few dollars per annum. They are all appointed indirectly by the President, and hold office during his pleasure. Next to these come the custom-house officers, who, including all grades, number not less than five thousand employés; after these comes another large body, whose business is to collect the Internal Revenue of the country; and also a very extensive force engaged in carrying on the interests connected with the Public Lands, the Indian Tribes, and the Judicial business in the various States and Territories, as well as those interests prosecuted under the authority of the Patent Office, the Pension Office, and the Agricultural Department. Now, as the people here mentioned, numbering in the gross not far from sixty thousand persons, obtain their positions through political influence, it is natural that they should take a special interest in politics, and do their utmost for the success of the particular party to which they belong. Hence the great excitement which invariably prevails at all the elections. As before intimated, the President and Vice-President are voted for once in every four years; and the Representatives in Congress once in two years;—the Senators being chosen by the State Legislatures. It would appear, therefore, that as the people are intelligent and honest, so must be the office-holders; but this is not always the case, because of the existence of what are called mere politicians or demagogues. This class of citizens has greatly multiplied of late years, and it is safe to say that nearly all the troubles which befall the country are the result of their petty schemes and selfish intrigues. There is not a village in the land where they do not congregate, or pursue in secret their unpatriotic designs. Of course there are many exceptions to this state of things, but the rule is as we have stated it; and the evils resulting from the power thus obtained and prostituted, have come to be universally recognized and deplored by the honest people of the land. The loss of dignity, and the decline in public morals on account of politics is, to-day, a source of mortification and alarm among the virtuous and patriotic citizens of the country. The philosophy of government is a subject to which the people of America have devoted but little attention, and very few books have been published on the subject, and yet it is claimed that they are in advance of all other nations, in the practice of self-government. To what extent this is true, the present writer is not called upon to decide. It is too true, however, that the opinion is frequently expressed by foreigners that the unbridled system of a Republican government leads to many political troubles. The two or three crowning features of the American Government would seem to be as follows: That the nation is a peculiar organism, having a life and destiny of its own, founded on the idea of humanity, and like the individual person, but in a more continuous degree; that its authority to govern the people is derived from their actual or implied assent; and that, in asserting its prerogatives, it looks to the least possible interference with the free action of the individuals composing the community. This form of government involves the idea of contract, tacit or expressed, and no matter how it may be carried out, must rest upon the understanding of the people, not only as to the end to be pursued, but also as to the methods. As one circle within another, so does the government of each State and Territory revolve within the circle of the Union, and the State, county, and town elections, for offices which are subject to State patronage, are precisely similar in character and results to the National elections. While deprecating the abuses to which the American people are subject, on account of what is called universal suffrage, there are many social features which are to be highly commended, and are peculiar to the country; among these is the absence of pauperism, and the universal respectability in personal appearance among all classes. This fact is apparent to all observers, and has been fully conceded by the best English writers on this country. There is no beggary here except such as arises from profligacy or causes beyond the control of human nature. Another peculiar feature of American life is, the equal distribution of wealth, acknowledged as remarkably characteristic of the nation. In all the large cities and occasionally in the country, may be found a man possessing enormous wealth, but among the millions of our population wealth is diffused, and there is a wonderful equality in the material condition of the population. Another phase of American life, to which we have already alluded, and which has astonished the governments of the Old World, is, the doctrine of universal suffrage. It is this which lies at the basis of all her institutions, and it is this, more than anything else, taken in connection with the superabundant resources of the country, that tends to an equal distribution of wealth. It is not, as a noted English statesman has said, so much a man's wealth, which the American people recognize, and to which they pay homage, as the energy and ability which may turn wealth to account. In theory, as well as in reality, they regard equality and brotherhood as of the *essence* of the Constitution under which they live, and of their social well-being and existence. As the official and political classes heretofore touched upon, are either the law-makers of the land, or engaged in carrying out the laws, it may be well enough to notice their rights and privileges under those laws. While it is true that members of Congress, and some few dignitaries besides, are exempt from arrest for civil misdemeanors, when engaged in their public duties, all persons of every position are amenable to the criminal laws. A leading dignitary, when he violates the law, is as promptly brought to trial as the humblest man in the community; but the misfortune is, that the influence possessed by the former is too apt to keep him from deserved punishment, while the latter is compelled to meet a less happy fate. The titles which accompany the possession of office are of no special value, and, except in the Army and Navy, terminate with the office. At the same time it must not be supposed that the Americans are without the sentiments which grow out of association with old and honored families. In some parts of the country there is a very decided feeling of aristocracy, but it is peculiar to the regions which have been the longest settled. The privilege of receiving and sending letters free of postage, and without limit, is enjoyed only by the President, his Cabinet, the heads of Bureas, and Congressmen; under certain official restrictions, the postmasters may frank their letters, but, beyond that, all men in office have to pay postage like ordinary people. When a young man has determined to lead a political life, his first desire is to be elected to the State Legislature, then to become Governor of the State, and from that position he thinks himself entitled to go into the United States Senate; but there is no uniformity in these promotions. Generally speaking, the career of public men in this country is measured more by their cunning or success in managing the people who have votes, rather than by their abilities. Nor does their political success depend upon their antecedents—upon wealth or family position. Ten years before he became President, Ulysses S. Grant was a leather-merchant; it was the boast of Andrew Johnson, the late president, that he had been bred a tailor; and of Abraham Lincoln, that he had earned his living in early life as a common chopper of wood, or rail-splitter. The present Minister to England was once a tutor in an academy; and the Ministers to France and Spain were both printers; but at the same time it does occasionally happen in these latter days, as it frequently did in former times, that the diplomatic representatives abroad have attained high positions, notwithstanding the fact that they have been men of culture and quiet scholarship, as in the case of Motley and Bancroft, the historians, and Marsh, the distinguished scholar and author. The present Secretary of the Treasury was, for many years, a merchant's clerk; and among the Senators and Representatives are men who once sold drygoods for a living, or were engaged in various mechanical employments, but who are not on those accounts less esteemed than they would otherwise have been. But when a notorious gambler or profligate is elected to Congress, as has sometimes been the case, it must not be supposed that the American people are indifferent to his antecedents. The most striking fact, perhaps, which can be mentioned, by way of illustrating the wonderful elasticity of the American Government, is this, that among the Representatives now sitting in Congress and engaged in moulding the laws, are several persons, members of the negro-race, who were once slaves, employed upon plantations, both of which could alike, at one time, have been sold for a specific sum of money. Although there are many instances among the State governors, where men have risen to eminence from obscurity, the people have generally been more careful in selecting their State executives than in selecting their Congressmen; and what we have said in regard to the changes effected by politics in the case of prominent officials, is equally true, in a less degree, of all the subordinate office-holders. And now the question arises, how about the servants of the public after they have been superseded in their official position? It cannot be said that any of the Presidents have ever gone into any unbecoming employment after leaving the Executive chair; but it is not uncommon for Ex-Congressmen and other ex-officials of the so-called higher grades, to go into all sorts of inappropriate employments, from a government clerkship to a claim agency. The only one of the presidents who consented to enter Congress after leaving the Executive Chair was John Quincy Adams; but his character stood so high as a man and a statesman, he could afford to do as he pleased; and to die, as he did, in the harness of public life. As before stated, the total number of men who have served the country as law-makers, is about five thousand; of these, the legal profession has sent the largest proportion: the men of letters have numbered only one in every fifty: the eloquent speakers, or orators of special note, have not been more than two hundred; less than one-half graduated at learned institutions; while the balance have been farmers and planters, merchants, and members of various professions. The total number of men who have held Cabinet appointments is one hundred and eighty-two, of whom one hundred and thirty-three have been Congressmen: of the forty-four Supreme Court Judges, one-half of them served in the Senate or House of Representatives: out of five hundred and twenty-seven Foreign Ministers, one hundred and seventy were members of Congress; and of the seven hundred and sixty-eight State and Territorial Governors, three hundred and forty-nine were Congressmen. The treaty which has recently been made between the American and English Governments, consummates a long-wished-for condition of affairs, viz.: a cordial good-will with all the great Powers of Europe—Great Britain, France, Germany, Italy, Russia, and Spain. It is claimed, indeed, by the best thinkers, that the American

Government was never more powerful and influential for good than it is at the present time. Intercourse and trade between the two continents, over the Pacific Ocean, are growing rapidly. The friendship of Japan for the United States, and its thorough reciprocation on their part, are universally acknowledged. The latter seem to watch attentively the movements of England and other European Powers, in the far East. And while the British Government may deem it wise to use force in its dealings with the eastern nations, the American policy appears to adhere resolutely to the principles of peace, justice, and equal rights to all, notwithstanding the late unwarrantable operations of the American Navy on the coast of Corea. The changes for good that have taken place in Japan during the last few years, are a matter of wonder and satisfaction to the whole civilized world. The American people have been, since the memorable visit of Commodore Perry, taking great and special interest in the affairs of Japan. The President of the United States has justly echoed the prevailing sentiment among the Americans, when he said to the Prince Fushimi, member of one of the Imperial families of the Mikado, that he had seen with pride the young men of Japan coming over to receive their education, and that he would take the greatest pleasure in contriving to make their residence in this country both agreeable and useful to them. There rests upon Japan a great hope, as well as high responsibility, for the success of bringing about a healthy and exemplary civilization, which must take the lead among all the Asiatic nations.

P. S. In view of the changes which are constantly taking

place among the officials of the American Government, to which allusion has been made in the foregoing pages, the writer must express an opinion. They are, beyond all question, a great disadvantage to the Republic. They naturally interfere with the proper and regular working of the machinery of the Government, and are the primary cause of the bitter political dissensions which have long prevailed, and continue to prevail, among the American people. And what is more, they lead to all kinds of corruption; and at the very time of our writing these lines, the people of New York are greatly convulsed over the discovery that the Treasury of the City and State has been robbed to the extent of many millions of dollars, growing directly out of the evils of office-seeking, and rotation in office, from party considerations. On the other hand, it must be confessed that where the people have it in their power, as in America, to regulate the conduct of the men they elect to office, so long as they are truly honest, they can always prevent a long continuance of the evils brought upon them by unscrupulous demagogues. Hence the great importance of their being both virtuous and truly patriotic.

# LIFE AMONG THE FARMERS AND PLANTERS.

In the present paper we propose to give a comprehensive account of the agricultural population of the United States, and shall speak of farm-life in New England (the Eastern), the Middle, and Western States; and of plantation-life in the Southern States. It is now generally acknowledged that the prosperity of America depends chiefly upon its agriculture, and that it has come to be considered the granary of Europe. The area of land susceptible of cultivation has been estimated to be about two thousand two hundred and fifty millions (2,250,000,000) of acres, more than half of which is owned by the Government; five hundred millions (500,000,000) having been surveyed, and is now ready for occupation; while the lands under cultivation amount to more than two hundred millions (200,000,000) of acres. It has also been estimated that seven-eighths of the entire population of the country are engaged in agricultural pursuits, or in the various professions and trades naturally dependent thereupon. The largest wheat crop ever produced in the States was in 1869, when the yield amounted to two hundred and sixty-four millions (264,000,000) of bushels, and, as the average price was one dollar and forty cents ($1.40), the total cash value was not less than $369,600,000. The quantity of corn was 1,100,000,000 bushels; rye, 22,000,000; barley, 28,000,000; buckwheat,

17,000,000; oats, 275,000,000, and potatoes, 111,000,000; hay, 22,000,000 tons; tobacco, 310,000,000 pounds; cane-sugar, 120,000,000 pounds, and cotton, 1,767,000,000 pounds, valued at $147,380,000. And, as to domestic animals, including young cattle, horses, sheep, and swine, their value was $978,872,785.

With these few leading facts before him, the reader may obtain an approximate idea of the agricultural wealth of the country: and he must remember, that the very numerous unmentioned articles would swell the agricultural supplies to the extent of many additional millions. It is claimed by English farmers that, in some particulars, their method of farming is superior to that practised in this country, and that is undoubtedly true; but, on the other hand, it has been demonstrated that the leading grains can be produced at a much lower cost in the United States than in England. As this is pre-eminently an agricultural country, it follows that here the most numerous attempts to produce labor-saving implements have been directed to facilitate the labors of the farm. The extent to which new agricultural inventions have been patented is so great, that in 1869 they reached the number of nineteen hundred (1,900), and all of them for saving muscular power on the farm and in the household. A particular account of them is as follows: Churns and churning, 130; Corn-shellers and huskers, 40; Cultivators, 150; Diggers and spaders, 30; Fertilizers, 6; Forks (hay, manure, etc.), 100; Harrows, drays, and pulverizers, 80; Harvesters and attachments, 195; Hay-spreaders, 25; Hoes, 25; Mowing and reaping machines, 30; Planters, 150; Ploughs and attachments, 255; Pruning, 15; Rakes, 90; Seeding and sowing,

80; Separators and smut-machines, 50; Straw, hay, and fodder-cutters, 30; Threshing-machines, 35; and Yokes, 15. In the more settled parts of the country the old-fashioned varieties of the hoe, the spade, and even the ploughshare, are now looked upon as barbarous contrivances, and in their place the farmers use what are called Steam-ploughs, the Rotary Spade, the Sulky-plough, Horse-Cultivators, Shovel-ploughs, as well as Reaping, Mowing, and Threshing machines, of many varieties. The improvements that have been made in such tools as the shovel, spade, hoe, and fork, are so great that they may almost be considered entirely new inventions. With regard to these and many other implements of husbandry in America, lightness, simplicity, and comparative cheapness are absolutely essential to their perfection. One of the effects, if not the most important, of these labor-saving machines has been, that, while one man has been kept in the field, three have been sent to the great towns to prosecute other enterprises of profit, or have entered upon the cultivation of other farms. The organization of Agricultural Societies, which have done much to perfect the science of tilling the soil, was commenced shortly after the establishment of the Government in 1775, and their influence, in connection with annual fairs, has been wide-spread, and of the greatest advantage. There is not a State in the Union which does not boast of one of them, organized for the benefit of all the inhabitants at large. Nor ought the fact to be forgotten, that there are already many Agricultural Colleges in the country, and that they are annually increasing in numbers and influence. And then, again, the agricultural periodicals are numerous and of high repute.

But notwithstanding all these facts, experienced men have expressed the opinion that the condition of agriculture in this country is not what might be desired. The great trouble is the want of proper method. The art is as yet imperfectly known and practised, and the American system is full of deficiencies. The domain of the United States embraces soil capable of yielding the richest and most varied productions, in the greatest abundance; and it is a peculiar feature of the country, that all the lands which have been sold by the Government, or are still owned by the same, are surveyed upon a system of squares, and divided into townships of six miles square, subdivided into sections and quarter sections, whereby the farms are generally regular in shape, and disputes are avoided in regard to boundary lines. The lands belonging to the Government are sold at the uniform price of one dollar and a quarter ($1.25) per acre, so that for one hundred dollars a new settler can receive a farm of eighty acres; but, under existing laws, a foreigner, as well as a native, if of age and intending to become a citizen, obtains a homestead substantially as a free gift. The total quantity of land owned by the Government was 1,834,968,400 acres; of which 447,266,190 acres have been sold; and the amount now for sale is 1,387,732,209 acres. That the National Government takes a deep interest in the welfare of the agricultural population is proven by the fact that a Department of Agriculture exists in Washington, which annually publishes a very valuable volume of miscellaneous information, and supplies seeds and cuttings for all who may apply for them, while the postal laws of the country allow their transportation through the mails free of expense; the same laws making only a small charge for the exchange of seeds, cuttings, and plants between private parties: but more than all that, the National Government has recently made a grant of seven millions (7,000,000) of acres of land for the benefit of Agricultural Colleges, and propositions are now pending for giving away nearly twenty millions (20,000,000) acres of land for objects directly or indirectly connected with the farming population of the Republic. The total number of farms in the United States is about three millions, which gives a farm for every thirteen of the entire population; and the largest proportion of these farms range from twenty to one hundred acres.

And now we propose to give a description in general terms of farm-life in the New England States (the six Eastern States), viz.: Maine, Massachusetts, New Hampshire, Vermont, Connecticut, and Rhode Island. In this region the farms are almost universally small, ranging from ten to one hundred acres, and stone-fences predominate above all other kinds. The agricultural season is short, winter lasting through half the year. No verdure but that of evergreens resists the annual cold, and an unmelted mass of snow covers the ground for months. The soils, excepting in the more extensive valleys, are poor and rocky, and aside from those farms which are given up chiefly to the grazing of cattle or the production of hay, the products of the earth are only obtained by the severest kind of labor. Along the sea-shore, kelp and fish are popular manures, but in the interior, guano, calcareous manures, and the yield of the barn-yards are employed. The owner is, himself, the foremost workman, and his sons, his principal assistants: and all household matters are performed by the females of the family. The farmers live in comfortable frame houses, very frequently surrounded with flowers, use both coal and wood for fuel, and are noted for their frugality and neatness. Their barns are spacious and substantial. They produce nothing for exportation, but a greater variety of crops than the more extensive farmers, and are quite content if they can obtain a plain, comfortable support. In Vermont, the raising of superior breeds of horses has been a specialty, but for farm-work, oxen are more popular than horses. If the farmers happen to have a small surplus of any commodity, they dispose of it in a neighboring town; and thus provide themselves with luxuries, or put aside a little money for a rainy day. In some localities agriculture is often joined to other employments, such as fishing and shoemaking. The farmers in New England, as well as throughout the country, are generally a reading people, and profit somewhat by the published theories on the science of agriculture. Their children have access to the country schools, but the sons are often obliged to help their parents in the field during the vernal months, so that their principal time for study is in the winter. They are a church-going people, and, to the extent of their means, liberal in furthering the cause to which they may be attached. They take an interest in politics, and are decided in their opinions. They are social in their dispositions, fond of visiting their friends, and on winter evenings have what they call apple-paring and bed-quilting frolics, when their homes are cheered by such refreshments as mince and pumpkin pies, as well as cider, walnuts, and apples. Their amusements are as various as their tastes, but the perpetual struggle with mother earth for the means of living, makes them careful of their time, and is apt to induce and keep alive the most serious views of life. On farms lying in the vicinity of villages, it is often the case, that certain members of the family obtain positions in the factories or other manufacturing establishments, whereby they are enabled to increase their means of support. As soon as the boys attain the age of manhood, they find their fields of operation circumscribed, and leaving the paternal roof, wander forth into the world to make their own fortunes:—some of them to the turmoil and strife of the large cities, and others to the more inviting regions of the great, and not yet fully developed, West. In New England, farm-life is to-day very much what it was a generation ago; and from the very nature of the cold and barren soil, will so continue without any marked progress. The farmers have done their best, in fact all that could be done; everything is finished, and they are contented. It is not that the spirit of competition has died out there. That the agricultural interests of New England have reached and passed the period of culmination is undoubtedly true. The farmers of this region are more truly the yeomanry of the land than any other class, and a large proportion of them are natives of the soil they now cultivate, and, like the venerable oaks and elms which adorn many of their farms, they are content to live in the present as in the past, hoping that any family offshoots that may have been planted in more congenial and productive soils will be, as they have been in unnumbered instances, a blessing to their descendants.

We now pass over into what are called the four Middle States of the Union, viz.: New York, Pennsylvania, New

Jersey, and Delaware, where we shall find a somewhat different condition of affairs, but with the stamp of New England manners and customs everywhere visible. There the average size of farms is between one hundred and one hundred and fifty acres, and, generally speaking, the soil is productive. The fences are usually made of rails, and every variety of manure is employed. If not rich, the farmers are in easy circumstances, and count upon annually laying up something handsome in the way of profits. Though well posted in their business, by years of practical experience, they employ a needed supply of hands, who do most of the hard work, while their own time is occupied with the lighter duties of the farm and a general supervision of affairs. Their houses are comfortable and often elegant, and afford ample accommodation for the proprietor, his family, and his assistants. While those of New York, where the native American element prevails, fare sumptuously on the food of their own raising, and have become celebrated for their superior butter and cheese, the farmers of Dutch descent, located in Pennsylvania, are charged with never eating what might be readily sold at the nearest market. It is to the credit of these farmers that their barns are unequalled in this country, oftentimes better than the houses they live in, and that with them, the profits of their style of farming are always satisfactory. With regard to the cheese business, it has come to be so extensive that we may allude to it more particularly. The entire produce of last year was about one hundred millions of pounds, three-fourths of which was made in the Middle States, but the largest amount in New York.

From time immemorial the Dutch have had control of

this business, but the exports from this country are now about double of the exports from Holland. Formerly it was the custom of the farmers to make cheese upon their respective farms, but it is now made in regularly established factories, which are supported by the farmers located in their vicinity. The total number of these factories now flourishing in this country is thirteen hundred, and they are supplied with milk from not less than three hundred thousand cows. In New Jersey and Delaware, and on Long Island, where the chief attention is devoted to fruits and vegetables, and where are to be found the most beautiful gardens in the country, the hired hands are more numerous than elsewhere, in proportion to the size of the farms or gardens, but their positions are not so permanent. Various kinds of berries are here raised in the greatest abundance, and the surplus hands left unemployed after the annual gatherings have to seek other employment.

In the great majority of cases, the proprietor joins his hired men in the work to be done, whether in casting the seed, driving the machinery employed, or gathering in the harvests; they all occupy the same platform as citizens, whether naturalized, or natives of the country: free access to schools and churches is enjoyed by all, without regard to family or fortune; and the man who is working to-day as a hired hand, knows full well, that if he continues to be true to himself and his opportunities, he will yet be respected as a proprietor. By means of newspapers and books, they keep up with the spirit of the age; and, though generally disinclined to participate in the partisan squabbles of the day, they are by no means indifferent to the welfare of the country, and are frequently called upon to fill offices of trust and honor. They rise early, eat a frugal meal at noon, and retire at the coming on of darkness, excepting in the winter, which is their time for visiting and home enjoyments; and this is true of the farming classes generally throughout the country. What are called fancy farmers are probably more numerous in the Middle States than in any other region, but these men are apt to spend more money than they make; and an idea of the wealth which some of them attain, may be gathered from the fact that there is one family in the Valley of the Genesee, in New York, who own not less than thirty thousand acres of land, and all of it in the highest state of cultivation. It is this class of the more wealthy farmers, residing in all the States, who greatly benefit the country by introducing the best kinds of stock from foreign countries, who have been known to pay twenty thousand dollars for a single stallion (horse), two or three thousand for a heifer, a ram, or a bull, or one hundred dollars for a trio of fowls, consisting of one male and two females. It was one of these extensive farmers who inaugurated the plan of issuing printed cards with the following regulations, for the guidance of his men: "Regularity in hours. Punctuality in cleaning and putting away implements. Humanity to all the animals. Neatness and cleanliness in personal appearance. Decency in deportment and conversation. Obedience to the proprietor, and ambition to excel in farming." Extensive and various as are the farming interests of the Middle States, and so great are the temptations to go farther west, the demand for farm-hands and female servants is always greater than the supply, and while the men receive from fifteen to thirty dollars per month, with board, the women receive from eight to fifteen dollars per month for home-work, and of these, by far the largest proportion are from England, Ireland, and Germany. The secret of the unparalleled growth and the daily increasing power of the United States is, that the Government, in its practical working, is confined to the narrowest limits; that it is the agent, not the master, of the people; and that the latter initiate all changes in its political and social life. It is, therefore, the condition of the success of a settlement that the immigrant relies on his own strength, acts on his own responsibility, and seeks by his own efforts the prosperity which he is sure to find, if undisturbed. In spite of obstacles and disappointments, he will make his way, and ultimately attain his objects. In the States now under consideration, as well as in all the States of the Union, excepting New York and a few others, a married woman may not convey her separate real estate, except in a joint deed with her husband; and yet, in most of the States, the separate property of the wife is recognized. There is no imprisonment for debt in any part of the Republic; and, when a farmer has become involved (in more than half the States), his homestead is exempt from execution; and in all of them, household furniture to the extent of five hundred dollars, wearing apparel, tools, and books necessary to carry on business, one to five cows, one yoke of oxen, ten sheep, carts, and farming implements, and the uniform and arms of any man who is or has been in the public service, are also exempt from the grasp of the creditor. When the head of a family dies without making a will, his property is equally divided among his children or their offspring, except that the wife has a life-interest of one-third, called the widow's dower;

and when there are no lineal descendants, the estate goes to the next of kin.

The next division of farm-life we have to consider, is that of the Western States. Of these there are sixteen in all, thirteen in the valley of the Mississippi River, and three on the Pacific Ocean. Their extent is so immense, and their products so numerous, that it is difficult for the mind to comprehend their importance and influence. Four of them were, until recently, classed among the Slave States; and because the system of slave-labor therein has become greatly modified by free-labor, they can hardly be, with propriety, embraced in our present review. As a wheat-producing region, the Western States have progressed in a manner perfectly amazing, until they now stand unsurpassed by any other region of like extent in the world. Although the population has increased about fifty per cent. in the last twenty years, the increase of produce has greatly exceeded that of population. But the relative value of all the other cereals and other farm productions in these States is quite as extensive and remarkable as that of wheat. That the people who are annually bringing out of the soil such immense wealth are wide-awake and industrious, is self-evident. Generally speaking, the farms are much larger than those in the Middle States, and the farm-hands very much more numerous. Very many of the farmers with whom we come in contact, seem to have settled in the country with limited means. Some bought land with no more money than would pay the first installment on it, and had to work for others to make money to pay the other installments as they came due. They are able, in this way, in a few years to settle down and cultivate their own soil: and this method of operating is in progress to-day. When farms are rented, which is often done, the system adopted is as follows: If the tenant is not able to provide stock, implements, and seeds, the proprietor supplies him with all these, and then allows him one-third of the grain-crops. In this way many a man works himself into a farm of his own. The ordinary rate of interest on borrowed money is ten per cent., but even at this high rate it usually pays a farmer well, and there is every facility given to respectable and industrious men. There are often cultivated farms in the market for sale, but persons desiring to purchase cannot always be present; and, in buying second-hand farms, it is well to be certain that it has not been previously mortgaged. As is the case in all other branches of business, the man who has the best capacity is likely to be the most successful, and the operations of some of the more famous farmers in the West sound more like romance than reality. For example, there was lately one farm in Illinois which contained about forty thousand acres, with one pasture-field of eight thousand acres; its chief production was corn, all of which was consumed upon the farm itself; but in one year the proprietor sent to New York City cattle enough to bring seventy thousand dollars, while his home-stock was valued at one million of dollars; and yet, the man lived in a small house, in the most simple and unpretending style, and habitually sat down at the same table with his hired men. But the farming exploits of this man were eclipsed subsequently by those of another, who is now carrying on a farm of fifty thousand acres. With regard to another of the model farms of Illinois, we may state, that it contains thirty-six thousand acres, and last year had one cornfield of five thousand five hundred acres, yielding two hundred and twenty thousand bushels, three thousand tons of hay, four thousand head of cattle, and gave employment to eighty-five ploughs, fifteen planting machines, and fifteen mowing machines. The hedge fencing on this farm measures about one hundred and thirty miles, and contains also about eighty miles of board fencing. There is, however, still another farm, located in Illinois, which ought to be mentioned in this place, as it is reputed to be one of the most extensive and successful in the world. It is called the Burr Oak Farm, and is owned by a man named Sullivant. It embraces sixty-five square miles; and although the owner commenced work upon it only four years ago, he has at the present time growing upon it not less than eleven thousand acres of corn, and five thousand acres, besides, planted in miscellaneous crops. The hedges which cross, re-cross, and surround the farm, measure three hundred miles, the board fences six miles, and the ditches one hundred and fifty miles. The workingmen employed on this farm are mostly Swedes and Germans, number two hundred and fifty, and are constantly employed from the first of April to the first of January. They work ten hours per day, report to the proprietor every evening, and are not allowed the use of intoxicating drinks. The working animals of the farm consist of three hundred and fifty mules, fifty horses, and fifty yoke of oxen, and it is amply supplied with the ordinary stock of an extensive farm; and the leading machinery employed consists of one hundred and fifty steel ploughs, seventy-five breaking ploughs; one hundred and forty-two cultivators; forty-five corn-planters, and twenty-five harrows; and it has one ditching plough which is drawn by sixty-eight oxen and managed by eight men. The house in which the proprietor resides is a common wooden structure, comfortable, but without the least pretension. It will be understood, of course, that farms of this extent are not found in every county or State; but they give us an idea of the spirit that animates the farming fraternity generally.

Let us now, on the other hand, look at the operations of one or two small farmers in Illinois. One man, for example, purchased eighty acres of prairie land for $360; spent $500 on improvements; his crops for the first year brought him over $1,500, and at the close of the third year his farm was sold for $2,000. Another man, with a capital of only $700, bought one hundred and sixty acres: his annual produce for six years was $2,000, at the end of which time he was worth about ten thousand dollars. And such instances as the above have occurred by the thousand in the great West. As we glance over the immense number of farmers who are toiling throughout the western States, it is quite impossible to depict their manners and customs with anything like accuracy. So many are the nationalities which compose the great mass of inhabitants, the mere mention of these is indeed a kind of description. In Illinois and Ohio, the Germans, Irish, and English are about equally divided, in Wisconsin the English and Germans predominate, and Missouri is most extensively settled by the Germans. In the States bordering on the Great Lakes and the Upper Mississippi several Scandinavian colonies have been established; and there has been a considerable immigration of Chinese into California, but this latter class has not manifested any strong predisposition for agricultural pursuits. The great variety of nationalities which sometimes congregate in one region, was strikingly exemplified a few years ago, when the State of Wisconsin was obliged to publish its Governor's message in not less than eight languages. The amount of money sent across the ocean by immigrants, to friends left behind, principally to pay their passage to America, is surprising. From the official returns of Emigration Commissioners of England, it appears that in 1870 there were sent from this country to Ireland, principally, $3,630,040 in gold, of which $1,663,190, was for pre-paid passage. In the twenty-three years from 1848 to 1870, the amount of money sent was $81,670,000 in gold, being an average of about $3,889,047 yearly. But this amount is probably somewhat below the actual amount, as it only includes what has been sent through banks and commercial houses. And these sums, large as they are, are made up by careful savings from the wages of servant-girls and farm-laborers. In California, Missouri, and Ohio, the grape has been so extensively cultivated as to give them the reputation of being the wine-producing regions of the United States; and among their vineyards we find many of the habits prevailing which are common to the wine districts of Europe. In California a farm is called a ranch, and one of the most noted ones in that State may be described as follows: It contains eighteen thousand (18,000) acres; and last year sixteen hundred (1,600) acres were devoted to wheat, eight hundred (800) to barley, two hundred (200) to oats, two hundred (200) to meadow, and about fifteen thousand (15,000) acres to orchards, vineyards, and pasturage. The fruit-trees number eight thousand (8,000,) the grape-vines fifty thousand (50,000); and the live stock consists of two hundred (200) horses, one thousand (1,000) head of cattle, three thousand (3,000) sheep, and two thousand (2,000) swine; and the entire domain is surrounded with good fences. From the above and other facts already narrated, it will be seen that the United States are supplied with all kinds of farmers; some cultivating their thousands of acres, and others their half dozen; and yet they all seem to live comfortably, and the great majority are independent. And there are numerous instances of American women who have been, and are to-day, quite successful in the management of farms; and what will be the result upon the agricultural and industrial interests of the extensive emigration from China to this country now going on, is a problem which can only be settled by the future.

Our next subject for consideration is the plantation-life of the Southern States. Only about six years have now passed away since the close of the civil war, which resulted in the emancipation of more than four millions of slaves; and a glance at the condition of the South, before the great event, would seem to be necessary. In 1860 there were fifteen States in which slavery existed, and all of them, excepting five, made war upon the General Government—four of them having already been mentioned as among the Western States. They contained a population of 4,334,250, of whom only 383,637 were slave-owners. The number of plantations under cultivation was estimated at 765,000, comprehending about 75,000,000 of acres : and as to the cotton and sugar, rice, wheat, corn, and live stock, which were produced upon them, they can only be appreciated by consulting the publications of the Census Office. The planter was the owner, not only of broad acres almost without number, but also of from ten to one thousand menials or slaves, whom he fed and clothed for his own exclusive profit; and who, for the most part, did his bidding without a murmur or thought beyond the passing hour. He lived at his ease, among books and in the dispensation of a liberal hospitality, leaving all the labor on his plantation to the direction of an overseer, who spent most of his time on horseback, issuing orders to the working men and women, and watching the regular progress of affairs. According to his wealth, the planter lived in a house, or an elegant mansion, while his slaves were domiciled in rude but comfortable cabins. They received a supply of provisions, but no compensation in money; although it was customary to allow them the use of a patch of ground for their own benefit, and a fragment of time out of each day or week to cultivate it. But all this is now changed: slave-labor has no existence on the soil of the United States: and the opinion is universal, that the suppression of slave-labor will ultimately add greatly to the national advancement of all the States in which it formerly existed. Among the results following the late rebellion, was the fact that much of the property in the Southern States passed into new hands. Many old plantations were abandoned by their owners and have never been reclaimed; others have been confiscated, and others sold at a ruinous sacrifice. Many of the soldiers who went South, who had been raised among the rocky hills of the North, became in love with the rich and beautiful fields and valleys of the South, and thousands resolved to settle in the new country. They married Southern women, formed new alliances and associations, and have opened up a new career for the South, which is rapidly becoming more and more salutary in its influences. The great landed estates which have been cut up, may be purchased by all new comers at a very small cost, while the black race, to a great extent, have settled upon small patches of land, where they can maintain themselves in comfort, and enjoy an independence of thought and feeling which they did not know under the old order of things. Whole plantations have been settled by families of owners, who were formerly slaves upon the same estates. Men who were formerly overseers or superintendents, are themselves settling down upon their own newly-acquired farms. Although attempts to obtain laborers from China and Sweden have been made, the principal cultivators of the Southern States are the Freedmen, who, indolent by nature, do as little work as possible, will not hire out for more than a single year, and one of the results of their freedom is, that they will not let their wives work, as in the olden times. To retain their services, the planter is obliged to praise and humor them in many ways. The terms upon which the negroes are hired is generally to let them have one-half of what they produce, but when supported by the planter they receive but one-quarter of what they produce. When the planters are attentive to their business they almost invariably succeed, and when unsuccessful as farmers, they are apt to help their pockets by keeping small country stores; and in all the towns are located men who are called warehouse-men, whose business is to receive, store, and sell all the cotton or other produce which may be consigned to their care. What the people of the South now need is help—not lands; and in many of the most fertile regions, every inducement is thrown out to invite emigration from the North. But, after all, it is idle to suppose that the griefs, the passions, and animosities engendered by the late rebellion, will die out while the present generation survives. Too many brave men have perished, too many homes made desolate, too many families broken up and reduced to beggary, to expect anything of that sort. Men whom it has impoverished will live and die poor, remembering constantly the cause of their poverty. Widows will long mourn over husbands, children over fathers, slain in battle. A new and happier era is in store for the rising generation; but its advance will be slow. The people of the North and of the South, it is fondly hoped and believed, will again become a happy, a united, and prosperous people; united in interests, in pursuits, in intelligence, and in patriotic devotion to their united country.

Of all the products grown in the Southern States the most important and universal is cotton, and it has been asserted that it was this single commodity which prevented that portion of the Union from relapsing into abject poverty. Everything was sacrificed to slavery, and slavery sacrificed everything to itself; and as there were not slaves enough to cultivate the soil as it needed, cotton-raising was all that saved the country. The principal States where cotton is now grown are Mississippi, Alabama, Louisiana, Georgia, Texas, and Arkansas, and in all of them efforts are being made for the introduction of Chinese labor. The cultivation of rice is limited to three States, South Carolina, Georgia, and Louisiana; sugar-cane and its products,—in the way of sugar and molasses, —to Louisiana. In Florida considerable attention is paid to the cultivation of oranges, lemons, and other tropical fruits: wheat and tobacco have occupied the chief attention of farmers in Virginia and the neighboring States of Tennessee and Kentucky: North Carolina has acquired a reputation for its sweet potatoes and ground-nuts. Indian corn is an important product in all the Southern States; while the mountain-lands, which in all directions are covered with grass as well as extensive forests, are devoted to the grazing of cattle in great numbers, where they flourish throughout the year without shelter or any special care. In all the States lying directly on the Gulf of Mexico the climate is mild, the winters short, open, and delightful, and farm-work can be done every month in the year. They begin there to make their gardens in December, and until the following December there is a continuous succession of crops. The people live easily, and produce more for the same amount of labor than in any of the Northern States. Lands are cheap, and may often be paid for by a single crop. The timber is everywhere magnificent, and the lands are irrigated by numerous streams, and adapted to an unlimited variety of products. And for the raising of cattle there is not a region, probably, in the world, better suited for that purpose than the extensive State of Texas. In some localities, the cattle may be counted by the thousand, and it is an amazing fact that droves of them are annually sent by the stock-raisers as far off as California; and Texas cattle have even been butchered in the city of New York, and even cargoes of Texas beef have been shipped in ice to Philadelphia. From ten to twelve men are required for a herd of a thousand cattle, with two horses or mules to each man, for day and night duty; the cattle needing to be herded at night to prevent stampedes. For those who have never witnessed its operations, it is difficult to realize the extent of this cattle traffic, and it is sometimes the case that the whole earth seems to be covered with the herds, as far as the eye can reach over the vast prairies. The class of people commonly known as the "Texas Cow-boys" are indeed a power in the land, whose exploits and lives of adventure are more like romance than reality. And here, in passing, we may with propriety devote a paragraph to the various modes employed by farmers in fencing. In those regions where loose rocks are abundant, stone walls are almost universal: where both stone and wood are scarce, they have a fashion of planting trees and shrubbery: as a matter of taste, wire fences are occasionally employed. In all localities where wood is abundant, they make what are called post and rail, and worm fences. It is said that the fences of New York have cost $144,000,000, those of Pennsylvania $120,000,000, Ohio, $115,000,000, and South Carolina, $20,000,000, while the fences of the whole Union are estimated at $1,300,000,000. These figures are enormous, but they tend to exhibit the extent of the farming interests of America.

Having now taken a general survey of the agricultural population of America, we shall conclude what we have to say, with a few remarks on their manners and customs, as exemplified by certain amusements, which are, for the most, peculiar to this country. And first, as to the *sugar-making frolics*. In various parts of the Union, large quantities of sugar are annually made from the sap of the maple-tree. The moment Winter breaks, and the sap begins to ascend in the Spring, the trees are tapped, and the liquid thus obtained is boiled down until it becomes a rich syrup or granulated sugar. All this takes place in the dense woods, and most of the work is performed at night. At the close of the season the farmers invite their friends and neighbors to a kind of jubilee, which is held in the sugar-camps, and where, with sumptuous fare, followed by music and dancing, the entire night is given to enjoyment; and when the last cauldron of sugar has been made, and daylight has appeared, the company is dispersed, and the sugar utensils are packed away until the coming of another season. Corresponding to the above, in most of the corn-growing regions they have what are called "*Corn-Huskings.*" This entertainment occurs when a farmer is anxious to prepare for market an unusual quantity of the yellow maize; and in the North or West, when the young men and country lasses have met, they are piloted to the spacious and sweet-smelling barn, and for a stated time all work without ceasing, until the allotted task is performed; an adjournment then takes place to the farm-house, where feasting and dancing continue all the night long. When this frolic occurs in the South, the colored people there do the work, and enjoy themselves in their own rude but amusing ways, while the white people for whom they may happen to be working, act as the hosts, content to enjoy the laughable scenes brought to view. In the New England States, especially those regions bordering on the sea, they have what are called "*Clam-Bakes.*" These are usually attended by men only, who congregate from various quarters, for the purpose of exchanging political opinions, and having a systematic good time; when speeches are delivered, and large quantities of cheering beverages are imbibed, as well as clams eaten, after a primitive fashion. The shell-fish are roasted in an open field, and duly prepared with the desired condiments. These affairs take place in the summer, after the leading harvests have been gathered in. In the Southern States certain festivals are common, but more so before the late war than now, which are known as "*Barbecues.*" They are political, and sometimes bring together very large numbers of the planters and their families, and the time is generally devoted to speech-making, happily varied by eating and drinking the good things of the land. The principal food on these occasions consists of beef or mutton, and the oxen or sheep are roasted entire, over a pit duly prepared, and filled with burning coals. The cooks and caterers are generally negro men and women, and, as they have the privilege of inviting their own friends, the groves where they assemble present a varied and fantastic scene. The young people have it all their own way, and there is no end to the variety of their amusements. Another rural custom is known as a "*House-Raising.*" This occurs after some farmer has prepared his timber for a new house or barn, when he invites his friends and neighbors to come and help him to lift the timbers and crosspieces into their proper places. This invitation is always cheerfully accepted, and most of the time is devoted to downright hard work. But after the task has been accomplished, the men have a substantial feast, and a good long talk about their farms, their crops, and cattle, and commonly separate with a warm brotherly feeling for each other, and for their fellow-men everywhere. In some of the fruit-growing regions, large quantities of apples are stripped of their skins, cut into quarter pieces, and hung up to dry for winter use, and in that condition become a source of revenue. Out of this variety of business has grown an autumnal festival called an "*Apple-Paring.*" This takes place in the evening: the guests are invited as to an ordinary party, and after a few hours' attention to business, the night is given up to feasting and dancing, or the playing of innocent games by the young people, who compose the majority. *Ball-playing* and *Sleigh-riding* are two other pastimes in which the Americans indulge with rare gusto. By the rural population Saturday afternoon is usually assigned to the former, on which occasions the young men are as active and expert in throwing and catching, or striking the ball, as if they had been idle all the previous week, instead of having had to work in the fields with the utmost energy. Sleigh-riding, of course, takes place in the winter only, when the ground is covered with snow, and then it is that the young farmers bring out their best horses, fill their sleighs with lady friends, enveloped in gayly trimmed furs, and, to the exhilarating music of the bells, start off on all sorts of expeditions over the neighboring country. From time immemorial it has been the custom among the negroes of the South to devote the last week of the year, commonly called *Christmas Holidays*, to every variety of amusement. When slavery existed, those prolonged festivities were freely accorded to the slaves, and were full of romantic interest; but now that they are free, the colored people claim their old privilege as a right, but do not find the same unalloyed enjoyment as of old in their annual frolic. They have not as yet arrived at that stage when they can enjoy the blessing of supporting themselves. About the close of the year they have in various parts of the country what they call "*Shooting Matches.*" These are of two kinds, one, where turkeys and other birds are tied to a stake, and made a target for men who like to shoot the rifle, and experienced shots sometimes win a sufficient quantity of large poultry to supply all their friends. Another kind of match is, when two parties pit themselves against each other, and go upon a hunt for a day or a week, for squirrels or birds of game, when the victors are rewarded with a prize of some kind, paid for by the losing party. And then they have throughout the country such rural jollifications as *Sheep-Shearing*, *Ploughing Matches*, and, to the discredit of the participants, *Cock-Fightings*, which need not be described. But of all rural assemblages none are so generally popular as country Fairs. They occur in the Autumn in numerous localities, and bring together thousands of the agricultural population. The first agricultural Fair ever organized in this country by any of the colored population, was recently carried through with success in the State of Kentucky. Farm products, animals, and country fabrics are exhibited to a marvellous extent, in many of these Fairs. All sorts of friendly competitions are entered into, and *Horse-racing* has become an important adjunct to all these Fairs, whether patronized by the State at large or confined to the counties where they are held. But the crowning custom, and the one most universally recognized by the American people, is the celebration of what is known as *Thanksgiving Day*. It is an annual festival, honored by proclamations from the President and the local Governors, who specify the particular day; and of all places to enjoy it, none can be compared to the house of a successful farmer. The primary object of this festival is to recognize the goodness of the Almighty in crowning the labors of the field with prosperity, and the occasion is made especially joyous by the gathering together, under one roof, all the scattered members of the family in the old home. There are some other rural customs which might be mentioned in this place, but as they are of a religious character we shall defer them for a subsequent chapter of this volume.

# COMMERCIAL LIFE AND DEVELOPMENTS.

The inland and coast-line navigation of the United States is not surpassed, in extent and character, by any country on the globe; and the industry and enterprise of the Americans, in developing their commercial and shipping interests, has been, until within the last few years, equal to their superior advantages. Passing by all statistics in regard to the tonnage of the country, let us take a brief survey of the vessels and navigators which have given the country its reputation. By far the largest proportion of American vessels are run upon inland waters, and are called small craft; but the sea-going vessels, if less numerous, are generally as large as those of any other nation, and have been constructed on unsurpassed models. The ships called "Liners," which, a few years ago, ran between New York and Liverpool, acquired wide celebrity, and have never been surpassed for beauty and speed. But they have been superseded by steamers, and ships of that class now transact the same business. The burthen of those sailing-vessels was about two thousand tons; they were splendidly equipped, swift, were commanded and manned by the best metal, and did an immense business in bringing merchandise and immigrants to America. But, with the calamities that have befallen the mercantile marine of this country, they have nearly all passed away.

During the fiscal year of 1870, there were less than one hundred thousand tons of sea-going vessels built in the United States, and less than three hundred thousand tons of all descriptions of vessels, which amount was about equalled by the vessels built on the Clyde alone, while the tonnage of steam-vessels, built all in England, was sixty times greater than that of America. One result of this falling off in American ship-building has been that large numbers of men, who were brought up on the ocean, are seen turning their attention to a variety of pursuits connected wholly with the land. The inland waters of the country are most abundantly supplied with steamboats, and all the varieties of the smaller sailing-vessels; the coasting trade and fishing interests are quite as important and extensive as heretofore, but new vessels are by no means now turned out with the rapidity that they were a few years ago. It was the late war, also, which helped to put back the carrying trade of America, but with the return of peace and the final restoration of the Union, the old order of things began to be restored. When the great rebellion, or rather the British cruisers sailing under its flag, drove American shipping from the seas, and thus transferred the carrying trade to foreign bottoms, the commerce of Philadelphia suffered in common with that of other cities. The substitution of iron for wood, at about the same time, as the material for first-class steamships, left the country not only without ships, but behind other nations in facilities for making them. Boston, New York, and Baltimore soon recovered in good part their former commerce, through the help of foreign subsidized steamship lines. But Philadelphia, more thoroughly imbued with American ideas, made little effort to secure such foreign lines, but waited to build a line of her own, which will soon be established between that city and Liverpool. In 1860 the tonnage of the United States amounted to 5,353,868 tons, and in 1870, to 4,246,507 tons. Notwithstanding the above facts, however, the commerce of the country is very large and flourishing, since it appears that the American imports for 1870 amounted to about $600,000,000, and the exports about $400,000,000. The great variety of native productions exported from America gives assurance of the impossibility of failure in the resources of the nation. For example, from the sea, they have such products as oil, whalebone, spermaceti, and many kinds, in great abundance, of fish; from the forest, timber, shingles, staves, lumber, naval stores, and furs; from agriculture, every description of corn and vegetable food, and the products of animals, in the way of beef, pork, tallow, hides, bacon, cheese, butter, wool, lard, and hams, with horned cattle, horses, and other animals. From the Southern States they have cotton, tobacco, rice, and sugar; from the factories, every variety of useful goods; while their exports of specie and bullion have never been exceeded by any other nation. And as to their imports, they are simply enormous—silks, woolen goods, tea, coffee, and sugars being the most important, and for which there has always been a demand. But the crowning element of American commerce is its internal trade; and in this connection we cannot, perhaps, mention a more remarkable fact than this, that the production of spirituous liquors in 1870 amounted to $600,000,000 —the persons engaged in selling it by retail, numbering not less than 150,000; while the importation of opium, from China, amounted to nearly $2,000,000. The distances in America are so great, that the internal trade and traffic of the country has been, and must always be, a business of vast importance. And the extent of territory implies great diversity of productions. The growths of tropical regions are exchanged for the field-crops and forest produce of cooler latitudes; and in another direction, the products of the coast and of extensive interior districts are exchanged. The tide of emigration sets from east to west, while the tide of commerce flows from west to east; and we can only obtain an adequate idea of the inland commerce, by considering the enormous extent of the inland shipping and the railway facilities of the country.

But it is with the social aspect of American commerce that we have to do at the present time. The grand business centre of the nation is New York City. Having direct and constant intercourse with all parts of the world, the nationality of its merchants is as varied as the countries which they represent. Of the native-born merchants the most numerous and successful originated in the New England States, and are distinguished for their intelligence, ability, and elevated personal characteristics. They live in elegant houses, and, while surrounded by all the appliances of prosperity and wealth, are not prone to making a greater display than their less fortunate neighbors; they are plain in their manners, and hospitable; and if many of them happen to indulge in keeping up fancy residences in the country, the largest proportion are quite content to spend their summer vacations by the sea-side, or among the green hills of their native States. They devote themselves to business with ceaseless activity, and are the men who generally take pleasure in expending their surplus capital upon all sorts of benevolent, religious, and educational institutions. A type of merchants, allied to these, is also found in all the other cities of the country. Next to them come the English, French, and German merchants, who generally deal in the kind of merchandise sent out from their several countries. In their modes of transacting business, and of living, they adhere as closely as possible to the customs of their native lands, but with many modifications. The particular men who laid the commercial foundation of New York were from Holland, but their characteristics have been amalgamated with those of the various nationalities which have, latterly, made that city the most cosmopolitan in the country. While a very large trade is carried on between New York and the Oriental nations, the merchants of Boston have long considered themselves the special patrons and friends of the far East, and that city has always been a noted mart for the commodities of India, China, and Japan, in which particular it is now finding a rival in San Francisco. Its coasting trade is also very extensive, and it is the port whence various manufactures are shipped in immense quantities. The whaling business, which was formerly divided between several cities, is now almost entirely confined to New Bedford; the merchants of which city, like those of Boston, are proud of their descent from what is called the Puritan stock. In Philadelphia, where the coasting trade is almost unparalleled, they have what is called a Quaker element of population, which has always been noted for its integrity in matters of business; but this city is now vying with

New York in the cosmopolitan character of its merchants,—and in the person of Stephen Girard produced one of the wealthiest and most eminent merchants in America. With regard to Baltimore and Charleston, Mobile and New Orleans,—all these places are the natural outlets of the entire Southern half of the United States, and in all of them may be found an abundant supply of merchants from the four quarters of the globe. And corresponding with the cities just named, there are, throughout the interior of the country, very many cities which have grown into centres of trade and commerce with marvellous rapidity; among them may be mentioned Chicago (whose merchants are now building up a large tea-trade with China, by way of San Francisco), Detroit, Cleveland, St. Louis, and Cincinnati, Louisville, Buffalo, and Pittsburg, in all of which may be found the principal nationalities of the globe. Looking at the commercial classes, in the aggregate, it is quite impossible to give prominence to any nationality; and it would seem as if, after a brief residence in America, the whole mercantile population, with one exception, becomes permeated with the characteristics of the native-born inhabitants. The exception alluded to is the Jewish race. They are found in every city, and almost in every hamlet—always engaged in bartering and selling, and never in producing, and they are pre-eminently a wandering people. With them, the one great end of life would seem to be to make money, but where they settle down to enjoy it has always been a mystery.

In America, as elsewhere, permanent success in business is chiefly dependent upon character; honest and upright men are sure to command the respect of their neighbors, and when unfortunate, always find their fellow-merchants ready to assist them; and when men of bad repute happen to make fortunes, they generally find it convenient to settle down among strangers, to enjoy their ill-gotten gains. One of the effects of the late war in this country was to enrich a large number of adventurers and unscrupulous men, who made money by imposing upon the General Government, through political intrigues; and it was because of their foolishness in spending their money and putting on airs to which they were not accustomed, that they came to be known by the opprobrious title of *shoddy*, in remembrance of a spurious cloth which some of them palmed off for the use of the army. But the average American merchant of to-day is a man who deserves and receives universal respect. He is intelligent, but not addicted to the profits and pleasures of literature. Engaged all day in the excitement of commercial speculation, he has but little time to devote to reading, and improving his mind. He works so hard and so constantly, that work becomes a second nature to him, prostrating his energies and making him indifferent to proper recreations; he considers his word as good as his bond, and, to protect his credit, will make the greatest sacrifice of property; he is liberal in his feelings, and gives freely to all objects which have the sanction of his good opinion; he is hospitable, but would prefer to have his wife and daughters attend to the honors of his house and table; and when overcome by reverses, he takes a new start, changes the character of his business, perhaps, and will not acknowledge himself as overwhelmed, and proves his mettle by attaining final success. Perhaps there is no feature in the character of the Americans which is so remarkable as their spirit of enterprise. It is indeed wonderful, and is the cause of their success. But it does not follow that this enterprise is all native-born; a portion of it is undoubtedly brought into the country by intelligent men from the leading countries of Europe.

But let us now take a glance at some of the phases of their commercial life, or rather, at the classes of men who transact the mercantile business of the country; and first, as to the shipping merchants. To carry on their business a large capital is required, and as individuals or organized companies, they are generally the leading patrons of the great ship-yards. They have vessels built to order, and also buy them in open market; they establish lines of communication between home ports, by way of lakes and rivers, and between the United States and foreign countries; and they are the men who so frequently obtain valuable contracts from the Government for carrying the mails, as in the case of the Pacific Steamship Company, which receives not less than five hundred thousand dollars for conveying a semi-monthly mail from San Francisco to China and Japan. One of the most famous of these men is named Cornelius Vanderbilt. Another class of shipping merchants are those who simply direct or superintend the business for other parties. They are indeed what might be called, more properly, brokers. The wealthiest man who ever lived in the country, John Jacob Astor, and who left about $25,000,000, was at one time engaged in the shipping business, and made a great deal of money by sending his ships to China; but he was pre-eminently a trader in furs.* Then come the

---

* Since this was printed it has been stated that W. B. Astor, A. T. Stewart, and Cornelius Vanderbilt, are each worth sixty millions of dollars.

importing merchants. They have their agents located in foreign countries, purchase and sell their merchandise only in the bulk, and are the men who give the greatest impetus to the home trade. Some merchants of this class, engaged in trade with the Oriental nations, have followed the same business for nearly a century; many of them, located in New York and Boston, have acquired immense fortunes, and it was the son of one of these, James Lenox, who lately made a donation of a million of dollars for the establishment of a Library and Gallery of Art in New York. With some few of these importers the custom prevails of selling their goods by auction, soon after their arrival; and in this manner whole cargoes of tea from China or sugar from the West Indies were sold within the space of half an hour. But this business has well-nigh been absorbed by the class known as brokers. Another important class of merchants are the wholesale dealers or jobbers. They receive their goods in the bulk from the importers, and sell them by the piece or in broken packages. They sell on credit, and usually confine themselves to a particular class, or a few classes of goods. One house, for example, will sell only silk goods; another, all sorts of cotton fabrics; another, the several varieties of woolen goods; another, hardware; and others, wooden or fancy goods and groceries of every description. And then there are what are called the retail merchants. They constitute the most numerous class, and are to be found in every city and village of the land. In the larger towns there is no mingling of drygoods and groceries, but, in the hamlets, the merchants find it necessary and to their advantage to keep for sale everything that the people can possibly require—from a yard of calico or a piece of ribbon, a paper of buttons or needles, to a pound of tea or coffee, or sugar or shot, or a cake of soap. It is sometimes the case, however, that the importing, jobbing, and retail trades are carried on by the same firm, and there is one man located in New York City, Alexander T. Stewart, who is reputed to be the wealthiest and most influential merchant of this sort, in the world. His establishments are on the most stupendous scale; he employs agents and clerks by the hundred; and his passion for business is so strong that he is among the first, as well as the last, in his daily attendance at his enormous warehouses. This man began his career a poor and friendless boy, and, besides building a palace for himself, giving away millions for the comfort of the poor, he is now engaged, at an immense outlay, in founding a model town in the vicinity of New York. The commission merchants form another very extensive class of the business men. To carry on their business, less capital is required than for those already named, but it is important that their credit should be unimpeachable. They receive goods or produce from the manufacturers, or farmers, and sell them to the best advantage, receiving for themselves merely a certain per cent. on the amount of sales, in the way of commission, for trouble and expenses. With regard to the subordinates, who are employed by the more important merchants, they consist of drummers, who devote their time to hunting up customers; of clerks, who sell goods and keep the books; of porters, who pack the goods and do the manual labor; and of draymen, who carry the merchandise to the vessels, of every description, and to the railway stations. But there are certain other classes of business men in all the commercial marts, whose duties are important and whose influence is extensive. First among these are the auctioneers, who sell to the highest bidders, real estate, furniture, books, works of art, and everything, in fact, which the owners desire to turn rapidly into money; then come the brokers, who usually devote themselves to one commodity, such as cotton or money, tea and coffee, sugar or grain, who have come to be a numerous and useful class, and who sell only by samples, receiving their pay like the commission merchants. They transact the business which was formerly performed by one class of auctioneers. The class of men known as bankers are those who conduct the moneyed institutions of the country, albeit large numbers follow the business on private account, many of whom, in all the leading cities, have acquired immense fortunes. Of these, perhaps the most successful and celebrated is now a retired citizen of Washington, and who, within the last few years, has given away for purposes of charity and culture many millions of dollars. And still another class of the business men who are very numerous and constantly increasing, are known as Insurance men. They are the managers of extensive corporations, who insure, in stated sums of money, all kinds of property from fire and marine disasters, as well as the lives of men who desire to secure a competence for their families in the event of death. From the foregoing statements it will be seen that the machinery of commerce in this country is fully organized and very complete.

But, fully to comprehend the extent and range of the commercial interests, we must now turn our attention to the system of railways, as it exists in the United States. This is a subject which increases in interest and importance every year. In 1860 this system had already reached a development which was justly regarded as amazing. It was the product of but a short time; every mile of road had been built within the recollection of men who had not yet passed middle life, and three-fourths of it all within ten years. Yet there were in operation more than thirty-one thousand miles of road, which, with their equipment, had absorbed of the capital of the country not less than twelve hundred and fifty millions of dollars, or ten per cent. of the entire assessed value of property in the United States. There were men, however, who protested that this interest had outgrown the needs of the country, and was the result of speculative and artificial influences; that it diverted capital from more useful employments, and tended to retard the prosperity of the country. Nor have these men changed their opinion. But what a change has taken place in this business! From the official reports we learn that at the commencement of the present year there were railroad lines in operation to the extent of more than fifty-three thousand miles, which, with their equipment, cost nearly twenty-seven hundred millions of dollars, or twenty-two per cent. of the entire assessed value of property in the country. Of these more than eleven thousand miles have been built within two years, and at an expenditure of four hundred millions of dollars. In other words, the people of America have contributed during the last ten years more than half as much to build railroads as they have paid in taxes for the support of the Government, including the conduct of the war, and are now contributing yearly for the same purpose two-thirds as much as the whole revenue of the national treasury. The total earnings of these railroads in 1870 were four hundred and fifty millions of dollars; and the gross tonnage transported equalled one hundred and twenty-five millions of tons, having a value of more than *ten thousand millions of dollars*.

Prior to the late war, the American railroads were regarded almost exclusively in their relations to trade, and the comprehensive study of them was the concern only of the economist. But they have now become the centres of many forms of power in the hands of corporations whose management is concentrated, secret, and largely irresponsible; they hold vast accumulations of wealth; employ a large proportion of the scientific and practical ability of the nation; they exert an immense influence on all the markets, and on the social and material welfare of the whole people. They are also the favorite instruments of speculation, and sources of sudden profit; they wield political agencies and parties, in many places, and even dictate to the State Legislatures. They thus connect themselves with society, in so many relations, that their growth and influence are becoming an anxious study, not only for the economist and the trader, but for the politician, the statesman, and the moralist. Hitherto, a large part of the capital thus consumed has been borrowed from foreign nations, and the want is not felt in the United States. But it makes part of the debt on which the productive industry of the country must pay the interest. The subject, as it has been well said, thus presents important and difficult questions for discussion. But all men must acknowledge that the rapid progress of this enormous interest is as wonderful as its present magnitude; and it is plain that of the ultimate extent to which the construction of railroads in America will be carried, no estimate can be formed.

Before leaving this subject we must submit a few additional particulars. The average rate of speed, with the passenger-trains, in America, is thirty miles per hour, and the number of cars in each train varies from five to fifteen; while the freight-trains frequently number not less than one hundred cars. The locomotives are far more powerful and much larger than those on English roads, and wood is the common fuel. In front of the engine is generally placed a massive iron grating, called a "cow-catcher," intended to throw off any animal that may be upon the track; and in winter they are supplied with immense plows for the purpose of cutting through the banks of snow. They are supplied with bells as well as steam-whistles, to be sounded when starting, or used to give note of coming danger. They are generally managed by three men, one engineer and his assistant, and one fireman. The passenger-cars are large, and have from eight to sixteen wheels; some of them plain and open to all, and others, called palace cars, are very elegantly fitted up, and occupied only by those persons who are willing to pay an extra fare. On all the trains are also to be found such conveniences as "sleeping" and "smoking cars." The men who manage the trains while running, are the "conductors," who collect the tickets; at the end of each car is stationed a brakeman, who helps to regulate the speed; there are also baggage-men; while boys with books or papers, or fruit, are permitted to pass through the trains; and upon those which carry the United States mail, there is always an officer of the General Post-Office Department.

Tickets are purchased before entering the cars, and for every piece of baggage a metal check is given, so that a man may travel a thousand miles or more without casting a thought upon his baggage. The rails are made of iron and steel, and single or double tracks are in vogue according to the necessities of the route; and the longest continuous line of railway in America, running from New York City to San Francisco, is 3,200 miles.

As the primary object of commerce is to accumulate money, it is proper that we should conclude this paper with a general survey of the finances of the United States, and of the people to whom their management is intrusted. At the close of the last fiscal year, the debt of the United States amounted to $2,480,672,427; the reduction, since 1866, when it reached the highest amount, having been $292,563,746. The total receipts of the Government were $566,935,818, while the expenditures amounted to $417,433,346, leaving a balance in the Treasury of $149,502,472. The money spent for the civil service was $19,031,283; foreign intercourse, $1,490,776; military establishment, $57,655,675; naval establishment, $21,780,229; collecting customs revenue, $6,237,137; assessing and collecting internal revenue, $7,234,531; light-house establishment, $2,588,300; mint establishment, $1,067,097; Indians, $3,407,938; and pensions, $28,340,202; while the balance was devoted to miscellaneous expenditures. Turning from the operations of the national Treasury to the banking institutions, we find the following information: the national banks, which are conducted by private enterprise, but made perfectly secure by the General Government, number 1,627, and have a capital of $436,478,311; the chartered banks, which are disconnected from the Government, number 1,882, and have a capital of $503,578,000; the private bankers represent about $400,000,000 of capital; and the savings banks are estimated to hold about $195,000,000. The system upon which all these institutions is managed is quite uniform—each having a president and cashier, a board of directors, and as many clerks as may be required. Taken in the aggregate, the bankers of America are as upright and intelligent as any in existence; but no class, from presidents down to common clerks, are so liable to go astray, and therefore it is that the papers have occasionally to chronicle acts of dishonesty among banking men. On the score of success, it is also worth mentioning that the private bankers have at all times led the way in the more important financial negotiations between the United States and foreign countries; and the late rebellion, as well as the preceding war with Mexico, were both greatly indebted to the skill of two men, whose names as bankers have passed into history, viz.: William W. Corcoran and Jay Cooke. Of the various financial institutions, perhaps the most useful and truly American in its character is that known as the savings bank, the primary object of which is to keep in safety the savings of the poorer classes, for the use of which the bank pays a regular interest. Other banks make it their business to lend money for commercial purposes, but not so with the savings banks, which have more to do with real estate in making use of their funds. With regard to the circulating medium of the United States, we may remark that it is divided into paper money and specie. The former, which is also called currency, is all issued indirectly from the National Treasury, in denominations ranging from ten cents to $1,000, and $356,000,000 being a legal tender, while all the issues under one dollar are called fractional currency. The specie of the country is coined at a national mint, located in Philadelphia, and of course under the direction of the Treasury, and is composed of nickel, copper, silver, and gold; the copper forming one and two cent pieces; the silver, five, ten, twenty-five, and fifty cent pieces; and the gold, one, three, five, ten, twenty, and fifty dollar pieces; to all of which may be added what is called gold and silver bullion. There are also branch mints in operation at San Francisco, Denver, Charlotte, Carson City, and an assay office in New York. While it is true, that in all parts of the world money is considered a great power, there is probably no country where the people are so univerally imbued with the love of gain, or place so high an estimate on the possession of wealth, as is the case in the United States of America.

# LIFE AMONG THE MECHANICS.

In no way, perhaps, can the magnitude of the mechanical and artisan interests of America be better realized than by walking through the spacious apartments of the Patent Office in Washington, where are to be found over one hundred thousand models of American skill and enterprise. Of these, about five thousand have been deposited within the last three years. It might also be mentioned that the cost of supporting the Patent Office and publishing its records, down to the present time, has been twelve millions of dollars; that fifty thousand applications for patents have been rejected; and that no inventions, which are inoperative, frivolous, or mischievous can ever be protected by the Government.

Sixty years ago, the manufactures of the country were valued at $200,000,000; to-day, they are estimated at $3,000,000,000; while the people who are engaged in this enormous business are also counted by millions. Their character is varied and interesting. All labor is respected, but this is especially true of skilled labor. The American mechanics are partial to the higher grades of work, and this has a tendency to elevate them in society. They are ambitious to succeed, but often fail because of their attempting too much. As employers, they are faithful and punctual, and they who work as subordinates seldom have cause to complain. As fellow-laborers, they are not always considerate, but offences in that direction grow out of individual dispositions. Their minds are not given to abstract thought, but they are fond of industrial organizations. In dealing with men and things, and in surmounting obstacles, they are wonderfully ingenious; and perhaps their chief intellectual distinction is that of inventors. To use the language of another, their moral qualities are not striking, but generally sound. They are a good-natured people, and treat strangers with kindness. Fairness and honesty prevail among them. Discipline is weak. They respect their institutions, and deserve to be called a law-abiding people. Their homes are generally well ordered, and their domestic virtues are above the average among European nations. They are fond of amusements, but perhaps too willing to break through the rules of a wise restraint. Different sections and pursuits, however, bring about different results; and what is true of one neighborhood is not always true of another; and of course the inhabitants of the newly-settled regions are not generally as far advanced in culture as those located in the older cities and towns. A single brick or block of stone may give us a faint idea of the house to be built of that material; and in like manner, we may partially become acquainted with the manufacturing population by considering a few of its leading classes, who come under the head of mechanics or artisans.

And, first, as to the very extensive number of persons engaged in the production of flour and meal—the millers of the country. They are to be found in every part, and the business of transforming the various cereals into flour is carried on by steam-mills, as well as those propelled by water and wind power. The mills which are run by water power are the most numerous, and it is only in a few level districts that the old-fashioned windmill is in vogue. Many of the mills in question are of limited capacity, and only intended to grind the grain which is sent to them from the immediate vicinity; but in various parts of the country are located very extensive establishments, which send their brands of flour to various quarters of the globe. In these larger mills, which run both day and night, and employ two sets of hands, they grind and turn out from three hundred to one thousand barrels of flour in each twenty-four hours. Wheat is always a cash article; and to carry on the business, a large capital is required. Besides the regular millers and their immediate assistants, these establishments give employment to large numbers of coopers, who manufacture the barrels that are used; but within the past year, complaints have been made against these millers that they were in the habit of using old barrels, which had been used for other purposes. This kind of dishonesty, however, is not common, and will undoubtedly be remedied. The weight of a barrel of flour is always one hundred and ninety-six pounds, and it is universally inspected by a public officer before shipment from the place of its manufacture; so that the several classes through whose hands each barrel of flour is obliged to pass are the proprietors, the millers and their assistants, the coopers, the inspectors, and finally the book-keeping and shipping clerks. In the larger mills, moreover, regular millwrights are also permanently employed.

Excepting agriculture, there is no branch of American industry which gives employment to so many people as that of boot and shoe manufacturing. The New England States take the lead in this business, and Massachusetts is in advance of all the other individual States, the largest single establishment in that State giving employment to fourteen hundred persons, and paying out, in the way of wages, nearly one hundred thousand dollars per annum. And it is reported of one town that it turned out, in one year, boots and shoes enough to amount to five millions of dollars. The States of New York and Pennsylvania come next to New England, and it is estimated that the product of the whole United States is very much more than one hundred millions of dollars per annum; while the raw material in the way of leather has reached a similar amount. The finer qualities of boots and shoes are usually made in the cities, and chiefly by Germans, and the more ordinary varieties in the country-towns and villages. In some of these, almost every house has attached to it a shop for making shoes, and all the members of the family, when not engaged in household affairs, or in cultivating a garden, take part in the manufacture. Within the last year, quite a colony of Chinese shoemakers have found employment in New England, and every inducement is given to encourage their coming in greater numbers. Where the sewing-machine is employed, large numbers of shoes are turned out by some families, which are paid for on being delivered to the local dealers, who ship them to the wholesale merchants in the cities. A large proportion of the shoes made are fastened on the bottom by wooden pegs, thereby creating peg factories, in many of which shoe-lasts are made, the combined business amounting to many hundred thousand dollars. About one-third of the people engaged in making shoes are women, and it is said that the aggregate amount now paid to the shoemakers as wages is not far from fifty millions of dollars. With regard to the leather used in this enormous business, it is chiefly manufactured in the country, and its annual production reaches very nearly one hundred millions of dollars.

The manufacture of clothing for men, boys, women, and children has become a business, of late years, of great magnitude. It is confined chiefly to the large cities, and gives direct employment to nearly one hundred and fifty thousand hands, the largest proportion of whom are women. According to the latest published returns of the Census Office, they received in one year nearly twenty millions of dollars in wages, and produced merchandise which sold for about ninety millions of dollars. The general distribution of wealth in America enables the people of all classes to be comfortably and respectably attired, and it is seldom that one class is compelled to wear the cast-off clothing of another class. Out of this fact has grown the vast demand for ready-made clothing of moderate cost, which has developed into an immense and growing trade, giving employment to multitudes of women in the larger cities, who would otherwise find it difficult to support themselves in comfort. The cutters of common clothing are principally Americans, while the Germans and Irish are chiefly employed in the other branches of the business. The wages, both for men and women, are larger than those paid in Europe. The American women are noted for their fondness for dress, and carry the custom of clothing their children to a preposterous extent; and hence the demand for fancy articles of dress is probably greater than in any other civilized country on the globe. And while that wonderful invention called the sewing-machine has not only greatly increased the means of producing, it has at the same time created an increased demand for every variety of clothing.

Of the class of artisans who are engaged in the manufacture of machines, the number is not far from fifty thousand. The machines made by them are well-nigh countless in numbers and variety, ranging from steam-engines and locomotives down to printing-presses and sewing-machines. There is no country in the world where hydraulic machinery or watermills are so abundant as in America, and its water power is practically unlimited. Taken as a whole, the machinists of the country are noted for their superior intelligence, and turn their attention more to what is useful than to what is ornamental. Among the articles which they produce of special importance may be mentioned clocks and watches, firearms, cabinet furniture, cutlery, and all sorts of implements and tools, musical instruments, including organs and piano-fortes, carriages, soap and candles, bricks, tobacco in all shapes, with articles of unnumbered varieties made of iron, copper, brass, glass, and wood. Within the bounds of the Republic may be found the raw material for almost every branch of manufacturing industry. The intellectual power and skill of the American mechanic may be partly appreciated by the fact that the manufactories of the country, when last officially published, numbered one hundred and forty-one thousand, besides the machine-shops of great value and capacity, yielding products to the value of two thousand millions of dollars. These immense results, which include the products of the cotton and wool manufactories, whilst measurably affected by the wealth of the soil and its successful cultivation, are yet traceable to the artisan skill, energies, and industry of the American people. It has been said that the manufacturing and mechanical capacities of the Northern States of America were the primary cause of their success in the late rebellion, and that a more striking illustration of the power and value of such resources is not to be found in history. In looking over the official lists, we find that the mechanics and artisans of the United States might be arranged in classes which number about one hundred, and of course, in a paper like the present, it is impossible to describe them with minuteness.

But let us now take a glance at the subject of compensation. Common laborers in America earn from one to two dollars per day, without board. The wages for skilled labor are considerably higher, but they cannot be precisely specified, because the workmen make their own contracts with their employers, the prices being regulated by ability, the season, and the nature of the business. By way of illustration, however, we append the following selection, as about the rate of full monthly wages in vogue at the present time, viz.: bakers, fourteen dollars; blacksmiths, ninety dollars; bricklayers, one hundred and twelve dollars; book-binders, eighteen dollars; butchers, twenty dollars; cabinet-makers, ninety dollars; carpenters, one hundred and twelve dollars; cigar-makers, sixty dollars; confectioners, forty dollars; coopers, one hundred dollars; engineers, ninety-two dollars; machinists, ninety-two dollars; masons, one hundred and twelve dollars; millers, ninety-two dollars; painters, sixty dollars; printers, ninety-two dollars; harness and saddle makers, sixty dollars;

shoemakers, sixty dollars; tailors, eighty dollars; stonecutters, one hundred and twelve dollars; watchmakers, eighty dollars; wheelwrights, eighty-four dollars; wagonmakers, ninety-two dollars; spinners and weavers, forty-eight dollars; and wood-carvers, eighty dollars. The above are only about one-fourth of the trades followed in America, but they are among the most important. Generally speaking, the lowest wages are paid in the cities along the Atlantic seaboard, and they increase as the immigrant passes westward, reaching their highest point on the Pacific.

We come now to speak of some of the incidental circumstances connected with that portion of the laboring population devoted to mechanical employments. The hours for beginning and ending a day's work vary according to the seasons of the year. Hitherto, it has been customary to labor ten hours, but this has generally been regulated by agreements between the employer and his hired men. Within the last two years, however, this business has been mixed up with politics, and Congress has been induced to pass a law limiting a day's labor to eight hours so far as the public service is concerned. Whether these regulations have resulted to the advantage of the employed or the employer is not yet settled. It is alleged that they have tended to make discord in the more important establishments, causing the employers to lower the wages paid, and at the same time making the employed restless and more disposed than formerly to demand unreasonable terms. Looking at the mechanics of the United States in the aggregate, it may safely be said that they live in comfortable houses, have the best of plain food, husband their money with care, and are less addicted to intemperance than are certain classes who think themselves their superiors. They are not so driven in their employments that they cannot enjoy a suitable amount of recreation, and their amusements or entertainments differ according to their nationalities. If the Germans have their gardens, where they congregate at stated times to play games and drink beer; the Irish have their festivals in honor of their patron-saints, as well as their wakes or hilarious funerals; while the native-born inhabitants amuse themselves with pastimes peculiarly American, including picnics, steamboat excursions, and athletic games—but seldom omitting to read the daily papers, or have something to do with politics. While it is true that there may here and there be found artisans who have a hard struggle to get along comfortably, yet a large proportion who are industrious and frugal succeed in laying up money and surrounding themselves with the elegancies of life. Indeed, in many parts of the country very marked changes are going on among the people, and successful mechanics are pushing aside the older and more aristocratic families, and giving tone to society. If called upon to say from what sphere the largest number of moderately wealthy men have arisen, our observation would incline us to answer, the mechanical and artisan classes. There are men in all the larger cities, who were once engaged in the most ordinary employments, but who have amassed fortunes that are truly regal, and who are using their wealth in helping the poor, building hospitals, and founding institutions of learning, thereby proving that all the wisdom and benevolence are not possessed alone by the cultivated and intellectual classes.

By way of illustrating the wonderful changes that have taken place in mechanical employment, through the inventions of machinery, we may direct attention to the simple affair called a button. The first manufacturer, in America, of these useful articles, was one Samuel Williston. He was a country merchant, and while selling buttons made of wood, he conceived the idea of covering them with cloth, and he invented a machine for that purpose, which was the first one invented in the United States. From this humble beginning sprang up a factory, until this man was found to be making one-half of the buttons made in the whole world. Several factories which he established are coining wealth for their proprietors, and are known to the dealers in all climes. This man Williston is now nearly eighty years of age, and is worth about five millions of dollars; he is also a very liberal man, and has endowed several institutions of learning with more than a million of dollars, one of them being Amherst College, where several Japanese students are at the present time receiving their education.

The inventive talent of the Americans is universally recognized, and its special power is derived from the existing facilities for education. Among these, the most important, undoubtedly, are those afforded by the great mechanical exhibitions, which take place in some of the leading cities every year. One of them, which occurs in New York, has come to be considered as a national institution. The total number of laboring men, women, and children in the United States has been estimated at thirteen (13,000,000) millions; and it is said that the steam machinery of the country is equal to two millions

2,000,000 of horse-power, or twenty-eight millions (28,000,000) of grown men; so that while one-third of this work is done by laboring men, two-thirds are performed by laboring machines. According to the opinion of a leading British statesman, there are few countries in which the workingman is held in such repute as in the United States. The laboring classes may be said to embrace the entire American nation. American artisans prefer those occupations in which the exercise of brain is in greater demand than that of the elbow, and their chief ambition is to attain the positions of master-workmen. Being educated, they perform their duty with less supervision than is required when dependence is to be placed upon uneducated hands. It rarely happens that a workman who possesses superior skill in his craft is disqualified to take the responsible position of superintendent by the want of education and general knowledge. The true mechanic toils at his trade under the conviction that manual labor, to be effective, must adapt itself almost wholly to the direction of science; and that under that direction, unskilled labor necessarily becomes skilled, and limited trusts enlarge into influential responsibility.

As already intimated in this paper, the records of the Patent Office bear witness to the effects of general education in the development of mechanical ingenuity in the American people. Nowhere in the world, it has been justly said, does it exist to the same extent; and yet, in some of the most important departments of manufacture, the people are now nearly stationary, while in others they make but little progress. A few years ago, Germany sent to Massachusetts for machinery to manufacture woolen cloth; but to-day there is scarcely any broadcloth made in any of the United States. Many of the most important improvements in the cotton manufacture are of American origin; and yet the amount of cotton-wool now consumed hardly exceeds that which was required eight years ago. The same is true of various other articles of manufacture. In the last ten years the population has increased about nine millions; and yet the number of persons engaged in many of the manufacturing establishments is not now greater than it was then. The whole increase, therefore, is forced into agriculture and trade; and a new class of men, called "middle-men"—who neither produce, nor sell at their own risk—has sprung into existence, whose influence upon the prosperity of the country is thought to be of doubtful character.

# RELIGIOUS LIFE AND INSTITUTIONS.

Under this head we propose to submit a general account of religion in the United States.

There is no state religion, and the Government undertakes only to maintain order and administer justice to all, and they are entirely free to choose any kind of religion, save those which are contrary to its civil laws. Men associate themselves, according to their preferences, under separate organizations called churches. They all believe in one eternal and incomprehensible Deity, and in the immortality of the soul. All these churches have a book called the Bible. This book is believed to be a revelation from the Deity, or God, and is divided into the Old and New Testaments, the former being called the Hebrew Scriptures, and the latter the Greek Scriptures. They claim that the Old Testament contains the most ancient writings known, and gives a history of the world and of man from the creation, and also prophesies the coming of Christ at a given time, which is fulfilled in the New Testament, wherein there is a history of the birth and ministry, death and resurrection of Christ, contained in its principal portion called the gospel, the meaning of which word is "good news," and is applied to the story of Christ. Christ is believed to have been "God manifest in the flesh," and all who believe in Him are called Christians.

As specimens of each of these parts of the Bible, we quote here some of its leading features. From the Old, the "Decalogue," containing the Ten Commandments or precepts, written on two tables of stone, claimed to have been delivered by God to an inspired man called Moses, at Mount Sinai, in Asia; they will be found in the following words:

"And God spake all these words, saying, I am the Lord thy God, which have brought thee out of the land of Egypt, out of the house of bondage. (1) Thou shalt have no other gods but me. (2) Thou shalt not make unto thee any graven image, or any likeness of anything that is in the heaven above or in the earth beneath, or that is in the water under the earth; thou shalt not bow down thyself to them nor worship them; for I the Lord thy God am a jealous God, visiting the iniquity of the fathers upon the children unto the third and fourth generation of them that hate me, and showing mercy unto them that love me and keep my commandments.

(3) "Thou shalt not take the name of the Lord thy God in vain, for the Lord will not hold him guiltless that taketh His name in vain. Remember the Sabbath day to keep it holy. Six days shalt thou labor and do all thy work; but the seventh day is the Sabbath of the Lord thy God; in it thou shalt not do any work, thou, nor thy son, nor thy daughter, thy man-servant, nor thy maid-servant, nor thy cattle, nor thy stranger that is within thy gates;

(4) "For in six days the Lord made heaven and earth, the sea, and all that in them is, and rested the seventh day: wherefore the Lord blessed the seventh day and hallowed it.

(5) "Honor thy father and thy mother: that thy days may be long upon the land which the Lord thy God giveth thee.

(6) "Thou shalt not kill.

(7) "Thou shalt not commit adultery.

(8) "Thou shalt not steal.

(9) "Thou shalt not bear false witness against thy neighbor.

(10) "Thou shalt not covet thy neighbor's house, thou shalt not covet thy neighbor's wife, nor his man-servant, nor his maid-servant, nor his ox, nor his ass, nor anything that is thy neighbor's."

From the New Testament we quote a part of Christ's Sermon on the Mount, as follows:

"Blessed are the poor in spirit, for theirs is the kingdom of heaven.

"Blessed are they that mourn; for they shall be comforted.

"Blessed are the meek; for they shall inherit the earth.

"Blessed are the merciful; for they shall obtain mercy.

"Blessed are the pure in heart; for they shall see God.

"Blessed are the peace-makers; for they shall be called the children of God.

"Blessed are they which are persecuted for righteousness' sake; for theirs is the kingdom of heaven.

"Blessed are ye when men shall revile and persecute you, and shall say all manner of evil against you falsely for my sake."

After thus declaring who are blessed, he goes on to say who are the salt of the earth, the light of the world; and that he came to fulfill the law; what it is to kill, commit adultery, and to swear. He exhorts man to suffer wrong; to love even his enemies; to labor after perfectness; to give alms; teaches him how to pray, how to forgive, how to fast, where to lay up treasures, how to serve God and not to serve mammon, not to be careful for worldly things, to seek God's kingdom. He reproves rash judgment, forbids to cast holy things to dogs. He warns them to beware of false prophets; to be doers of the word, and to be like houses built upon a rock. He then teaches the following prayer:

"Our Father which art in heaven, hallowed be thy name, Thy kingdom come, Thy will be done in earth as it is in heaven; give us this day our daily bread; and forgive us our debts, as we forgive our debtors, and lead us not into temptation, but deliver us from evil, for thine is the kingdom, and the power, and the glory, forever. Amen."

In another place he says: "Thou shalt love the Lord thy God with all thy heart, and with all thy soul, and with all thy mind. This is the first and great commandment, and the second is like unto it: Thou shalt love thy neighbor as thyself. On these two commandments hang all the law and the prophets."

And still in another part of the Gospel we find this assertion: "Not every one that saith unto me, Lord, Lord, shall enter into the kingdom of heaven; but he that *doeth* the will of my Father which is in heaven."

In view of the fact that Christ was crucified on a *cross*, and the same has ever been considered a symbol of suffering, we quote the following mandate: "And when he had called the people unto him with his disciples, also, he said unto them: Whosoever will come after me, let him deny himself, and take up his *cross*, and follow me. For whosoever will save his life, shall lose it; but whosoever shall lose his life, for my sake, and the gospel's, the same shall save it. For what shall it profit a man, if he shall gain the whole world and lose his own soul? or what shall a man give in exchange for his soul? Whosoever, therefore, shall be ashamed of me and of my words in this adulterous and sinful generation, of him also shall the Son of man be ashamed, when he cometh in the glory of his Father with the holy angels."

What is called the "golden rule" is contained in the following words: " Therefore all things whatsoever ye would that men should do to you, do ye even so to them: for this is the law and the prophets."

These specimens will show how the Christian religion accords with the Bible.

Both the Old and New Testaments contain, as most of such books do, many wonderful and strange stories, hard to be comprehended. The present writer deems it best not to allude here to any of them, as they appear to him to be of no grave importance, in regard to their real religious essence. The increasing influence of the Bible is marvellously great, penetrating everywhere. It carries with it a tremendous power of freedom and justice, guided by a combined force of wisdom and goodness.

Education, industry, and benevolence are also other strong agents of the Bible influence. The believers in it have schools, and preaching, and missionary enterprises. For the care and help of all the unfortunate they have institutions. These are of three general kinds:

First. Schools for the masses, supported by the State,

though this does not exclude schools supported by those directly partaking of the benefit.

Second. Institutions of mercy, asylums for the blind, the deaf and dumb, and the insane. These, because of the great expense attending them, are general, and are supported by the State; while hospitals and infirmaries and lying-in establishments are denominational or belong to churches, and are supported by charitable contributions.

Third. Penal institutions, which include houses of correction for young persons, jails, and penitentiaries—all these being conducted more upon the principle of reforming the evil-doers than upon the principle of punishing them.

Having now given a general outline of the system of religion, we will give a few particulars connected with the separate organizations.

There are three great divisions of the Christian Church throughout the world,—Protestant, Roman Catholic, and Greek Church,—the latter being organized in the United States only to a limited extent.

The name Protestant was first given in Germany to those who, under the leadership of Martin Luther, an Augustine monk, protested against a decree of the Emperor Charles V. to support the doctrines of Rome. The Pope, Leo X., had granted indulgences for sins, on the payment of certain sums of money into the church treasury, and this was deemed wrong by Luther, who soon founded a religion in opposition to such teachings, and the name Protestant now comprehends chiefly all those Christians who are opposed to the Roman Catholic Church.

Numerous denominations or sects have since sprung up among the Protestants, and they may be named as follows:

Methodists, Presbyterians, Congregationalists, Baptists, Episcopalians, Lutherans, Moravians, Quakers, Dutch Reformed Church, Universalists, Unitarians, and a few others. The sacred volume, or Bible, in which all these sects believe, although some of them interpret it differently from others, is chiefly printed and circulated by special Bible Societies, which, in connection with other Societies established in Europe, have issued the book, or parts of it, in one hundred and sixty-five different languages, and circulated it to the extent of one hundred and one millions of copies during the present century. With regard to the leading principles just mentioned the great multitude of Protestants are agreed; but the sects, in their modes of worship, are somewhat different from each other, and must be mentioned separately. Of these, the most extensive class are the Methodists.

This sect was founded in England, and is known by the names of Methodist Episcopal and Methodist Connection. It receives its name Methodist from the fact that its members profess to be guided in their living by the methods laid down in the Bible, and the name of Episcopal marks that branch whose power is vested in bishops. They have arranged their doctrines of belief into twenty-five articles; they recognize the two great sacraments of Baptism and the Lord's Supper, in common with all Protestants. They are ruled by what is termed a Conference, and their principal officers are called bishops, preachers, deacons, and elders. Their churches are plain, and usually built without steeples or towers. Many of the preachers spend their time in travelling from one part of the country to another as missionaries.

They own an extensive book establishment, and annually give large sums of money for the support of missionaries in various parts of the world. In 1870, their preachers numbered 19,170; regular members, 2,623,201; colleges, 23; academies and seminaries of learning, 85; while the total amount of their property was about $7,000,000.

Presbyterians are governed by *presbyteries*, or associations of ministers and ruling elders; several adjoining presbyteries meet under the name of *Synod*, and their *General Assembly*, which is their highest tribunal, is composed of delegates from each presbytery; this body meets annually, and attends to the interests of their church throughout the country. Although known in various parts of Europe, this sect was introduced into America from Scotland, where it is the Established Church. The doctrines which they profess are purely evangelical on all points. They give the name of bishop to each minister, and hold them equal in power; the meaning of the word bishop being overseer. In 1870, the total number of ministers was 4,877; the churches, 5,342; and the members or communicants, 524,945. The amount contributed and expended for church and missionary operations was about $8,000,000. One of their customs is to have *protracted meetings*, which continue for several days at a time, and often terminate in what are called revivals of religion, usually bringing many new members into their congregations.

Closely allied to the above is the sect called Congregationalists. It is the same as that known in England as the Independents, and they have been identified with America ever since 1620, when the Pilgrims first landed on the shores of New England. The essential peculiarity of this church is, that it maintains the independence of each congregation. It is associated with Presbyterians in missionary and publishing enterprises; its colleges are numerous, and its chief strength lies within the New England States; its ministers number 3,043; churches, 2,341; its members, 306,518; and in the last forty years it has expended for religious purposes nearly $6,000,000.

Next to the Methodists, in point of numbers, are the Baptists. They differ from all other sects in regard to the rite of Baptism; they not only exclude infants from the rite, but in case of all adults, insist upon immersion, or subjecting the entire body to the influence of water; hence they have in most of their churches a large tank or basin, built behind their pulpits, in which the ceremony is performed; but in some parts of the country it is quite common to perform the rite in rivers or natural pools of water, and at such times the congregated spectators help to make the scene impressive: the officiating pastor leads the person to be baptized into the water, and dips the head under, while pronouncing the necessary form of words. There is a loose dress worn on the occasion by the pastor and the person to be baptized. They do not use the title of bishop, and they recognize no officials higher than pastors and deacons. One branch of this sect call themselves Close-Communion Baptists, and will not allow members of other denominations to commune with them; another branch are called Seventh-Day Baptists, because they consider Saturday,—or the seventh day of the week,—the true Sabbath. Still another branch are called Free-Will Baptists, because of their more liberal opinions. According to the latest records the members of this church number 1,221,349; the churches, 15,143; and ministers, 8,784. They publish thirty-five periodicals; and support twenty-five colleges and fourteen seminaries of learning.

We now come to the Protestant Episcopal Church. It consists of thirty-nine confederated dioceses under the care of bishops, to whom their priests and deacons are subordinate. Each bishop has charge of a diocese or circuit, which is the extent of his jurisdiction and generally comprises one State. These representative bishops meet in a General Convention, composed of the "House of Bishops," consisting of all the diocesan and missionary bishops, and of the "House of Clerical and Lay Deputies," consisting of four laymen from each diocese. This convention meets triennially. Each diocese has its Annual Convention, composed of its bishop and assistant bishop, if there be one, and the priests, deacons, and laity from each congregation; and all disputed questions are referred to the House of Bishops. This sect has a written form of worship, called a Liturgy, which is embodied in a book called the "Common Prayer;" it is founded upon the one used by the Church of England, with such alterations as were deemed expedient upon its adoption in the United States. There have been several dissensions in this church growing out of the use of this book, and these have caused the division of the sect into High and Low Church. They are the only Protestants, excepting the Dutch Reformed, who wear robes or gowns while performing their priestly office. This gown is of black silk, fitting loosely, and is worn while preaching and at funerals. A white gown is used for all other services, which is made of white muslin; bishops wear only the white gown. They have 52 bishops, and their priests and deacons number 2,786; their parishes, 2,605; and members or communicants about 220,000.

The denomination known as Lutherans claims to be more especially Protestant than any other, and takes its name from Martin Luther, although that celebrated reformer was opposed to its use in that connection. Another name for this church is that of the United Evangelical Church. They believe in the actual salvation of infants, dying unbaptized.

In other respects the Lutherans substantially agree with all the denominations hitherto mentioned. It has long been an influential body in America; its ministers number 1,933; its churches, 3,417; and members, 387,746. Closely allied to the sects already mentioned are those known as the Dutch Reformed and the Moravians. The first of these has its seat of power in New York; its ministers number 974, and its members, 175,091. The Moravians, though not numerous, have also been noted for their devotion to missionary labor, especially in the northern parts of North America.

All the denominations described above are commonly styled as Orthodox or Evangelical. The following are those which in some degree are in opposition to the others in both faith and principle. They are regarded very liberal and broad in their views.

The sect known as Universalists claim that their doctrines were preached in the United States, as far back as one hundred years ago. They reject the doctrine of the Trinity, giving to Christ the second place, and making him subordinate to the Father; and while declaring that God is infinite, they believe in the final destruction of evil and the restoration of all human souls through Jesus Christ. They do not believe that any of the human race will be finally lost. Their government is representative and ecclesiastical; and they have 1,279 societies, 998 churches, and 724 preachers; publish about twenty periodicals, and hold property to the value of about eight hundred thousand dollars.

And next come the Unitarians. They oppose the doctrine of the Trinity, which is held by the great majority of Protestants, and believe in the absolute unity of God. They do not reject the existence of Christ, but believe him to have been only a man. The manner of their worship is simple, and each church manages its own affairs separately. This sect originated in the United States in 1825, and is more popular in Massachusetts than in any other State of the Union. The number of societies which they support is 334, and they have 396 ministers, a large proportion of whom are not permanently settled. They support two Theological Seminaries; seven or eight periodicals; and fifteen charitable institutions. The population connected with this denomination is variously estimated at from fifteen to thirty thousand. Within the last few years they have accepted the co-operation of the Universalists in their efforts to do good; and they have made the following agreement:

"Reaffirming our allegiance to the Gospel of Jesus Christ, and to secure the largest unity of the spirit, and the widest practical co-operation, we invite to our fellowship all who wish to be followers of Christ."

Having now given a general description of the various Protestant denominations, it is proper that we should be a little more explicit in regard to the sacraments of the Evangelicals. They admit as essential to membership only two sacraments, which are considered of Divine institution. These are the rite of Baptism, and the Lord's Supper, called the Communion. Baptism is a representation or seal of the new covenant, and is the appointed ordinance for their introduction into the church, and is a sign of profession, whereby the promises of remission of sins and adoption into the family of Christians are said to be visibly sealed by the Holy Ghost. All the denominations mentioned above, excepting the Baptists, believe in the efficacy of infant baptism, and that it has an influence on all the periods of life; and all administer the rite by sprinkling with water the face of the child or adult believer, and sometimes, as in the Episcopal Church, making the sign of the cross on the forehead while the minister pronounces the words, "I baptize thee in the name of the Father and the Son and the Holy Ghost," showing by these words that the person baptized, or the person bringing the child, believes in the Trinity or Triune God, the Father as Creator, the Son as Redeemer, and the Holy Ghost as Comforter. The water is used as an emblem of purity, and it is not generally supposed that the outward sign will profit those who live and die without the inward grace, but is to be an adoption into the family of God, by being consecrated to his service, and is a safeguard from evil, so far as the remembrance of this consecration has its influence. Baptism, therefore, is supposed to commemorate the fact that Jesus Christ revealed God to be the Father, himself the Son, and the Spirit the

Holy Ghost, or three persons in the one Godhead, all of which are acknowledged by them to exist as a mystery, understood by God alone.

The Holy Communion, or Sacrament of the Lord's Supper, commemorates the fact that Jesus Christ lived and died; and it derived its institution from the fact that, on the evening before his death, he had a supper, commonly called the Last Supper, and he gave bread and wine to his disciples, saying, "Take and eat this bread in remembrance of me, and as often as ye drink this cup ye do show forth the Lord's death until He come." These words are found recorded in their Bible, and are believed by all Protestants; so that this Sacrament is revered by all who believe in Christ's sacrifice on the cross to atone for the sins of the whole world. The Episcopalian and the Methodist form of partaking of the Lord's Supper is by kneeling around the chancel in front of the pulpit, while the minister passes before them, first with the bread, which he gives to each one, saying, "The body of our Lord Jesus Christ, which was given for thee, preserve thy body and soul unto everlasting life. Take and eat this in remembrance that Christ died for thee, and feed on him in thy heart by faith, with thanksgiving." He then gives the cup to each one, saying, "The blood of our Lord Jesus Christ, which was shed for thee, preserve thy body and soul unto everlasting life. Drink this in remembrance that Christ's blood was shed for thee, and be thankful."

Right here we may pause for a moment to look at a passage in the New Testament, wherein Christ declares himself to be the bread of life to all believers, and addressing himself to the doubting Jews: "Then Jesus said unto them, 'Verily, verily I say unto you, except ye eat the flesh of the Son of man, and drink his blood, ye have no life in you. Whoso eateth my flesh, and drinketh my blood, hath eternal life; and I will raise him up at the last day. For my flesh is meat indeed, and my blood is drink indeed. He that eateth my flesh, and drinketh my blood, dwelleth in me, and I in him. As the living Father hath sent me, and I live by the Father; so he that eateth me, even he shall live. This is that bread which came down from heaven; not as your fathers did eat manna, and are dead; he that eateth of this bread shall live forever.'"

The Presbyterians partake of the Sacrament sitting either around a table, which is placed in some churches, or in the pews of the church; the bread and wine being handed to them by the Elders of the church; the minister at the same time repeating words nearly allied to those used by Christ at the Last Supper. The Congregationalists and Baptists use nearly the same forms.

The next rite of importance is that of marriage. It is considered by all Christians to have been ordained by God, and therefore it is a holy rite, not to be engaged in without the sanction of the proper authorities, which make the tie binding and lawful. The ceremony, after a license has been granted, is performed either in the church or at the home of the bride, always by a clergyman, if one can be procured, but in some cases of emergency it can be solemnized or performed by a justice of the peace. The Episcopalians have a written form contained in their Prayer-Book, and the other denominations use also a set form of words, although every one in conclusion makes use of the Bible text: "Those whom God hath joined together, let no man put asunder," which was the injunction used by Christ at the institution of the ordinance.

The burial service for the dead is also a written form with the Episcopalians and Methodists, and is generally performed at the house of the deceased, but members of the church are frequently buried from the church, where the body is carried, for the purpose of having the burial service performed. It is then borne out of the church by persons selected by the family, called pall-bearers, and followed by the relatives and friends to the grave, which has been previously prepared, and is there committed to the earth by the clergyman, lowered into the grave by the pall-bearers, and the earth thrown upon the coffin, and the grave is then closed.

But there are some other religious classes that must be mentioned, who are noted for their peculiarities.

The sect called Quakers or Friends was founded in England by a man named George Fox, and the recognized head in the United States was William Penn. The epithet Quaker was given to them, because they often trembled under an awful sense of the infinite purity and majesty of God. While professing to be guided by the Protestant Bible, they have the following peculiarities: They are very plain in their manner of dress, and in their church buildings; have no special reverence for the Christian Sabbath; speak in public assemblies only when prompted by the Spirit; and they allow women to speak at their meetings. They are to some extent Unitarians in belief, have always been opposed to slavery, and also to war, and never participate in military affairs; and, in consequence of a division that once took place among them, a portion of them followed the lead of a man named Elias Hicks, and became known as Hicksites. The city of Philadelphia was founded by them, and Pennsylvania and New York have been their principal fields of labor. Of late years, they have increased in numbers in the western States of the Union, and the sect now claims about one hundred and thirty-five thousand members, while they have four colleges, and quite a number of large boarding-schools.

The people called Shakers originated in England about one hundred years ago, but are now confined to the United States. The order was founded by two women named Ann Lee and Jane Wardley, the former having professed to receive divine light directly from heaven. They believe that God is dual, there being an eternal Father and Mother in the Deity; and the same of Christ. They are ascetics; live in secluded communities; take no part in earthly governments, and are virtually opposed to the marriage relation. They look upon idleness as sin, and are noted for their neatness and plainness of dress. There are twelve societies or settlements of them in the United States, and they have not increased in numbers in the last fifty years, their total number being less than two thousand. They are famous for their knowledge of gardening, and in their principal community, called Mount Lebanon, in New York, which they own in common, they carry on an extensive business in the way of selling seeds and certain articles of domestic manufacture, often yielding an annual income of fifty thousand dollars. In their religious services they frequently resort to dancing, and they believe that their members have the power of healing diseases by means of prayer and abstinence from food.

Another class of religionists are called the New Jerusalem Church, and was originated by Emanuel Swedenborg of Sweden, whose name it sometimes bears; its doctrines are founded upon the Bible, but are considered by Protestants as very symbolical. Its followers in America are not numerous, but generally cultured people. Another sect is known as Mormon, whose founder was Joseph Smith, and whose disciples have built up a city in Utah; they are the advocates of polygamy, which they practise to a large extent, and Brigham Young is the name of their present leader, but who, within a short time, has been prosecuted by the General Government as an offender against the criminal laws of the country.

Next come the Millerites or Second Adventists, founded by one William Miller, who preached that the world was to be destroyed on a particular day, when his disciples dressed themselves in white robes and waited for the great event in open fields; and although the predictions of this pretended prophet were not fulfilled, the sect still survives to a small extent. And then there are the Tunkers or Harmless People, who profess to be animated in their religion by fraternal love; the Spiritualists, so called, who boast that they are infidels and heretics; the Perfectionists, who advocate a new and perfect way of society; the Socialists, the Fouricrites, the Trappists, who believe in a "community of goods," and finally the Female Seers, who claim that women are superior to men, and that some of their sect have been ordained to be prophetesses and seers.

The Roman Catholic Church comprises that society of Christians whose members acknowledge the Pope as the visible head of the church. Its followers claim it to be coeval with the commencement of the Christian era, although it does not appear to have been fully organized until the fourth century. The pope is also called a Sovereign Pontiff, and the word pontificate is used to denote the reign of a pope. He resides in Rome, and his power extends over all his followers, wherever they may exist, and all the churches of this sect in the world are under his supervision. All rules for government and discipline emanate from him, and he is supposed by them to be the present representative of St. Peter, one of Christ's apostles, from whom the popes have in a successive line proceeded; thus founding their belief in *Apostolical succession.* After the pope, the next in order of rank or power is the archbishop, who presides over the bishops of the dioceses over which he has jurisdiction; then follow the bishops, priests, deacons, and sub-deacons, with similar powers to those mentioned in the Episcopal Church.

But that which chiefly distinguishes Roman Catholics from Protestants, is their belief in the Virgin Mary as an intercessor between God and man, and also in the intercession of the saints or the good persons who have died, and are supposed to be in the enjoyment of heaven. These, they think, can hear and transmit the prayers of the faithful on earth, to Christ, and that the prayers of the Virgin Mary are especially efficacious with her son, Jesus Christ. They believe in the use of images and relics of saints and the Virgin, and generally wear these and the crucifix, or image of Christ, about their person, as a supposed safeguard from evil, and as reminders of their dependence upon these persons for salvation.

Roman Catholics also believe in the prayers of the church

for the dead, and what is called High Mass is said in the church, after death. These prayers are said for the dead, believing that there is a middle state, called Purgatory, between Heaven and Hell, into which persons pass for purification before entering heaven, and therefore that the prayers of the church, and good people, will avail to get them from the transition state into Heaven. Their chief reliance for salvation is in the blood of Christ, but they believe that their good works of prayer, fasting, and almsgiving are meritorious. They believe in the saving grace of baptism, and that after the form has been used, the person is regenerate, and delivered from all sin: besides the use of water, they anoint with oil and use salt, and the rite is performed somewhat after the following manner: The priest blows three times upon the face of the person, saying, "Depart out of him, O Unclean Spirit, and give place to the Holy Spirit, the Comforter;" he then makes a sign of the cross on the forehead and breast, and a grain of salt is put into the mouth of the person, and he is admonished to keep the soul from the corruption of sin. Oil is used to anoint the breast and between the shoulders, and water is then poured upon the head three times in the form of the cross—saying, "I baptize thee in the name of the Father, and the Son, and the Holy Ghost;" then a white linen cloth is put upon the head, and a lighted candle is placed in the hand, the priest saying, "Keep the light of faith ever burning by the oil of good works." He finally pronounces the blessing: "Go in peace; the Lord be with thee."

They believe in the sacraments of confirmation, marriage, penance, extreme unction, and holy orders, but that of the

Lord's Supper, or Eucharist, as they call it, and Baptism, are the only ones held in common with Protestants, and we will only give these to show how they differ from that body of Christians. They believe in the Real Presence of the body and blood of Christ in the Lord's Supper; or that the bread and wine are changed by the consecration of the priest into the real body and blood of Christ; this they term Transubstantiation, or the change of the substance from bread and wine into flesh and blood. In performing this sacrament the priest blesses the bread, or wafer, as they call it, and then the people go up to the rail before the altar and kneel down, holding a towel, or white cloth, before their breasts, so that if a particle of the bread should fall it may be received into the towel and not fall to the ground. Then the priest distributes it to them, making the sign of the cross with the consecrated bread upon each one, saying, "The body of our Lord Jesus Christ preserve thy soul unto everlasting life." They do not give the cup to the people, but the priest takes all the wine, believing that after consecration, the whole body and blood and divinity is substantially contained in the wafer or in the wine, and that it is not necessary to give both, and the bread is distributed instead of the wine, as there is danger of spilling the blood of Christ if all receive the cup.

Their church service is called the mass, and it is in the form of a liturgy or manual. It is read in Latin, that being the original language in which it was written, and the translation accompanies each part, and is thus comprehended by those who can read, while the ignorant accept the form and hear it in a devout manner, believing in the power of the priest to present it to God for them, although they may not understand the words. Their faith in the priesthood is extreme, and they have frequent access to them for spiritual advice; the special guide of each individual is the priest who presides over the congregation of which he is a member, and according to his dictation are performed outward acts of contrition, satisfaction, and confession, called penances, by which those sins into which they may have fallen after baptism can be remitted; some of these penances are very severe, sometimes requiring much bodily suffering and great sacrifices of time and pleasure, and often much fasting before absolution is given by the priest. They have what is called the confessional, and the apartments devoted to this purpose are small closets or curtained places in the church or chapel, wherein the priest stands, outside of which the person who confesses kneels with head covered, and repeats his sins, and receives the admonitions of the priest; it is not necessary that the individual be known personally to the priest; all that the priest is required to do, is to hear and absolve as he may deem proper. This constitutes one great hold which the priesthood have upon the people, and they are willing to accept from them all advice upon matters of conscience. The priests wear robes and vestments while officiating in the church, and these are sometimes very elaborately embroidered and enriched by lace and other materials. This sect denounces as heretics all who do not believe in their teachings, and they believe that none can be saved outside of their church, excepting by a special providence of God, in cases of ignorance of their doctrines.

The Bible is interpreted by their priests for the people,

and Roman Catholics are said to be opposed to the free schools of America, because the Bible is permitted to be read and taught in these schools. They exclude it from their own schools, as a whole, believing it to be wrong to place it in the hands of those who may be led to interpret it for themselves. That portion of it which they allow for general use contains only the New Testament; the Old Testament being given in the form of a Bible History which has been compiled for this purpose. This question has caused a great deal of discussion in the political world, as free schools are a government institution, and it has influenced many political elections throughout the country, when it has been made a test question whether the candidate under consideration would vote for or against free schools. This plan of interpreting the Bible is another bond of union for Romanists, all being made to adopt the interpretation of this church before becoming a member of the same; while Protestants differ and are divided into sects, just as men will naturally differ on any subject they are allowed to discuss freely. While the Roman Catholics are all united under one head, there is, however, a secret society among them known as Jesuits, whose special object is for its propagation. It was this society, as our readers will remember, who established themselves in Japan in 1549, but who were destroyed or driven from the Empire in 1595. This sect had, in 1870, seven archbishops; forty-five bishops; seven vicars-apostolic; thirty-five hundred and five priests, and, according to the best authorities, three millions three hundred and fifty-four thousand members.

The most devoted people in this denomination think it incumbent upon them to make certain sacrifices of time and service, and voluntarily go into entire seclusion from the world. For this object they have institutions called nunneries, to which the women retire and take certain vows, and live within their enclosures during the remainder of their lives; of course, these women never marry. There are also monasteries where the men retire from the world and also take the vow of celibacy, which means never to marry; they devote themselves, generally, to teaching young men, and there is a college for that purpose connected with most of these institutions; as there are also female academies connected with the nunneries.

Another class of religious people who occupy a position peculiar to themselves, are the Jews or Israelites, whose history is identified with ancient and modern times, and more replete with incidents than any other. Although unable to give the extent of their population in America, we may safely state that they are to be found in almost every city and town in the country, and they claim to have about two hundred congregations. Though standing alone in their religious beliefs, they have the credit of manifesting great energy in prosecuting works of charity in behalf of the sick, the needy, and the widows and orphans of their own people. A large proportion of them are wedded to the doctrines of their illustrious father, the patriarch Abraham, with whom the recognition of One Supreme Being originated, and has been cherished to the present day by Bible believers. A party has sprung up among them, of late years, called the Reformed or Christian Jews, and they advocate a religion of progress, in which they have been somewhat successful. They never intermarry with people not of their own race, and from time immemorial have been noted for their sagacity in accumulating money. Their history, which occupies a large space in the Bible, is considered the most wonderful in the annals of religion throughout the world.

Of all the rites or ceremonies which are practised by the Jews, the most strict and solemn is that which annually occurs on what they call the Day of Atonement. It is marked by a rigid fast, which commences at sunset on one evening, and ends with sunset on the following day, during which time the more faithful of the sect will not permit a morsel of food or water to pass their lips. During all this period they offer up prayers, clad in such garments as are used in burying the dead; and until the close of this special season for religious worship their synagogues are crowded with worshippers, who, like the Quakers, invariably wear their hats in all public assemblies.

In looking at the people of the United States in the aggregate, it has been estimated that about seven-eighths of them are either allied to the Protestants, have no religion at all, or come under the head of miscellaneous sects, while the remainder are Roman Catholics. Nearly all the denominations are amply supplied with theological institutions, which number more than one hundred, and those who are educated in them are always expected to become the advocates of the doctrines in which they have been instructed. As to the benevolent institutions for the relief of suffering humanity, they are to be found in nearly all the individual States, and are chiefly supported by the Protestant sects, or by the people, through their legislatures. In their internal arrangements all these asylums and hospitals are in keeping with the advanced improvements of the age. By means of raised letters the blind are enabled to read; by wise treatment the insane are made docile, and contented with their unhappy condition; and by personal kindness and sign-alphabets the deaf and the dumb are instructed and made to forget their misfortunes. The total number of these unfortunates in the United States is nearly one hundred thousand.

To give an account of the hospitals, the homes for the orphan and widow, and other charitable institutions of the country, would occupy more space than can be afforded in this work, but we can state that they are very numerous, liberally endowed, and as efficiently conducted as any in the world; and when necessary, people from every clime can find a convenient place where they may be cared for, whether their troubles are the result of poverty, of accidents, of sickness, or any other misfortunes.

Of all the visible evidences of prosperity among the religious people of America, the most impressive and extensive are the churches or temples of Christian worship. Not only are they to be found on almost every street in the larger cities, but they are the leading architectural attractions in the towns and villages of the whole country. Bricks and every variety of stone are employed in their construction; every school of architecture is called upon to beautify them with their designs; and the money expended in building them ranges from ten or twenty thousand to one or two millions of dollars. The current expenses of these churches are paid by voluntary subscription, or with the money received through the renting or sale of pews or seats.

The ministers who preside over these churches, excepting

the Roman Catholics, who are supported in a different manner, receive by way of compensation from five hundred to ten thousand dollars, according to the wealth of the congregations. These churches are open for public worship twice on every Sunday, and occasionally on weekdays; are never used for mere secular purposes; and in many of them, elaborate music, consisting of singing combined with magnificent organs, forms an important part of the services. It is from these churches, moreover, that the money goes forth for the support of charitable and benevolent institutions, and for spreading the religion of the Bible, by means of missionaries, throughout the world. There is also attached to most of these congregations what are called Sunday Schools, in which children, both rich and poor, are instructed in the ways of Christianity. While it is true, as we have already stated, that there is no State religion in America, it is also true, however, that the religious denominations of the country occasionally exercise a decided influence in public affairs; and when a man of mark puts himself forward as a candidate for an elective office, his chances of success very frequently turn upon the nature of his religious belief, and hence we find a perpetual warfare going on in America between the Protestants and Roman Catholics, which is anything but creditable to the parties, an honor to the country, or a blessing to the world.

Although only indirectly connected with the foregoing subject, we deem it quite proper to append in this place a few words in regard to the noted secret societies known as Free-Masons and Odd-Fellows. The first, which is identified with the history of architecture, is claimed to have originated in the religious mysteries of the ancient world—and especially in Asia Minor. Members of the fraternity are found in every quarter of the globe, but it is perhaps more flourishing in the United States than elsewhere. They have what they call a Grand Lodge in all the States of the Union, and many of the most distinguished men in this country have been members of the Order. Their highest officer is called a Royal Arch Mason: in the exercise of charity, particularly towards their fellow-members, they are eminently liberal; and their houses, which are called temples, are numerous, and often very handsome; and their publications are highly respectable, if not abundant.

The fraternity known as Odd-Fellows bears a general resemblance to the Free-Masons, traces its origin to the fourth century, and has, until recently, been confined to Great Britain and the United States, in which latter country it is exceedingly prosperous. Like the Free-Masons, they have their Lodges and many officers, and it is said that in the last forty years they have expended for charitable purposes not less than fifteen millions of dollars. The relief furnished to its members during sickness, and to their families after death, is accorded to them as a right. Connected with this Order is an institution which they call the Grand Encampment, whose members are known as patriarchs and priests, and which consists of past officers of the several subordinate Encampments. The State Grand Lodges consist of the past officers of the subordinate Lodges; and the Grand Lodge of the United States, which is the highest body of the Order in this country, is formed of Representatives elected by the several State

Grand Lodges. Some years ago, by the action of the present Vice-President of the United States, Schuyler Colfax (who is a distinguished member of this Order), women were admitted to a partial fellowship in it; and since then, at stated periods, the different subordinate Lodges confer upon such wives and widows of Odd-Fellows who may desire it, what is termed the "Degree of Rebecca."

But there is one feature connected with religion in America which is peculiar to this country, and must not be forgotten in this summary. We allude to the *Young Men's Christian Associations.* There are one thousand of these societies in the United States, and they are conducted by an active element in the various churches, and without any denominational distinctions. They are supported by the free-will contributions on the part of their members, and their buildings, in the larger cities, are frequently quite splendid and beautiful. They are generally so arranged as to afford, under one roof, a library of the best books, a Reading-Room, supplied with the leading newspapers and periodicals of the day, a General Receiving-Room, where religious services are held for those who wish to attend them, and a Lecture-Room, where able men are invited to lecture. To all of these privileges, excepting the lectures, the public are admitted without any charge, and the good which these associations have already accomplished, in elevating the tone of society, is considered in the light of a national blessing.

It is proper, before concluding this chapter, that the writer should submit a few particulars respecting its arrangement, which are somewhat personal to himself.

After his return to Japan from Europe, some years ago, he was frequently questioned by his countrymen as to his opinions about the Christian religion. In his replies, he took the ground, that, so far as he could understand it, the Bible was a good and a wise book, but that it contained many things he did not understand. That while the people who called themselves Christians claimed to have the only true religion, and pretended to be better than all other men, they did not, in that particular, differ from the Chinese or Japanese, who assert the same claims for their religions. He thought it advisable that those who desire to form any opinion on Christianity, should acquaint themselves with it by close and attentive study, and then to judge for themselves. Hence, in the present chapter his desire has been simply to give facts, and in the plainest possible terms. Whatever may be his private opinions on matters of such great importance, he has not thought it proper for him either to oppose or advocate them. According to his observations, a very large proportion of the American people are known by the name of Christians, and yet a great many things are said and done by them which do not accord with the principles of their own Bible; but, is not this true of every nation upon the earth? Where men think that they know everything, and boast of their superior wisdom, the presumption is that they have yet much to learn; and all human experience, as well as the Bible of the Christians, inculcates the idea that before men can be wise and good, they must be humble. It would be a very wonderful thing, should the time ever arrive, when the so-called Christians, who profess the faith, but do not live up to it, shall cease to boast of the superiority of their religion, and regard themselves as worse than all other people, because of their guilt in making insincere professions. True Christianity may not be considered as identical with the general sense of civilization—in which the good and the bad participate,—but true philosophy would seem to teach that it should be a leading element in such civilization.

# LIFE IN THE FACTORIES.

The term factory, as employed in America, means a place where men and women are engaged in fabricating goods. In this paper it is proposed to speak of those establishments, especially, where the staples of cotton and wool are turned into the woven fabrics commonly known as calicoes, sheetings, carpetings, cloths made of both materials, as well as hosiery and worsted goods, blankets, shawls, table-covers, felted cloths, and bed-spreads.

The largest amount of cotton ever produced in this country in one year was in 1860, the year before the late rebellion, when the figures reached 4,669,770 bales, each bale weighing 465 pounds; and the factories numbered 1,091. According to the last published statistics, the supply of cotton reached only 2,500,000 bales; the number of cotton-mills or factories is 831, of which 444 are in New England, 86 in the Southern States, 220 in the Middle States, and the balance in the Western States. The total value of the cotton crop was $270,000,000, and it is said that the people producing it sold and exported the whole of it, excepting the value of $10,000,000 kept for home consumption.

But, however we may arrange the cotton statistics of America, the fact remains that its cotton manufactures, though still very large, have declined of late years, and are greatly excelled by those of England.

## LIFE IN THE FACTORIES. 247

The annual production of wool in the United States is estimated at about $100,000,000, while that of Great Britain, in 1868, was, in pounds, 260,000,000; Germany, 200,000,000; France, 123,000,000; Russia in Europe, 125,000,000; Spain, Italy, and Portugal, 119,000,000; Austria, South America, and South Africa, 157,000,000; British North America, 12,000,000; North Africa, 49,000,000; and Asia, 470,000,000; making the aggregate of wool produced in the world, 1,610,000,000 pounds, or one pound and a quarter to each inhabitant on the globe—on the supposition that the total population is 1,285,000,000. As is the case with cotton, the most numerous woolen factories of America are found in New England. With these few particulars in view, we may proceed to speak of the peculiarities of factory-life in the United States, which, of course, must be done in very general terms.

Wherever, in the northern portions of the country, is to be found the best supply of water, suitable for running machinery, there do the manufacturing establishments mostly congregate. And it is because New England is rocky and not well suited to agriculture, and also because its rivers are numerous and well adapted for mills, that its manufactures have become especially celebrated. The villages which have sprung up out of this kind of business are to be found in every part of the land; and while some of them consist only of the houses collected around one factory, others contain a number of factories, and are proportionally large. In one place the ownership may be vested in one man; at another place in an organized company of men; and then again, a single man or family may be the proprietor of several factories, employing thousands of hands to carry them on, and requiring millions of money for their support. In this connection, a few such men as Amos and Abbot Lawrence and William Sprague have acquired national reputations. In many instances the small villages alluded to are located in the midst of beautiful scenery, and the necessary surroundings of the mills, which give them existence, are pleasant little churches, comfortable school-houses, shops for the sale of household merchandise, and appropriate houses for the shelter of the operatives. Men, women, and children are all employed in these factories, and, generally speaking, they absorb all the laboring population to be found in the country immediately surrounding them, as well as many persons from abroad. The idea of strict discipline is recognized and carried out, from the overseer down to the humblest workman, and it is in these small villages that a greater amount of comfort is enjoyed by the persons employed than in the larger manufacturing cities. Of course, the facilities for obtaining the raw materials of cotton and wool, and for transporting the manufactured goods to market, are commensurate with the necessities of the case; and the establishments where the goods are sold are generally located in the larger cities.

But a truly comprehensive idea of factory-life in America cannot be had without considering its character as we find it in the larger towns or cities; and no better example can be selected for that purpose than the city of Lowell, in Massachusetts. What may be said of this place is also true, only in a different degree, of all the factory-towns throughout the country, and especially such places as Lawrence, Providence, Norwich, and Worcester; and it may safely be said, that the aggregate number of persons who obtain their living by means of the cotton and woolen factories of the country, is not less than three hundred thousand. The growth and prosperity of Lowell, as a manufacturing town, are without any parallel in America. It lies on the river Merrimac, and the water-power is formed by dams that are thirty feet high. It has not less than fifteen manufacturing corporations, with about sixty mills, which employ a capital of fifteen millions of dollars, and support about fifteen thousand hands, from the beginning to the close of the year, while the entire population of the city is nearly fifty thousand. All the mills are heated by steam and lighted by gas. The women who work in them far outnumber the men; and although, a few years ago, much the larger proportion of these were native Americans, so great a change has taken place in this particular, that the majority are now foreigners, and chiefly Irish. The men are without ambition, and the women work for the sole purpose of making money, and not because they like the employment. Widows are there, toiling for the education of their children; and daughters are there, hoarding up their wages to pay the debts of improvident fathers. The labor of the women is essentially on an equality with that of the men; but while the former receive from two to three dollars per week, in addition to their board, the latter receive from four to six dollars for the same period. The time for labor ranges from ten to twelve hours per day, and extra sets of hands are often employed for night-work. The hands are summoned to their work by the ringing of bells; a brief time only is allowed for meals; and the only opportunities which the operatives have for recreation or study are at night, when worn out with the fatigue engendered by the jar and whirl of the machinery in the mills. When the American element prevailed in these factories, an earnest effort was made to elevate the minds of the thousands of girls employed, and for a time these efforts were successful. A monthly periodical was established, called the "Lowell Offering," which was supported entirely by the productions of females working in the mills, and in which many valuable papers were published. For a time this magazine was very successful, and excited much wonder and comment among the factory-people of New England, but the novelty soon wore off, and the work was suspended. A leading American writer, while mourning over this fact, and also over the fact that there was so little comfort to be found in these large manufacturing towns, said, that the patron-saint of Lowell was *Work;* that the "Factory Girls" might be counted by the acre; that the motto over the gateways should be, "Work or Die;" and that the fifty factories in the city were each larger and more imposing than the temples of worship in Japan and China. In the largest of these mills from one thousand to fifteen hundred women or girls are constantly employed, and from three hundred to five hundred men. Each manufacturing company owns from twenty to thirty dwellings, which are leased to responsible persons as boarding-houses, for the exclusive benefit of the hands employed in the factories. These dwellings are large enough to accommodate from forty to fifty inmates, and the sexes are kept entirely separate. The corporations also provide hospitals in which the work-people find attendance in sickness, for which, if they be unable to pay, the employers are responsible. While it is true that the young people who are obliged to work in the factories have little or no time to cultivate their minds, the younger children of the married people have every facility afforded them to obtain knowledge; the common-schools of the city are numerous, well conducted, and chiefly under the direction of competent female teachers. There is also a good library in the city, where all who are fond of reading, no matter how poor, can be furnished with useful and entertaining books: and the religious privileges enjoyed by all, by means of numerous churches, and the weekly day of rest, which is called Sunday, are all that could be desired. But notwithstanding these many advantages, recent writers on this subject have declared that the extinction of the educated American operative has become an accomplished fact, and the mills of Lowell, as well as those of the Atlantic States generally, are now worked, as already stated, by immigrants from Europe—from Ireland, Wales, and Germany. But these, as they grow in intelligence, and begin to go westward, like their predecessors, demand higher wages, shorter hours for work, and more freedom. They have learned the European lesson of fighting employers by combinations; and, altogether, the problem has become so confused that the manufacturers are beginning to look for relief to the Chinese, a number of whom have already been induced to enter the factories of New England. American girls are said to be growing dissatisfied with the restraints of factory-life, where they have to compete with the more rugged and experienced women from European countries; hence they go to the larger cities, and become domestic servants; but that kind of employment they find irksome, and so they make another effort to succeed according to their wishes, and emigrate, as best they can, to the western States.

In the further elucidation of this subject, it is proper that we should consider the opinions of the manufacturers themselves. They assert that the opprobrious epithet of "white slavery," which has sometimes been applied to the labor in the New England factories, is wholly unwarranted. They claim to have purged it of every element of feudalism; that they have avoided the English plan of employing whole families in the mill, often including children, who should have been at school,—the families being kept in a state of absolute dependence upon the mill, and exposed to suffering whenever business was not prosperous. They claim also to have abolished the custom of payment by orders on a factory-store, which tended to involve the workpeople in debt, and they instituted the practice of weekly payment of wages in money; and that they have done all that could be done, to secure the independence as well as comfort of the American operatives.

And here, it occurs to us, we may furnish a further illustration of factory-life in America by submitting a brief description of what may be termed a model New England establishment, as follows: It is located in the city of Lawrence; is a joint-stock company, with 150 stockholders and 9 directors; has 100,000 spindles; and has a capital of $2,500,000, while its property is valued at a considerable advance on that sum. The manufactured goods, consisting chiefly of fabrics for the wear of women, made both of cotton and wool, which are annually sold, amounting to about $7,500,000; and the total dividends declared, during the last twelve years, was more than $3,000,000.

The total number of work-people employed in this factory is 3,600, of whom the men number 1,680; women, 1,510; boys between ten and twelve years of age, 80, and between twelve and eighteen, 140; girls between ten and twelve, 40, and between twelve and eighteen, 150. The lowest weekly wages, according to gold rates, are as follows: for men, $6.75; women, $2.48; boys, $2.85; and young girls, $1.82; while spinners, weavers, and a few others, receive according to the quantity of goods produced, and some of them large wages. Very many of the operatives are frugal with their money, and have invested their earnings in the stock of the company itself, deposited it in Savings Banks, or purchased the bonds of the General Government; some of them have been so successful as to be elected members of the City Government; and not a few are the owners of comfortable houses. Where men are obliged to hire houses, they pay only one-eighth of their wages for rent; and for the comfort and accommodation of the unmarried females a large building has been erected, holding not less than eight hundred persons, who pay for food, lights, and washing, only one-third of their regular wages. Connected with the establishment is what they call a "Relief Society," organized for the care and support of the sick among the work-people. Every possible attention is paid both to the morals and intellectual culture of the operatives. No men are employed who are intemperate in their habits, and the use of profane language and the ill-treatment of subordinates strictly prohibited. All females are compelled to be at their lodgings by ten o'clock at night, and none of them are permitted to attend improper places of resort. No child under ten years of age, according to law, is allowed to work in the factory, and all the boys and girls must be furnished with from eleven to sixteen weeks of schooling, in each year, and all the schools are paid for by the company. Of the persons employed, less than fifty in every thousand are unable to read, and for the benefit of all there is a well-conducted library, with pleasant reading-rooms for both sexes, and every facility is afforded for attending lectures, and places of profitable amusement. A week's labor in this establishment will produce more yards of cloth than is produced in any European mill, but it is claimed that a yard of cloth costs less in Europe, which latter point, however, is not conceded by the Americans.

But let us now look for a moment at some of the local results of the cotton and woolen manufactures of recent times. It has been said, that where one person, a century ago, consumed one yard of woven goods, the consumption, per head, has since risen to about twenty-six yards. This vast difference in the comforts of every family, by the ability which they now possess of easily acquiring warm and healthful clothing, is a clear gain to all society, and to every individual as a portion of society. It is more especially a gain, they say, to the females and the children of families, whose condition is always degraded when clothing is scanty. The power of procuring cheap clothing for themselves and for their children, has a tendency to raise the condition of females more than any other addition to their stock of comfort. It cultivates habits of cleanliness and decency, which are considered, in America, great aids to virtue, if not actual virtues themselves. There is little self-respect amid dirt and rags, according to the American belief, and without self-respect there can be no foundation for those qualities which mostly contribute to the good of society. The power of procuring useful clothing at a cheap price has tended to raise the condition of women in America, and the influence of the condition of women upon the welfare of a community can never be too highly estimated. If there be one thing more remarkable than another in the visible condition of the people of the United States, it is the universality of good clothing. The distinction between the rich man and the artisan, or between the lady and her maid, is oftentimes almost imperceptible. Perhaps the absence of mere finery, and the taste which accompanies good education, constitute the chief difference in the dress of various ranks; and this feature of the present time is a part of the social history of America.

The history of the cotton and woolen manufactures has occupied the minds of many of the ablest men in the world, and their developments are of vital interest to the whole human family. The arts of spinning and weaving were slowly developed from the time of the simple distaff, and it was just as they had reached something like completion, that an American, named Eli Whitney, invented the cotton-gin, in 1793, which at once gave a new character and impulse to the growth, as well as the manufacture, of cotton. This invention was the final step, by which the whole process of manufacturing cotton into cloth was effected by machinery; and just about that time, steam was introduced to the world as an agent of limitless power, in driving machinery of every kind; new channels of internal communication were opened between the different parts of the world; chemistry furnished the means for rapidly bleaching the fabrics produced from cotton; and all the resources of science and skill, of invention and industry, seemed combined to create an immensely increased demand for the raw material upon which all these labors were to be expended. And if something like this enterprise can be transported to Japan, what may we not expect, in the future, from that Empire?

There are many wonderful inventions connected with the manufacture of cotton, but nothing is perhaps more astonishing than the rapidity with which some portions of the machinery is employed. Notice the fact, for example, that the very finest thread which is used in making lace is passed through the strong flame of a lamp, which burns off the fibres, without burning the thread itself. The velocity with which the thread moves is so great, that the motion cannot be perceived. The line of thread, passing off a wheel through the flame, looks as if it were perfectly at rest; and it appears a miracle that it is not burned. The primary object of the extensive and complicated machinery employed in the manufacture of cotton has been, of course, cheapness of production, and in that particular the advance, from the time of the distaff, has been wonderful, and success complete. Nor has this been done at the expense of the working classes. Ten years after the introduction of the machines, the people employed in the trade, spinners and weavers, were more than forty times as numerous as when the spinning was done by hand. It was thought that the newly discovered power might supersede human labor altogether, but such was by no means the case. It only gave a new direction to the labor that had previously been employed at the distaff and spindle; but it increased the quantity of labor altogether employed in the manufacture of cotton, at least a hundredfold. What is here said of the machines for manufacturing cotton, is also true of those employed in the woolen, the silk, and the linen manufactories, and to the uneducated eye and understanding they are all wonderful, and of incalculable value to the commercial world.

But there is another curious machine which we may, with propriety, mention in this place, and that is one for making needles. Hitherto the largest number of needles used in America were made in England; but there is a machine in New Haven in which the whole process is performed without the manual labor of a single person. A coil of steel wire is put into it; then the machine cuts it off at the required lengths, punches the eyeholes, countersinks the eyes, and then sharpens the needle, when it drops out a perfected thing. They are also arranged and put up in paper by another machine; and the number of needles thus manufactured per day by each machine is about forty thousand.

But before dismissing the subject under consideration, we would submit to the Japanese reader a few remarks on the art, whose object is merely to beautify the very numerous fabrics which are made in the various factories already alluded to,—the art of printing cloth in colors. It applies to the most common as well as to the finest productions of the loom; and the science of the dyer, the beauty of his patterns, and the perfection of his machinery, have become universally celebrated. As an experienced writer has said, there is a striking, although natural parallel, between printing a piece of cloth and printing the sheets of a book or newspaper. Block-printing is the impress of the pattern by hand, as block-books were made four centuries ago. There are no block-books now, for machinery has banished that tedious process. But block-printing is used for costly shawls and velvets, which require to have many colors produced by repeated impressions from blocks covered with different colors. Except for the most expensive fabrics, however, this mode is superseded by block-printing with a press, in which several blocks are set in a frame. Then again they have what they call cylinder-printing, which resembles the rapid working of the book-printing machine, each producing with great cheapness. As the pattern has to be obtained from several cylinders, each having its own color, there is great nicety in the operation; and the most beautiful mechanism is necessary for feeding the cylinder with color; moving the cloth to meet the revolving cylinder; and giving to the machine its power of impression. But those who witness this operation can hardly realize the ultimate effect subsequently obtained by the process of dyeing. Fast colors are produced by the use in the patterns of substances called mordants; which may be colorless themselves, but receive the color of the dye-bath, which color is only fixed in the parts touched by the mordants, and is washed out from the parts not touched. Other processes are also employed, which enhance the beauty of the fabrics.

It is thus seen that the chemist, the machinist, the designer, and the engraver, set the calico-printing works in operation, so that the carrying on of this complicated business can only be profitably done on a large scale. Very numerous also are the employments required merely to produce the dyes with which the calico-printer works. The mineral, vegetable, and even the animal kingdom, combine their natural productions in the colors of a lady's dress; there is the sulphur from Sicily, salt from Austria or Turk's Island, peculiar woods from Brazil, indigo from the East and West Indies, madder from France, and insects from Mexico. The discoveries of science, in combination with experience and skill, have set all this industry in motion, and given a value to innumerable productions of nature which would otherwise be useless or unemployed; and they also create modes of cultivation which are important sources of national prosperity. But of all the discoveries of chemistry, in this connection, was that of chloride of lime, which has become the universal bleaching powder of modern manufactures. What was formerly the work of eight months, is now accomplished in an hour or two,—so that a bag of raw, dingy cotton may now be converted into the whitest cloth within the space of a single month.

As an appropriate conclusion to the foregoing remarks, we may now submit a few general facts on the American Tariff of duties on imported merchandise. This has been the means on which the Federal Government has chiefly depended for its support ever since it came into existence. It has also been amply sufficient for affording money to extend its territory, carry on wars, execute treaties, and accumulate a large property in lands, buildings, and materials for war. From the earliest times, however, the people have been divided into two great political parties on this subject, and yet the friends and opponents of the measure have in the main admitted that it is the best means for raising the public revenue, inasmuch as direct taxation has been thought impolitic for Federal revenue. There is a large class of people, moreover, who believe that the levying of duties is detrimental to the agricultural interests. These, and numerous questions of a similar character, have long occupied the minds of the leading statesmen of the United States, and they remain unsettled to this day. As the political parties have gained ascendency, so have the tariff rates been changed or modified, from time to time; and in looking back over the forty years prior to the late civil war, we find that the rates of duty have varied from eighteen to forty-eight per centum, and that the largest receipts from customs during the period in question were in 1854, and amounted to $64,224,190,—when the free imports reached $33,285,821, and the dutiable imports $271,276,560. The total imports at the port of New York, in 1870, amounted to $315,200,-022, and the exports to $254,137,208; while the figures for all the States for the same year were, imports, $373,894,-980, and the exports, $328,072,226; and for 1869, imports, $463,461,427, and exports, $394,644,335. That these enormous figures have an important bearing upon the success, or want of success, of the factory-system in the United States, must be apparent to all men who investigate these subjects.

In accounting for the excess of imports over the exports, it may be stated that the difference arises chiefly from the importation of articles of luxury. The American people are practical, and while they confine themselves chiefly to producing the necessaries and comforts of life, and to accumulating money, they are quite willing to obtain their fashions and articles of luxury from Europe. Notwithstanding the immense immigration from abroad, the American people have always had enough to feed all who come to their shores, and to provide employment for all ; and the strength of the nation is shown by the fact that, in spite of the large amounts which are expended for the mere elegancies of life, which the rich bring over from Europe, the country is constantly prospering.

But again. Statistics show that the trade of the United States has been regularly progressing, until interfered with by the late civil war. Generally speaking, the exports have exceeded the imports, and the balance of trade has been in favor of America. The export of grain does not depend upon the state of the crops so much as upon the wants of other countries. The great variety of the native productions exported gives assurance of the impossibility of failure of the resources of the nation. Figures also show that there is no industrial pursuit in which the people of the United States do not regularly progress, and that there is little demand for any class of produce which they are not able to supply.

As the revenue of the country depends in a great measure upon the customs duties, so does its prosperity chiefly depend upon the amount of its exports of bread-stuffs and all sorts of merchandise ; but as the theories which have been brought to bear upon this subject are widely different, and have occupied the minds of the ablest writers, they cannot be entered upon in this chapter. Upon one subject, however, all men are agreed, viz. : that the extension of commerce will do more than anything else to diffuse the blessings of civilization, to bind together the universal society of nations, by sharpening and at the same time gratifying their mutual wants and desires, and to maintain undisturbed that tranquillity so indispensable to its full development.

P. S. Since the foregoing chapter was sent to the printer we have received from the Bureau of Statistics and the Census Bureau some interesting particulars bearing upon the Factory, Mechanical, and Farm-life of the United States, which ought not to be omitted in this place. The following have reference to 1869. The hours of labor per week were sixty-six; and, omitting overseers, the average weekly earnings of operatives in the cotton mills was $5.56 in gold. The wages in the woolen mills ranged from $5 to $17 per week, including overseers; in the paper mills from $4.50 to $26; in establishments for making musical instruments from $15 to $31; in foundries and machine shops from $8 to $24; and in leather establishments from $9 to $25 per week. In 1870, the average daily wages for blacksmiths, $4.85; masons, $5.66; cabinet-makers, $4.99; carpenters, $5.03; coopers, $4.30; painters, $5.36; plasterers, $6.51; shoemakers, $4.49; stonecutters, $6.10; tailors, $4.58; tanners, $3.97; tinsmiths, $4.96; and wheelwrights, $5.37. The wages for farm-labor in the Eastern States ranged from 73 cents to $1.49 per day, but on the Pacific States and Territories, from $1.35 to $2.97 per day. As a subject of general interest, we also submit a list, showing the average retail prices for the leading necessaries of life, in 1869, as follows: Flour, $7.36 per barrel; beef, veal, mutton, and pork, 9 to 22 cents per pound; butter, 38 cents per pound; dried fish,

13 to 15 cents per pound; potatoes, per bushel, 75 cents; rice, per pound, 13 cents; beans, 11 cents; milk, 9 cents per quart; eggs, 29 cents per dozen; tea, $1.40 per pound; coffee, 28 to 35 cents; sugar, 15 to 17 cents per pound; coal, $10.80 per ton; and wood, per cord, $3.98 to $4.98. The prices for plain house-rent ranged from $10 to $15 per month; and plain board from $4.14 to $4.80 per week. And finally, for the want of a better place to print them, we submit the following aggregate of returns for the year 1870, respecting the agricultural resources of the country:

| | |
|---|---:|
| Acres improved, | 188,806,761 |
| Acres woodland, | 158,908,121 |
| Acres unimproved, | 59,366,633 |
| Cash value of farms, | $9,261,775,121 |
| Cash value of agricultural implements, | $336,890,871 |
| Wages paid, | $310,068,473 |
| Farm products, | $2,445,602,379 |
| Value of live stock, | $1,524,271,714 |
| Wheat, bushels, | 267,730,931 |
| Rye, bushels, | 17,000,000 |
| Indian corn, bushels, | 760,963,204 |
| Oats, bushels, | 282,095,996 |
| Barley, bushels, | 29,761,267 |
| Buckwheat, bushels, | 9,821,662 |
| Rice, pounds, | 73,635,021 |
| Tobacco, pounds, | 262,729,640 |
| Cotton, bales, | 2,999,721 |
| Wool, pounds, | 102,053,264 |
| Potatoes, bushels, | 143,230,000 |
| Sweet potatoes, bushels, | 21,634,000 |
| Wine, gallons, | 3,096,000 |
| Cheese, pounds, | 53,492,000 |
| Butter, pounds, | 514,002,460 |

Milk, gallons, .................................. 236,500,000
Hay, tons, ..................................... 27,416,000
Hops, pounds, .................................. 28,456,669
Sugar (cane), pounds, .......................... 87,043,000
Sugar (maple), pounds, ......................... 28,443,000
Molasses (cane), gallons, ...................... 6,600,000
Molasses (sorghum), gallons, ................... 16,041,000

# EDUCATIONAL LIFE AND INSTITUTIONS.

Although the cause of education in America has always been considered of primary interest and importance, there does not, after all, exist a regular and uniform system of instruction. The diversity of plans is almost as various as the several States of the Union are numerous; for each State, in its sovereign capacity, has a right to devise and execute, and does execute, such provisions for the education of the people as are deemed expedient. Setting aside, therefore, a detailed account of all the existing plans, we can only consider in this place the characteristics of the school systems of the States, in their collective capacity. It should be remembered, however, that the Federal Government is a most liberal patron of the schools in all parts of the country, and that a majority of the States have received large grants of land, to be used for the support of educational institutions, and that they have appropriate officers to look after and expend the revenue derived from the sale of those lands. Ten years ago, the aggregated amount of money realized from the liberality of the General Government was about $50,000,000, but this amount has been annually increased since then; and when to this fund we add the appropriations regularly made by the State Legislatures, we find that the total amount of money spent for educational purposes is truly enormous, and that, in this particular, if not in any other, the States of America are unequalled by any other nation. Hence it is that there is ample provision made by the authorities alone, without including the munificent gifts of private individuals, to furnish every child in the land with a good education; and the black race, or Freedmen, have the same privileges which are enjoyed by the whites. Prior to the late rebellion, there existed no provision for the education of the colored race, but as soon as they became free, measures were taken for their education, and in 1869 the total number who were known to be in attendance upon day, night, or Sunday schools, under the auspices of the Freedmen's Bureau, was upward of 250,000, and the freedmen paid out of their own earnings about $200,000 for tuition, and $125,000 for school-buildings.

But we must now proceed to submit a general account of the educational systems of the United States, and we begin with the common-schools, the principle of which is the free elementary education of every child in the community, and which underlies the whole intellectual fabric of the American Republic. The system, as formerly practised, originated in New England at the commencement of the present century, and was based upon the following ideas: First, the instruction of all the children in the State in the rudiments of an English education, viz., reading, writing, elementary arithmetic and geography, and grammar, this to be accomplished by schools in every district; Second, each district to be independent of every other in all financial matters and management; Third, that there should be a superintendent or board of visitors in each town, generally consisting of professional men, and especially clergymen, to examine teachers, inspect the schools, and prescribe text-books; Fourth, the support of these schools by taxation; and Fifth, the power of compelling attendance on the part of the town authorities. After an experience of nearly twenty years, it was found that the condition of the schools was not up to the demands of the time, and a revival in the cause of education took place, which resulted in greatly increasing the efficiency of the old system, until it was brought to a state of rare excellence, through the efforts of such men as Horace Mann and Henry Barnard. The school-system was again regenerated, and now possesses all the elements of the highest efficiency, the leading features of which are as follows: First, a system of graded schools for each town, embracing primary schools for the younger pupils; grammar-schools for the older, in which are taught, in addition to the common branches, philosophy, chemistry, history, drawing, music, algebra, geometry, and the French language; high-schools for the more advanced, in which are taught the studies necessary for a business education, as well as the languages and the higher mathematics. Secondly, the employment of regular visitors, who are paid for their services. Thirdly, the enforcement of uniformity of text-books, and regularity in attendance. Fourthly, regular and frequent public examinations. Fifthly, the establishment of school libraries in connection with all the schools. Sixthly, the introduction of blackboards, globes, maps, charts, and other apparatus for instruction. Seventhly, the proper construction of school-houses. Eighthly, the establishment in every State of normal schools for the instruction of regular teachers. Ninthly, the organization of State associations for comparison of methods of teaching, and the establishment of school periodicals. And, Tenthly, the extension of the privileges of these schools to all the children of the school-age in each State, either by supporting the schools entirely by taxation and the income of funds where they exist, or by taxation and small ratebills, which are abated where they are unable to pay, and the furnishing of necessary books to the children of the poor.

That the above is a noble groundwork for the education of the masses must be acknowledged by all, and yet we find it a subject of serious complaint that the teachers in the common-schools are not what they should be. In the great majority of cases, they are said to be too young and inexperienced, and that both the young men and young women employed look upon the office merely as a stepping-stone to better positions or more agreeable employments, and not as a permanent business. An office under the Government, or a profession, will allure the young man from the school-room; and so also will an offer of marriage, the young woman. Of course there are many teachers whose knowledge, discipline, and nobleness of character, eminently fit them for their responsible posts, but they are not sufficiently numerous to form a class; and it was this fact which caused a prominent writer on the subject to suggest that all badly-managed schools should be closed, and that the houses should bear this inscription: "Poor teachers worse than no teachers." In the one particular to which we have alluded, it is confessed by leading Americans, that Prussia is far in advance of the United States. But notwithstanding this drawback, the common-schools of the country are a great national blessing. They are free and open to the poorest children in the community; but because these advantages are not always accepted by the people, in some of the States of the Union, laws have been passed compelling a certain attendance at school. The houses are comfortable, and conveniently located in every district where they are needed. The teachers are generally intelligent and circumspect in their lives and morals, and where they make teaching a regular profession, are all that could be reasonably expected or desired. With regard to their compensation there is no uniformity, but it is estimated to range from $39 to $57 per month for male teachers, with board, and from $27 to $30 per month for female teachers, with board. But, perhaps a better idea, on this head, may be obtained by looking at the average of the annual salaries which have recently been paid in some of the leading cities, as follows: Boston, $798; Cincinnati, $769; New Haven, $577; New York, $649; New Orleans, $675; Philadelphia, $415; San Francisco, $829, and Washington, $507. Nor is there, as we have already stated, any uniformity in the management of the schools by the State authorities, and so, with a view of attempting to give a general idea of their condition, we submit the following figures in regard to four of the representative States of the republic: The number of scholars who attend school in the small State of Connecticut, is 124,000; amount expended in 1870 for school purposes, $1,269,152, and its school-fund is $2,046,108: in New York there are 1,000,000 children in the common-schools, and 120,000 in the private schools; the school-houses are valued at $20,500,000; the amount paid to teachers, is $6,500,000; amount expended in 1870 for instruction, nearly $10,000,000, and the school-fund is $11,300,000: in Pennsylvania, the scholars are 900,753; schools, 14,212; teachers, 17,612; school property, $14,045,632, and annual expenses about $7,000,000; and in Ohio, the scholars are 740,382, and the school expenditures in 1870 amounted to $7,771,761. Total amount of school-fund in all the States is estimated at $50,000,000. We give no figures in regard to any of the Southern States, first, because the system of common-schools has never flourished in that region of the country, and secondly, because the late war has so deranged all public matters in those States, that no statements at this time would do them full justice. Notwithstanding all that has been done in the United States for the cause of education, it has been estimated that the illiterate people of the country number about 6,000,000.

With regard to the much discussed subject of the Bible in common-schools, we may submit the following remarks by a distinguished professor of Harvard University: " To banish the Bible was to garble history, for there was much history of which it was the only source. Christianity is the great factor in the history of the world. If moral philosophy is to be taught, it must be Christian ethics. For the culture of the taste and imagination, the Bible transcends all other literature. Our English Bible has rendered important service in preserving our language. It is the key to the best English diction, and has helped to form the diction of every child. Our children should not be kept in ignorance of the fact that we are a Christian people. Sectarian religion should be excluded; but this can be done only by giving an unsectarian book, and the

Bible is such a book. The Roman Catholics, in opposing the introduction of the Bible in common-schools, do not so much object to the book itself, but rather desire that the school-funds should be separated, which course the Protestants think would be detrimental to the welfare of the whole system."

With a view of enhancing the efficiency of the common-schools in the United States, there have been organized within the last few years a large number of Normal schools, the sole object of which is to educate a class of persons solely for the business of teaching, whereby very great good has already been accomplished, in elevating the tone of instruction. At the present time there are fifty of these schools in successful operation in the Northern States, which are supported by the City or State Governments, and not less than thirty in the Southern States, for the benefit of the freedmen;—and the number of teachers already educated by them, including males and females, is estimated at two hundred thousand, and the pupils now being instructed about nine thousand. While there is no special uniformity in the management of these schools, we may obtain a general idea of their character by glancing at the features of a single one of them which has been particularly successful, viz.: the Normal University of Illinois. Candidates for admission to this institution, whether male or female, must have attained the age of sixteen; must produce certificates of good moral character; must sign a declaration that they intend to devote themselves to school-teaching in Illinois; and must pass a satisfactory examination in reading, spelling, writing, arithmetic, geography, and the elements of English grammar. The necessary annual expenses for each pupil range from ninety-seven to one hundred and eighty-eight dollars. There are five professors, and the term of study is the usual one of three years: and the course of instruction embraces the following subjects: metaphysics, history and methods of education, constitution of the State and the United States, school-laws, English language, arithmetic, algebra, geometry, natural philosophy, book-keeping, geography, history, astronomy, chemistry, botany, physiology, geology, vocal music, and writing and drawing. The total number of pupils is three hundred; and there is an appendage to the institution called a model school, which contains five hundred pupils, whose tuition is free, although they have to support themselves. While the Americans confess that their common-schools are not equal in efficiency to those of some other countries, they claim that this state of things cannot continue, and that their Normal schools, as at present organized, are unsurpassed.

Before an American youth can pass from a common-school into a college, he is obliged to go through a course of studies in what is called a high-school, or academy. These institutions are exceedingly varied in character, quite numerous, independent in organization, and very frequently originate in the liberality of private individuals. Although the instruction afforded by them is not gratuitous, the expenses are generally moderate. In some of them, however, provision is made by public appropriations for the education of such pupils as are too poor to pay. It often happens, however, that when young men are about to leave the academy or high-school, they conclude that their education has been sufficiently advanced for all practical purposes, and so relinquish the idea of passing through college.

And here, before describing the colleges and universities of America, we may with propriety allude to the present condition of the miscellaneous schools of the country. Of distinct schools of science, unconnected with colleges, there are none of any importance; but the Sheffield Scientific School, which forms a part of Yale College, and the Lawrence Scientific School, connected with Harvard University, are both flourishing institutions, and are doing much to meet the wants of the age; while there are departments, standing on nearly the same basis, belonging to Brown University, Rutgers College, and the University of Michigan. As to Industrial Schools, there is also a great dearth of these in the United States; especially is this true in regard to Engineering and Navigation; and about all that is accomplished in the country, in the way of art-instruction, is accomplished by the National Academy and Cooper Institute of New York, the Athenæum in Boston, the Academy of Arts in Philadelphia, and the Peabody Institute in Baltimore. In Massachusetts, New York, and Pennsylvania, they have Institutions of Technology; in California, a College of Mining and the Mechanic Arts, associated with Agriculture; and attached to Columbia College, in New York, they have a School of Mines. As to the advantages afforded by agricultural Colleges, they are quite numerous, and well-endowed institutions are to be found in the States of Delaware, Illinois, Indiana, Iowa, Kansas, Kentucky, Maine, Maryland, Massachusetts (where there are several Japanese students), Michigan, Minnesota, New Hampshire, Pennsylvania, Vermont, West Virginia, and Wisconsin. In none of the public schools of America are the foundation principles of commerce taught, and hence there have been established by private individuals what is called a "Chain of Commercial Colleges;"—they number not less than forty, and extend from Maine to Louisiana; their course of instruction is very complete, and covers all that is necessary for a commercial life; and because this association is under one head, the regulations are such, that a student, after completing a course of studies in one, may again take them up and pursue them at another school of the Chain, without additional expense. With regard to the theological institutions, they have already been mentioned in a previous part of this volume; and on a page which is to follow, we shall speak of the Army and Navy Schools of the country. The only schools remaining to be mentioned under this miscellaneous head are those devoted to the study of medicine and law. The Medical Colleges and Schools of the country number fifty-one, and, first and last, as a competent writer has said, there have stood at the head of them men of learning, genius, and eminent distinction. And so there have also been, in the ranks of the profession, many physicians and surgeons of great ability and skill. But hardly any one who is acquainted with the status of medical education in America, will claim that either the distinguished professor, author, or practitioner, has owed his success, in any considerable degree, to the training of the schools; for, as compared with the European standard, the training in America has been unsatisfactory to the last degree. The Law Schools of the United States number twenty-two; and it is said that, in at least one respect, they are superior to those of England:—in that, what they assume to do at all, they do more thoroughly and well. But it is no less true that they undertake very little in comparison with what is both attempted and accomplished in several of the European countries. In the form of departments, there are schools of law connected with many of the leading colleges; and in all of them the term of study is two years, the course of instruction being so arranged that a complete view is given during each year of the subjects embraced within it. The professors number from one to five in each of these schools; a majority of them, in many instances, being judges of the Supreme Courts and resident lawyers in regular practice, whose services are gratuitous or partially compensated. The terms of admission are simply good morals and the age of eighteen years, and the fees, payable in advance, amount to one hundred dollars. The lawyers of the United States, as heretofore mentioned, have much to do with the making of the national laws, and the affairs of the General Government; and a competent American critic has said, how few of them have been students of political economy, of civil polity, and of universal history, is painfully manifest from the legislative discussions they hold and the laws they enact.

We come now to speak, in general terms, of the Collegiate Institutions of the United States, known as universities, colleges, seminaries, and institutes, and which number in the aggregate not less than two hundred and eighty-five,—exclusive of eighty-two, in which theology is alone studied. While their courses of instruction embrace all branches of learning, it is almost invariably the case that something like a sectarian element pervades each institution, the only exceptions to this rule being those which are supported by the State governments. The number of institutions in America bearing the title of university is larger than in any other country, and a less number of them is said to have really any sort of claim to the title. On the other hand, there are several colleges which, though bearing that more modest name, are really entitled to be called universities. And then again there are seminaries and institutes which would seem, from their extent and high character, to be worthy of being called colleges. The precise meaning of the term university is a universal school, in which are taught all branches of learning, or the four faculties of theology, medicine, law, and the sciences and arts; a college is a school incorporated for purposes of instruction, where the students may acquire a knowledge of the languages and sciences; the idea of a seminary or an academy is allied to that of a college, only that the former are more especially designed for a younger class of students; and an institute is a literary or philosophical society, formed by persons for their mutual instruction and advantage in all matters connected with intellectual culture. The so-called universities of America number one hundred, while the other collegiate institutions are about equally divided between the three remaining classes. To give an account of all is, of course, not to be expected in this paper, but the reader may obtain a general idea of their character by glancing at a few of the more influential and prominent institutions.

Harvard College, located at Cambridge, in Massachusetts, and founded in 1636, is the oldest institution of learning in America. It has twenty-eight professors and about five hundred students; and although it has hitherto had a Liberal divinity school, arrangements have recently been made for incorporating in it an "Episcopal Theological School." It has a Law department, with three professors; a Medical department, with eleven professors; a School of Astronomy, with two professors; a Dental School, with seven professors; a Museum of Zoology, with lectures by four professors; and the Lawrence Scientific School, and School of Mining and Practical Geology, with seven professors. Its general and special libraries comprise one hundred and fifty thousand volumes, and its scientific collections are extensive and of great value. It is managed by one president, five fellows, and one treasurer, and by thirty overseers chosen by the State Legislature; its endowment fund, derived from numerous individuals and corporations, and independent of the college grounds, buildings, libraries, and collections, is somewhat over two millions of dollars; and its annual income is about one hundred and eighty thousand dollars. The term of study in the law school is two years; in the divinity school three; and candidates for the degree of doctor of medicine must have studied three years, and attended two courses of lectures.

The next oldest institution of learning in America is Yale College, founded at New Haven, Connecticut, in 1700. It has about sixty professors, and usually seven hundred students. Besides an academical department, it has five others, devoted to philosophy, theology, law, medicine, and the fine arts. Its miscellaneous collections are extensive and very valuable, and its libraries comprise about eighty-five thousand volumes. The total amount of its funds available for the support of the college is something over one million of dollars. This college differs from Harvard chiefly in the constitution of its department of philosophy and the arts, which has come to be known as the Sheffield Scientific School. Candidates for admission are obliged to be sixteen years of age, and to undergo a twofold examination, first in mathematical studies, and secondly in elementary literary studies. The charge for tuition is one hundred and twenty-five dollars, but students of chemistry have to pay an additional sum of seventy-five dollars. The term of study in each of the courses is three years; and in the divinity school no charge is made for tuition.

Another college of note and influence is Columbia College, founded in the city of New York in 1754, but prior to 1787 it was known as King's College. Its funds, derived chiefly from donations, amount to two millions of dollars; its professors about fifty, and the usual number of students is nine hundred. It has four departments, devoted to Letters and Science, Mines, Law, and Medicine. The charges for tuition range from one hundred to one hundred and sixty dollars per annum; several societies and municipal corporations are entitled to several scholarships free of charge; every religious denomination in the city of New York is entitled always to have one student free of all charges for tuition; and every school from which there shall be admitted four matriculants in any year, is also allowed to send one pupil free of charge.

The College of New Jersey, located at Princeton, is another of the venerable institutions of the United States.

It was founded in 1746; has about twenty professors, and nearly three hundred students; is supported by the Presbyterians, and has educated nearly nine hundred men for the ministry; charges a tuition fee of seventy dollars; and has a choice library of twenty-five thousand volumes. In Georgetown, District of Columbia, there is a Roman Catholic College, founded in 1792, with twenty professors, two hundred students, and a library of thirty thousand volumes; in Brunswick, Maine, is located Bowdoin College, founded in 1802, and possessing a library of thirty-seven thousand volumes; in New Hampshire they have Dartmouth College, founded in 1769, supported by the Congregationalists, and with thirty-eight thousand volumes in its library; in Pennsylvania, Dickinson College, founded in 1783, supported by the Methodists, and with twenty-five thousand volumes; in Rhode Island, Brown University, founded in 1764, supported by the Baptists, and having a library of thirty-eight thousand volumes; and in Virginia, a State University, founded in 1819, with thirty-five thousand volumes. But there are several institutions, which have more recently been founded, and which are growing with great rapidity and exercising a paramount influence in the educational world, viz.: the Universities of Michigan, Kentucky, and Illinois, and the Cornell University in New York. But there is another institution which deserves special mention, because of its extent and peculiar character, viz.: Vassar College, located at Poughkeepsie, New York. It was founded in 1861, through the liberality of one man, Matthew Vassar, and is wholly devoted to the education of women. The buildings are extensive and beautiful; the school offers the highest educational facilities to females at moderate expense, and admits as beneficiaries those who are unable to pay even that expense. Special attention is devoted to the fine arts, and it has a corps of instructors in the English language and literature, the modern languages of Europe and their literature, ancient languages, mathematics, all the branches of natural science, including anatomy, physiology, hygiene, intellectual and moral philosophy, political economy and the science of government, domestic economy, and the study of the Scriptures, without sectarianism.

Notwithstanding the fact that the educational records of the United States are very complete, and the amount of money annually expended in the cause is very large, it would seem that the requirements of the age and of America have not as yet by any means been attained. An American writer, in an elaborate report on this subject, published at the National expense, has summed up his opinions in a single paragraph, as follows: To tell the plain truth, he says, the very best of our many universities are but sorry skeletons of the well-developed and shapely institutions they ought to be and must become, before they will be fairly entitled to rank among the foremost universities of even this present day. And if we are not content always to suffer the contempt of European scholars, who properly enough regard us as a very clever, but also a very uncultured, people, it is time that all true lovers of learning, as well as all who desire the highest prosperity and glory of America, should awake to the importance of at once providing the means of a profounder, broader, and higher culture in every department of human learning.

As the education of women is a subject which possesses

a peculiar interest for the people of Japan, we here submit a few observations in that connection. In America, females possess precisely the same advantages for education that are possessed by the males. Boys and girls are admitted to the same schools; and the gentle influences of the latter are counterbalanced by the elevating influences of the former, whereby it is thought that both classes are improved. At the same time, there are thousands of schools in which the two sexes are instructed separately. The idea is universal that the women of the country are capable of receiving, and should receive, the highest kind of education; and as to the question of their right to take part in politics, by voting, which has been extensively discussed in America, it seems to be one of those problems which the future alone can establish. The important part which the women of America take in educational affairs is shown by the following facts,—that they are educated at the Normal schools for the express purpose of becoming teachers,—that they officiate as teachers in thousands of the common-schools,—that seminaries for the education of young ladies are to be found in every part of the country,—that they are admitted into several of the American colleges as regular students, and that a number of institutions of the highest character are exclusively devoted to the education of women, the most extensive and interesting, Vassar College, having already been mentioned. Not only are the libraries of the country regularly visited and used by ladies (in some of which they are employed as librarians), but in the leading cities are to be found libraries and reading-rooms designed for their use exclusively, and all of them in harmony with the idea of American civilization.

# LITERARY, ARTISTIC, AND SCIENTIFIC LIFE.

Under the head of literary life, we propose to submit some information on the book-publishing and newspaper interests of the United States. When an author has written a book, whether large or small, and desires to profit by its publication, he is obliged to take out a copyright, by which the Government promises to protect his rights, for a term of years, in the profits of the work, as his own property. The document in question is issued under the law by the Librarian of Congress, and two copies of every book or pamphlet published have to be deposited in the National Library, whereby the collection of volumes belonging to the Government is annually increased to a large extent. The books printed and the authors who write them are so numerous, that it would be quite impossible even to name them in this place. The best and most comprehensive work ever published on the authors who have written in the English language, was written by an American, named S. Austin Allibone; it is called a "Dictionary of Authors," and contains the names of not less than forty-six thousand authors, with an account of their publications.

As to the subjects upon which books are written, they are, of course, very numerous, the general heads under which they are arranged being as follows: theology and religion, poetry, history, biography, geography and travels, philosophy, science, social reform, school-books, useful and fine arts, fiction, literature, miscellaneous books, republications and translations from foreign authors. With many men, as well as women, the writing of books is a special business; and then again there are thousands of books written merely as a pastime by their authors, or from motives of personal vanity; generally speaking, the writers do not find the business profitable; but then again, there are authors who make a great deal of money by writing—especially is this the case with school-books, novels, and national histories. The men who print and sell the books which are written, are called publishers, and in all the principal cities are to be found establishments which do business on a very large scale. Some of them give employment to large numbers of people, such as writers, paper-makers, printers, binders, artists of various kinds, and machinists, as well as clerks and common workmen, and not a few have acquired very large fortunes by this branch of industry. They usually sell books by the quantity alone, and the retail merchants who purchase of them are to be found in every town and village in the whole land. When an author has written a book, he either sells his copyright to the publisher for a specific sum of money, after which he has nothing to do with his work, or else he allows the publisher the privilege of printing and selling his book, charging for the same a certain per centum on the price of each volume, retaining the ownership of the work in his own name. While many of the books published are so interesting or valuable as to be purchased by everybody interested in the subject, very many of them can only be sold by means of extravagant notices in the newspapers, and hence the custom prevails of sending most of all the new books to the newspapers, which pretend to give impartial notices, but often do the very reverse. The custom of reading books among the people of America is almost universal, far more so, it is said, than is the case in England or France; and in every home, from that of the rich merchant down to the poorest farmer, may generally be found such collections of books as they desire or can afford to buy. And for those who cannot afford to purchase all they may wish to read, in the cities and towns everywhere they have circulating libraries, where, for a small consideration, books may be read, or borrowed, to be read at home. In most of the leading cities collections of this sort have been established which are very extensive and valuable. The good which these libraries accomplish, by furnishing the people with information on every conceivable subject, cannot be estimated;— the money which some of them have cost would reach $1,000,000; and the largest in the country, which is called the National Library, and located in Washington City, contains not less than 200,000 volumes, and is entirely free to all who may desire to consult its treasures. In 1860, there were 27,730 libraries in the country, in which were collected nearly 14,000,000 of volumes.

But the most striking feature connected with the literature of America, is the universal circulation of newspapers and magazines, which are read by all classes of the people, and so conducted as to form, to a great extent, a substitute for books. According to the latest accounts, the whole number of periodicals issued in the United States and its Territories, is 6,056; of these 637 are published daily, 118 tri-weekly, 129 semi-weekly, 4,642 weekly, 21 bi-weekly, 100 semi-monthly, 715 monthly, 14 bi-monthly, and 62 are issued quarterly. Of this large number it is estimated that about four-fifths are political journals, the remainder being religious or literary. It is through these numerous publications that the mind of the nation is chiefly expressed, and its intellectual pulse may generally be measured by the success of the several journals. While very many of these have a circulation which is confined to their particular religious sect or political party, there are a few whose circulation is immense, and their influence proportionably extensive. For example, there is one weekly paper published in New York, which has a circulation of 175,000, and if we estimate that each paper is read by five persons, which is not unlikely, we perceive that each issue has the teaching of 875,000 minds; and then again, there are some daily papers which issue every morning from 100,000 to 200,000 copies. As far back as 1860, it was estimated that the circulation of the newspapers alone amounted to 100,000,000. Hence we perceive that the power of the Press is enormous, and it is a matter of the utmost importance that it should be conducted with honesty and wisdom. That portion of it which comes under the head of newspapers is by far the most profitable, so far as making money is concerned, but the profit does not come from selling the paper alone. In all of them certain columns or pages are filled up with advertisements, and as these are paid for on liberal terms, they become a source of profit. The ownership of these papers is generally vested in a company of men, who are the printers and publishers; and as some of these great establishments send forth books, as well as newspapers and periodicals, we can only obtain an idea of the extent of their business by resorting to figures. According to the latest published statements the capital invested in printing and publishing is about $20,000,000; cost of raw material used, $13,000,000; cost of labor, per annum, about $8,000,000; number of hands employed, more than 20,000; and the value of books, periodicals, and daily journals, nearly $32,000,000. With these figures before us, we cannot wonder that what is called the Press of America should be considered an element of almost incalculable power. As has well been said, it records with fidelity the proceedings of Congress, of all State and Territorial legislatures, and of judicial tribunals, holds the pulpit to a just responsibility, reviews the doings of business and social life, and watches with sleepless vigilance over the concerns of the people. It is the great representative of the people; a conservative power held by them to guard both public and industrial liberty; reflecting their opinions and judgments in all matters respecting the public weal; exposing wrong, and vindicating and encouraging the right.

In writing for the newspapers of America, many of the ablest men are employed, and the leading writer for each journal is called an editor. He is frequently the sole proprietor, sometimes only owns a few shares in the enterprise, and then again he may be hired to perform a specific editorial duty. He is responsible for the opinions expressed, and when necessary, as is always the case in the larger establishments, he is assisted in his labors by sub-editors, who look after all matters connected with commerce or literature; by reporters, who prepare the proceedings of public assemblies; and by correspondents, who furnish information on every subject of public interest. Weekly papers are commonly published on Saturday of each week, and daily papers in the morning or evening; and as most of the latest news is received through the telegraph, it is frequently the case that an evening paper will publish information of an event which may have taken place in Europe on the morning of the same day. With regard to what is called the liberty of the press, in times of peace, it is quite unbounded; so much so, indeed, that the rights of private citizens are not always respected; but while an editor may not be interfered with by the government for expressing his opinions, provided they are not immoral, it is too often the case that his real independence is materially affected by the allurements or dictation of the political party to which he belongs. And then again, the habit of dealing in personalities is perhaps more prevalent among the newspaper writers of America than among any other people; the excesses in this direction sometimes lead to bitter conflicts and even to untimely deaths; but it is certain that all the more notorious abuses of the press are frowned upon by the better classes in every community. Notwithstanding its many drawbacks, the conclusion is inevitable, that the Press of America is the leading civilizer of its multifarious population, and the particular engine which has brought about the present prosperous condition of the Republic.

Our next topic for consideration is the artistic life of America, as we find it developed in the pursuits of painting, sculpture, and architecture. The number of persons engaged in these various employments is not large, but they are necessarily men of culture; exert a great influence in developing the taste of the people generally; and they congregate and find employment chiefly in the larger cities. The painters are of several kinds, viz.: portrait painters, historical painters, landscape painters, and various subordinate classes who produce miscellaneous pictures. The materials most commonly used are oil-colors and canvas; and while the majority of these artists manage to support themselves in comfort, those who happen to become fashionable, or possess extraordinary ability, frequently meet with great success. While it is true that good portraits may be obtained for fifty or one hundred dollars, it is also true that five thousand dollars is not an uncommon price for very superior portraits; and, according to circumstances, the prices paid for pictures of scenery range from fifty dollars to ten thousand dollars. In these two departments, the American artists are perhaps equal to those of Europe;—but with regard to historical paintings, the English, French, and German artists are all in advance of the Americans. Generally speaking, before a man can become expert in the art of painting, he has to acquire a knowledge of drawing, and this study has come to be so common and popular that many artists confine themselves to drawing alone, and hence the kind of pictures known as engravings, which are merely copies of drawings, as well as paintings, have almost a universal circulation. They are executed on steel, on copper, on stone, and on wood, and used extensively in books, and weekly and monthly periodicals. To what extent this is true, is shown by the fact that a single illustrated journal, published in New York, is said to have a circulation of three hundred thousand copies. And then again, large numbers of engravings are prepared and published, which are used for the adornment of the houses of the people, as is the case with paintings, as well as photographs, and chromolithographs, which latter classes of pictures have come to be more popular than any others. The custom of hanging pictures on the walls of the houses is a leading characteristic among the Americans; and while the poor mechanic or farmer may be content with a few cheap engravings or photographs, men of wealth are very much in the habit of spending thousands upon thousands of dollars for works of art of the highest order. Many of the private collections thus formed are really of a princely character; and then, in all the leading cities, they have extensive public collections of pictures, with which are commonly associated certain schools for imparting a practical knowledge of the fine arts. The extent to which the General Government patronizes the art of painting is limited to a few historical productions, including compositions and portraits, to be found in the Capitol and Executive Mansion.

As the art of sculpture is far less popular among the people than that of painting, we find the sculptors reduced to a small number. Among them, however, are to be found some few men of great abilities and extensive reputations. It is claimed, indeed, that the United States has gained, in sculpture, a far higher rank than in any of the fine arts. The works here produced are generally executed in white marble, though sometimes in bronze, and in the great majority of instances represent the busts or full-length figures of distinguished men. This style of art is always expensive, and it is only the rich who can afford to perpetuate the features of their family-friends in this manner. When intended for exhibition in private dwellings, or in galleries of art, these productions are usually of the size of life, but when intended for the adornment of private gardens or public grounds, they are of colossal size, and noted military men are occasionally represented mounted on horses. The chief patrons of this kind of art are the National and State Governments, and hence busts and statues are to be found stationed, to some extent, in the public buildings in Washington, and in the capitals of the several States. In the National Capitol a large and handsome hall has been appropriated entirely to the reception of busts and statues of celebrated statesmen, and military and naval commanders;— and in this connection, a law has been passed, granting the privilege to each State in the Union, to send to this central exhibition-place, a portrait, in marble, of any two men which the State authorities may choose to honor in this manner. When copies of marble or bronze productions are desired by private individuals, and the means of the person wanting them are limited, it is frequently the case that a kind of white plaster is used as a substitute for the more enduring materials; and this composition is employed, to a great extent, in reproducing the ancient and more celebrated works of sculpture in Europe, which are brought to America to serve as models in the art-schools of the country.

We come now to speak of what has been done in the United States in the way of architecture. In the early years of the country the abundance of wood, and the ease of preparing it, made it the universal building material, and for a long time hardly anything else was used; although for buildings of importance brick was brought from England. The haste to get shelter, and the availability of wood, make this still the common material—almost the only one used—in the new cities of the Western States and Territories. The recent terrible fire at Chicago is an illustration, in part, of this fact, and of the evils of building with wood alone. But within the present century much brick has been made, and stone-quarries have been opened all over the country. In the older cities, brick and stone, in connection with iron, are now almost entirely employed, certain varieties of stone being used for all the most important buildings. The New England States furnish a great deal of granite and sienite, which are very strong and durable stones, but too hard and rough for finely cut or ornamental work. There is much sandstone in the Middle States, and in the West are many kinds of sand and limestone, which are easily cut, and receive readily the richest ornamentation. There is also throughout the United States a great variety of white and colored marbles, much used in ornamental and decorative work; and many elaborate buildings are built of them.

Before the present century architects were few in America and of little skill; buildings were designed, for the most part, by the men who built them. But the gain of the community in wealth and leisure has greatly developed the profession in the present generation. The earlier architects worked only by English traditions, which were, in their turn, derived from the Italian architects of the sixteenth and seventeenth centuries. The earlier architects of this country usually obtained their professional education in Europe, where the advantages were numerous; at the present time, however, young Americans find excellent opportunities in the offices of the better-trained architects at home. The multiplication of prints, photographs, and casts in plaster from the best old examples, have greatly facilitated study; schools of architecture have been established in several of the educational institutions of the country; and in New York they have an American Institute of Architects, which is represented in all the leading cities of the country by what they call "Chapters," and which are said to exercise an important influence within their proper sphere. The styles of architecture employed in America are as various as possible, but perhaps the kind of buildings in which the United States architects are most successful is that of wooden villas, which are often both beautiful and convenient. It has been charged against the Americans, that in regard to architecture, if nothing else, they lay more stress upon the idea of a conventional beauty, than upon substantial usefulness. A church may be beautiful to the eye, but filled with uncomfortable seats and a perpetual darkness; a public building may be very ornamental, but badly ventilated; and a dwelling may appear like a palace, and in reality be without a single comfort. Notwithstanding the immense amounts of money which are annually expended in America upon fine buildings, it is claimed that there is much room for improvement; and it is a creditable truth, that a great impetus has recently been given to the art of architecture by the patronage of the General Government, whose buildings are numerous, and among the most extensive and imposing in the Republic. In this connection, one fact which seems amazing, and is, indeed, a subject of remark, is this: that there now stands, in the city of Washington, a monument to the memory of George Washington, who is called the Father of his Country, which was commenced a quarter of a century ago, and is yet unfinished, and a painful spectacle to all the world.

We come now to speak of science in America, but before doing so it may be proper to make some remarks in regard to science in general. The term science, in its more restricted sense, is a knowledge of the laws of nature, or how the changes in the natural world are produced. In a more general sense, it is used to include descriptive natural history, from which it differs in this, that the latter classifies and describes things or objects in nature, as they exist, without considering their origin or the changes to which they are subjected. Science, then, although founded on the results of experiments and observations, does not consist in collections of isolated facts, but in general principles, from which special facts can be deduced when certain conditions are known. Thus, the phenomena of astronomy are all referred to principles which are denominated the laws of force and motion. By means of these laws, if the relative mass, position, and velocity of the heavenly bodies are known at a given epoch, their relative position for all times, in the remotest past as well as in the distant future, can be calculated. Other phenomena are referred to other laws, such as those of light, heat, electricity, navigation, chemical action, life, and organization. These laws are generally expressed in the form of theories, by which they can be more readily understood and applied, either in the way of practical inventions, or in the discovery of new truths. The knowledge of a law of nature enables the savant to explain, predict, and in some cases to control the phenomena to which these laws pertain. These characteristics of science afford the means of clearly distinguishing between the expressions of real truths or laws, and the mere vague speculations with which the principles of science are often confounded. It is by the discovery and application of these laws that modern civilization differs essentially from that of ancient times, and also from the civilization of China and Japan. In these countries the arts of life are based upon facts accidentally discovered, which lie, as it were, on the face of nature, are few in number, and soon exhausted; while in Europe and North America the various inventions which add so much to the material well-being of man are derived from the endless stores of facts deduced from scientific principles. It is by a knowledge of the law of gravitation, heat, electricity, and chemical action, that these powers are rendered obedient and efficient slaves, by which man emancipates himself from the bondage of brute labors, to which in ancient times he was universally subjected; while, by a knowledge of the laws of light and of sound, the infirmities of age are remedied, and the range of human senses indefinitely extended. By the constant study of the phenomena of nature, irrespective of the use which may flow from them, our knowledge is continually increased, while from the discovery of every new principle in science many applications in art usually follow. It is this which is understood by the Baconian aphorism—"Knowledge is power." There are at the present time, in all parts of the civilized world, men who are devoting their thoughts and time to the investigations of the various phenomena of nature; and through the intercourse which is established between all parts of the world, the discoveries made by each become the knowledge of all, and in this way science is rapidly increasing. Moreover, whatever is discovered in one portion of the domain of nature, as a general rule, tends to reflect light on various other portions, and also to furnish instruments for more extended and varied research.

It is evident, from the foregoing remarks, that the country is most highly civilized,—at least in one direction,—which makes the best provision for the investigation of abstract science. Of all nations at present existing, Prussia appears to be the most advanced in this respect. Whenever an individual is found capable of making original discoveries, in that country, he is at once consecrated to science. He is elected a higher professor in one of the universities, receives a liberal salary, is supplied with all the implements necessary for research in his special line, and is allowed full time for his investigations; being required to give but few lectures on higher subjects, while the teaching and the drilling of pupils are performed by men of inferior talents. In the United States, where so much is to be done in the way of subduing nature and developing the resources of a new country, there has been, consequently, a great demand for the application of science, and less attention has been given, until of late, to encourage and sustain original invention.

One effect of the general diffusion of education in the United States, especially in New England, has been to render the people impatient as to mere manual labor, and hence, from the scarcity of laborers, and the great demand for them, a large amount of talent has been devoted to the invention of labor-saving machines. There are no people in the world who make so many inventions as the Americans, which fact is evinced by the number and variety of models in the Patent Office. There is, however, a growing inclination on the part of the Government and of wealthy individuals to endow establishments for the advance of pure science. The Government has established the National Observatory, which is supported at an annual expense of not less than seventy-five thousand dollars, and in which the motions of the heavenly bodies are continuously studied, new facts observed, and new deductions from them constantly made. There has also been established a Bureau for the calculation of a Nautical Almanac, the object of which is to furnish mariners with the means for determining their position on the ocean, while it also contributes to the advance of science by original mathematical deductions from facts which have been observed. An extended work called the Coast Survey has likewise been established, the object of which is to furnish accurate maps, by means of astronomical determinations, of the whole coast of the country, but which also is developing, in its operations, new facts of the highest interest to science. Among those are the laws of the variation, direction, and intensity of terrestrial magnetism—the form and dimensions of the earth—the variation of the force of terrestrial gravitation on the different portions of the earth's surface—the knowledge of organized beings which live at the bottom of the ocean, within soundings—and temperature, motion, and magnitude of the Gulf Stream, which, in passing across the Atlantic ocean, moderates the temperature, and gives a genial climate to the north of Europe. Another of the Government establishments which advances science is the office of Weights and Measures, in which a series of investigations are carried on, for determining the expansion of bodies and the best manner of making accurate standards of measure, of length, weight, and capacity. The Government also has its schools of applied science; one at West Point, for the education of officers of the army in all things pertaining to military life and operations; and another at Annapolis, for the education of naval officers in all matters connected with the naval service. Of late years, moreover, numerous surveys and explorations have been made at the expense of the Government, across the Continent, which have tended, not only to develop the resources of the country, but have afforded means for the critical study of the geology, mineralogy, and natural history of the regions traversed, and which have resulted in the construction of the celebrated railroad between the Atlantic and Pacific oceans. In many of the older States of the Union there have been instituted geological surveys, which, while they have served to discover the peculiar mineral treasures within the State limits, have greatly added to the science of geology as well as to natural history. The ostensible object of all these establishments of the General Government, as well as those of the separate States, is practical utility, although abstract science is greatly advanced by means of them.

In various parts of the country astronomical observatories have been erected in connection with some of the principal universities and colleges, but in them, with but few exceptions, original investigations are subordinate to the business of education. There are also connected with the higher institutions of learning, scientific schools, the object of which is generally to teach the principles of science, as far as they are applicable to civil and mining engineering, and the various manufactures which depend upon a knowledge of chemistry and physics. The professors in universities and colleges are the principal contributors to the scientific journals of the day, in which the progress of science is recorded. There is no civilized country in which there appears to be a greater taste for a knowledge of general scientific results, or in which a greater number of popular scientific works are read than in the United States. At the same time, there is scarcely any country in which original talents, applied to pure scientific investigation, meet with less reward. In France and other European countries there are Academies of Science, consisting of a limited number of the most distinguished individuals, and supported by Government, each member receiving a salary, besides marks of social distinction. To become a member of one of these academies is an object of the highest ambition, to which is directed the best mind of the community. In Great Britain there are no such academies, yet the Government makes yearly grants for scientific investigations; and individuals, distinguished for their scientific discoveries, not only receive pensions, but are honored by the titles of barons and knights. No adequate inducements are yet held out in the United States, as a stimulus to scientific investigation, but for scientific invention or the application of science to useful arts, there is frequently an abundant remuneration. Notwithstanding these drawbacks, much has been done and is doing, in the way of advancing science, as is evinced by the transactions of the American Philosophical Society of Philadelphia, of the American Academy of Arts and Sciences of Boston, the publications of the Smithsonian Institution, and of the

Natural History Societies and Academies of Boston, Salem, Philadelphia, Chicago, San Francisco, and New Orleans. All these institutions were established and are sustained by private individuals. To the above may be added the American Journal of Science in New Haven, and the Journal of the Franklin Institute of Philadelphia.

A large portion of the scientific labor of the United States has been devoted to descriptive natural history, to which attention was invited by the almost unbounded field which was presented for study in the mineral, vegetable, and animal kingdoms, and because a knowledge derived from these was intimately connected with the development of the wealth and prosperity of the country. Science should, however, be studied for its own sake, without regard to its immediate application, since nothing tends more to extend the bounds of thought, to add to the intellectual powers of man, and to raise him in the scale of intelligence, than the study and contemplation of the operations of nature; and we are happy to think that, as we have said before, there is in this great country a growing appreciation of the importance of abstract science, and that many institutions in various parts of it will be established, through the enlightened policy of wealthy individuals, for its cultivation and advancement. A conspicuous example of what has been done in this line is the Smithsonian Institution, founded in Washington by James Smithson, of England, for the increase and diffusion of knowledge among men. The founder was devoted to scientific investigation, and, under the impulse of his ruling passion, bequeathed his entire property for a similar purpose. It is as yet the only well-endowed institution in America which is intended exclusively for the advancement of abstract science. But through the influence which it has attained by the persevering effort of its director, Prof. Joseph Henry, and the example which it has set, it is thought that other institutions of a similar character will be founded. Indeed, several wealthy individuals have already, independently of each other, made appropriations for scientific investigations. Foremost among these in liberality, and more especially as a man of science, may be mentioned Prof. A. D. Bache, the late Superintendent of the Coast Survey, who left the sum of fifty thousand dollars for scientific experiments and observations, the first proceeds of which are now being devoted to a magnetic survey of the United States, the results of which will be published and distributed to all parts of the world.

# LIFE AMONG THE MINERS.

It is now generally acknowledged that the mineral resources of the United States are more extensive and varied than those of any other country in the world. Indeed, to give anything like a minute account of them would fill many volumes; and therefore, with a view of being brief, we propose to submit a few facts on the leading mineral productions of the country, beginning with the precious metals.

Gold has been found in about one-half of the States of the Union. Prior to the year 1848 this metal, as well as silver, was chiefly obtained from Virginia, Tennessee, the Carolinas, and Georgia; at the present time the States of California, Oregon, and Nevada, and the Territories of Washington, Idaho, Arizona, Colorado, New Mexico, Montana, Dakota, and Wyoming, are by far the most productive gold-fields on the globe; and throughout all this region many other valuable minerals are found, but silver is the most important. At the time of the great discoveries in California, the annual production of the whole world was only $20,000,000, but in seven years from that time, California alone yielded $60,000,000, and its recent annual production has been fixed at $80,000,000. The total gold and silver product of the United States, down to the year 1868, was estimated at $1,255,000,000, and never before in the history of the world have so few people established so extensive a business. The region where gold is found covers an area of 1,000,000 square miles, and is chiefly the property of the nation. Hand-washing, as we have been informed by a man of experience in these matters, was the earliest mode of collecting gold, and the pan and the rocker were the first implements used in California mining. Quicksilver was soon employed to collect the fine particles, often lost in hand-washing. Hydraulic mining, now largely used in California, is done by throwing currents of water, from hose and pipes, with enormous force against banks of earth, cutting away whole hills. Down the face of the hills, also, pour artificial streams. At the foot, the waters all pass away in long flumes or wooden troughs, carrying the earth and stones with them. Slats on the bottom of the flumes catch and retain the gold; and where gold is found in hard quartz, the stones are ground to powder by machinery and stamp-mills, and the gold thus comes to the light, and quicksilver separates it from the dust. Silver is never found like gold, in grains among the sand, but in ores or quartz, from which it has to be reduced by stamping or grinding, or by smelting. It is found in a variety of ores, usually associated with gold, copper, or lead. Pure masses are occasionally found among the copper mines of Lake Superior, and also in Nevada and Idaho. The discovery of the rich deposits of gold and silver in California gave new impetus to the movements of population everywhere, stimulated all departments of industry, brought together into the same communities people from every part of the globe, settled the vast territories of the United States, facilitated intercourse between the nations, and, with the mining operations in Australia, has steadily changed values throughout the world.

But, notwithstanding the immense amount of treasure that has been taken from the soils and rocks of California and other Pacific States, the business of mining has not been profitable with the majority of miners. Indeed, it is said that during the last fifteen years, the farmers of Illinois have more frequently made fortunes than have the gold-hunters of the West. In 1865 a miner of California named Jules Fricot realized the sum of $182,511 by quartz mining, and since then a man named James P. Pierce, from placer mine obtained in one year the sum of $102,011,— but these were exceptional cases. The cost of living at the mines is always expensive, and the accommodations anything but comfortable. At the general eating-houses which are established among the mines, they commonly charge one dollar for a single meal, and twelve dollars per week for board,—the sleeping accommodations being a bare floor and a pair of blankets. According to the latest authentic data, the number of miners in California alone was 46,550, of whom 20,800 were Chinese, and the wages of these men ranged from three to five dollars per day. The national laws bearing upon the mining region of the Pacific Slope are not, as yet, what they should be; but those which have been enacted provide for two classes of miners,—those who are licensed to work upon the public domain, and those who become actual proprietors by purchase from the Government. The right is also granted to men, to purchase and work such mines as they may discover; and as to the mining customs,—mandatory edicts are passed, at twenty-four hours' notice, by from five to five hundred men, which, for the time being, are the law of the land.

And now, in closing these remarks, let us glance at what has been said in regard to the distribution of the precious metals. The drain of them has hitherto been toward the East, where they are used for hoarding and for ornaments, rather than for money. This is particularly true of silver. Between the years 1850 and 1864, there were exported to Asia from England and the Mediterranean, more than $650,000,000. The total amount of silver in the world is estimated at $10,000,000,000, or only enough to pay the debts of three or four of the leading nations of the present time. The coining of gold and silver, as well as copper, was commenced by the United States in 1793, and the total product of each metal, down to the middle of 1870, was as follows: Gold, $971,628,046; silver, $143,760,474; copper, $11,009,048; or a grand total of $1,126,397,569.

Of the baser metals which have hitherto been employed in the coining of money, copper is the most important. Its most valuable alloy is brass, out of which a very large number of useful things are manufactured. Another alloy, known as "French gold," is extensively used in the manufacture of cheap jewelry and watches. Copper is found in ores and in a metallic state, and was first mined on the American Continent in New England. It has been worked in seven or eight of the United States, but, practically, all the copper product of the Union comes from Lake Superior, which was almost an unknown wilderness as late as the year 1843. It is found in a ridge of trap-rock, on the shores belonging to Michigan, and masses of the solid metal have been discovered weighing several tons. The mines were opened there in 1845, since which time the total yield has been not far from 150,000 tons. It is extracted from its ores by smelting and calcination, and prepared for the market in ingots, which are converted into sheets by rolling mills, established chiefly in the Atlantic States. Situated as are the copper mines of Michigan, in a region where the winters are long and the summers short, the miners are subject to many hardships from the cold, and to many privations in the way of bodily comforts. A large proportion of them are men who have had experience in the mines of Great Britain and other countries, and their compensation is not on a par with their habits of industry and their experience, but the quantity of metal which they obtain from the earth and send to market is very large.

Next in importance to the precious metals, come the coal productions of the United States, the two prominent varieties of which bear the names of anthracite and bituminous. The largest producer of both is the State of Pennsylvania; and in the production of the former, Rhode Island stands second; and Ohio occupies the second position in regard to bituminous coal. The area of workable coal-beds in the United States, excluding Alaska, is estimated at 200,000 square miles, which is said to be eight times as large as the available coal area of all the rest of the world. The coal-veins are usually reached by vertical shafts, but when found in hills are worked by horizontal galleries. Notwithstanding the fact that perpendicular shafts are employed to secure thorough ventilation, and safety-lamps are used to prevent the ignition of the fatal fire-damp, many serious accidents have happened in the mines of Pennsylvania. The first railway for the transmission of coal from the mines was built in 1827, and the coal mines now give employment to more than forty railroads and canals. It is a common occurrence for a train of 100 cars to enter the city of Philadelphia, loaded with anthracite, and the same may be said of Baltimore, which is the principal exporting place for bituminous coal. The total product of the United States for the year 1868 was about 19,000,000 tons, valued at $26,000,000, since which time these figures have been increased, and are still increasing. It is now seventy years since anthracite coal was used as fuel in this country, and about forty years since it began to be extensively mined in the United States; and it has been stated by authentic writers on the subject, that the coal-fields of the United States are thirty-six times greater than those of Great Britain, while the annual production of Britain is five times greater than that of the United States. The reasons for this great difference are apparent. In many of the States of the Union, the climate is so mild that no coal is needed for domestic purposes, and when fuel is demanded for manufacturing purposes, there is always to be obtained an abundant supply of wood. And then again, excepting the New England, the Middle, and some of the Western States, where prairies abound, the forests are so numerous that it must be many years before coal will become a necessity among the people. Indeed, the very remarkable fact has been chronicled, that in some of the Western States, where agriculture is the chief source of wealth, the article known as maize, or Indian corn, has been employed as fuel. If, however, we find that a large proportion of the inhabitants in

America have no immediate interest in the production of coal, it is at the same time true, that a very large part of the population are consumers of what is called coal-oil, or petroleum. Although long known to the scientific world, this article did not become known to the commercial world until 1858. It is found in various parts of the country, but more extensively in western Pennsylvania than in any other region, where very large fortunes have been made by persons engaged in drawing the precious liquid out of the earth. It is obtained by means of artesian wells, which are sunk from one hundred to six hundred feet into the earth, and some of which have yielded, with the aid of forcing-pumps, as much as two thousand barrels of oil in a single day. The applications of petroleum are chiefly limited to purposes of illumination and lubricating machinery, and for the latter purpose the consumption is very large on the railroads and in the manufactories. A distillation of this oil is also used in the manufacture of certain kinds of leather, and in the preparation of paints and varnishes. This trade in rock-oil has become very extensive, and is every day becoming more and more highly appreciated as a servant of civilization; the revenue which it produces being of great magnitude, and the number of people which it supports very numerous.

The next important mineral product that we have to notice is iron, recognized as the most useful known to man. It is more widely distributed throughout the United States than any of the important metals; is found in abundance in New York, New Hampshire, Massachusetts, Connecticut, Maryland, and Ohio, Michigan, Wisconsin, Oregon, Virginia, the Carolinas, Alabama, and Missouri; but is chiefly mined in Pennsylvania and New Jersey, where the yield is more than one-half of the whole product in the United States, or about seven hundred tons per annum, from one hundred and thirty establishments. In Missouri it is found in great abundance, where there is a hill called "Iron Mountain," which is more than two hundred feet high, and is supposed to contain two hundred and fifty millions of tons of pure metal. Another well-nigh solid iron mountain is called "Pilot Knob," nearly six hundred feet high, and, it is thought, would furnish one million tons per annum for two hundred years. These two mountains, with another called Shepherd's Mountain, also in Missouri, are considered among the curiosities of America. And yet, with these figures before us, the astounding fact is proclaimed that nearly half a million tons of iron were imported from Great Britain in 1868, while the yield of the United States was about sixteen hundred thousand tons. But the fact that there should be any iron imported from England, grows out of the operations of the American Tariff. The great magnitude and importance of the iron interest, which can only be fully treated in elaborate volumes, is rendered difficult to notice in a paragraph like the present. The processes by which the ores are turned into metallic iron are as follows: In what are called bloomeries and forges the ores are converted directly into malleable iron, without passing through the intermediate stage of cast or pig iron; and by means of blast-furnaces, the ores are decomposed as they fuse, in vast quantities at a time, and produce the cast or pig iron;—and then they have what are called rolling-mills, which convert the iron into sheets and plates. With regard to the uses to which iron is appropriated in the United States, they are well-nigh infinite; and we can only obtain an idea of the extent of its consumption, by reflecting upon the quantity of it which is transferred into steel, for cutlery and machinery; upon the extensive lines of railway in the country and the great number of locomotives employed; and upon manifold uses in connection with shipping and house-building throughout the length and breadth of this immense country.

We come now to speak of the production of lead in the United States. The two most prominent deposits of this useful mineral are to be found in the States of Missouri and Illinois. The working of the former was commenced in 1854 and the latter in 1718. The largest supply comes from those two States, although it is also found in abundance in Wisconsin and Iowa. The American lead is remarkable for its softness and purity, and although obtained with comparative ease, excepting what is mined in Illinois and Iowa, it is not easily transported to market. The total production of the Union, during the year 1869, was estimated at thirty-eight millions of pounds, while Spain produced about sixty seven millions, and Great Britain more than one hundred and fifty-three millions of pounds;—and the imports into the United States greatly exceed the domestic product. The uses to which the metal is applied are very numerous and highly important. One of the most useful applications of lead is in the manufacture of the carbonate, which is extensively used as a white paint, and also as a body for other colors. The smelting of lead and the manufacture of the white paint therefrom, are considered prejudicial to health, and the workmen suffer much from colic and paralysis.

Another of the more important minerals found in the United States, in almost inexhaustible quantities, is quicksilver. It is chiefly mined in California, where the annual product is considerably more than half the yield of the whole world beside, the total annual yield having been about six hundred thousand pounds. Until recently the mines of Spain controlled the Chinese market, but the miners of California shipped a large amount to Hong Kong, where they sold it far below cost, and the supply from Spain was driven back to that country. The English market is now supplied by Spain and the Chinese market by California. Besides the countries named, Austria and Peru furnish a small supply of this valuable mineral. The chief demand for it is for mining purposes, and for the manufacture of calomel and vermilion.

With regard to the metals known as tin, zinc, platinum, nickel, antimony, cobalt, and other minor metals, they are all found in various parts of the United States, but none of them have as yet been mined to any great extent. With the increase of population and railways, it is supposed that the business of mining will grow into a gigantic national interest, and that America will lead the world in the value and variety of her mineral products. The National Government, within the last few years, has done much to develop the hidden resources of the land, by sending forth competent scientific expeditions, and publishing their results for the benefit of the public; and the people themselves have manifested their interest in the subject by establishing and supporting a number of well-conducted journals devoted wholly to Mining-Engineering.

In taking a general survey of the mining population of

America, we cannot but conclude that they are noted for their intelligence, and, in view of the hardship and privations which they undergo, are not as well paid as they should be, although better paid than the mining people of other countries. A very large proportion of them, however, are foreigners, and as they have generally improved their condition by emigrating to this country, they are contented with their lot. Those of them who are engaged in mining coal, iron, lead, and copper, in the older States of the Union, have facilities for the education of their children at common-schools, but in the frontier States and Territories, where the precious metals are chiefly found, family-men are not abundant, and the opportunities for making them comfortable, and educating the young, are few and far between.

# LIFE IN THE ARMY AND NAVY.

The standing army of the United States began with the foundation of the Government in 1789, but, when necessary, it has always been customary to employ what is called a volunteer force or army. During the war of the Revolution, the number of soldiers employed was 275,000; in the war of 1812, the combined troops numbered 527,631; during the Seminole war of 1817, 5,611; Black Hawk war of 1832, 5,031; Florida war of 1842, 29,953; war with Mexico in 1846, 73,260; miscellaneous troubles, about 20,000; and during the late Civil War, the forces in the field, at one time, numbered 2,688,523. The total amount of money expended by the United States in carrying on its various wars was $3,308,352,706.

The regular army of the United States is at present constituted as follows: 1 general, 3 major-generals, 16 brigadier-generals, 68 colonels, 83 lieutenant-colonels, 271 majors, 36 aides-de-camp, 532 captains, 40 adjutants (extra lieutenants), 40 regimental quartermasters (extra lieutenants), 682 first lieutenants, 455 second lieutenants, 34 chaplains, 29 military store-keepers, 5 medical store-keepers, 40 sergeant-majors, 40 quartermaster-sergeants, 40 chief musicians, 60 principal musicians, 10 saddler-sergeants, 10 chief trumpeters, 151 ordnance-sergeants, 362 hospital stewards, 430 first sergeants, 430 company quartermaster-sergeants, 1,947 sergeants, 1,837 corporals, 240 trumpeters, 654 musicians, 240 farriers or blacksmiths, 620 artificers, 120 saddlers, 430 wagoners, 300 privates of the 1st class (ordnance and engineers), 299 privates of the 2d class (ordnance and engineers), 22,100 privates, also one battalion sergeant-major, and one battalion quartermaster-sergeant; making the whole number of commissioned officers 2,263, and the whole number of enlisted men 30,000. There are, besides, at the United States Military Academy, 8 professors and 241 cadets, making the total commissioned and enlisted, 32,512. The army is sub-divided into 10 regiments of cavalry, 5 regiments of artillery, 25 regiments of infantry, and the Engineer Battalion. Each regiment of cavalry has 1 colonel, 1 lieutenant-colonel, 3 majors, 1 adjutant (extra lieutenant), 1 regimental quartermaster (extra lieutenant), 12 captains, 12 first lieutenants, 12 second lieutenants, 1 sergeant-major, 1 quartermaster-sergeant, 1 chief musician, 1 saddler-sergeant, 1 chief trumpeter, 12 first sergeants, 12 company quartermaster-sergeants, 60 sergeants, 48 corporals, 24 trumpeters, 24 farriers and blacksmiths, 12 saddlers, 12 wagoners, and 804 privates. The whole number of commissioned officers to the regiment is 44, and whole number enlisted is 1,013, making the aggregate 1,057. The regiment is sub-divided into 12 troops, each troop having 1 captain, 1 first lieutenant, 1 second lieutenant, 1 first sergeant, 1 company quartermaster-sergeant, 5 sergeants, 4 corporals, 2 trumpeters, 2 farriers and blacksmiths, 1 saddler, 1 wagoner, 67 privates; total commissioned, 3; total enlisted, 84; aggregate, 87.

There are 5 regiments of Artillery, each regiment having 1 colonel, 1 lieutenant-colonel, 3 majors, 1 adjutant (extra lieutenant), 1 regimental quartermaster (extra lieutenant),

12 captains, 24 first lieutenants, 13 second lieutenants, 1 sergeant-major, 1 quartermaster-sergeant, 1 chief musician, 2 principal musicians, 12 first sergeants, 12 company quartermaster-sergeants, 50 sergeants, 48 corporals, 24 musicians, 24 artificers, 12 wagoners, and 562 privates; total commissioned, 56; total enlisted, 749; aggregate, 805. To each regiment there are 12 companies, one of which is mounted, and is called a light battery. A company of artillery consists of 1 captain, 2 first lieutenants, 1 second lieutenant (light battery has 2), 1 first sergeant, 1 company quartermaster-sergeant, 4 sergeants (light battery has 6), 4 corporals, 2 musicians, 2 artificers, 1 wagoner, 45 privates (light battery has 67); total commissioned, 4 (light battery 5); total enlisted, 60 (light battery 84); aggregate, 64 (light battery 89).

There are 25 regiments of Infantry, each having 1 colonel, 1 lieutenant-colonel, 1 major, 1 adjutant (extra lieutenant), 1 regimental quartermaster (extra lieutenant), 10 captains, 10 first lieutenants, 10 second lieutenants, 1 sergeant-major, 1 quartermaster-sergeant, 1 chief musician, 2 principal musicians, 10 first sergeants, 10 company quartermaster-sergeants, 40 sergeants, 40 corporals, 20 musicians, 20 artificers, 10 wagoners, and 450 privates; total commissioned, 36; total enlisted, 605; aggregate, 641. Each regiment has 10 companies; to each company there are 1 captain, 1 first lieutenant, 1 second lieutenant, 1 first sergeant, 1 company quartermaster-sergeant, 4 sergeants, 4 corporals, 2 musicians, 2 artificers, 1 wagoner, 45 privates; total commissioned, 3; total enlisted, 60; aggregate, 63.

Another branch of the service is the Engineer Battalion,

which has 1 major, 1 adjutant, 1 quartermaster, 5 captains, 5 first lieutenants, 5 second lieutenants, 1 sergeant-major, 1 quartermaster-sergeant, 50 sergeants, 5 corporals, 10 musicians, 119 privates of the first class, 119 privates of the second class; total commissioned, 16 ; total enlisted, 350; aggregate, 366. In the battalion there are 5 companies, each having 1 captain, 1 first lieutenant, 1 second lieutenant, 10 sergeants, 10 corporals, 2 musicians, 24 privates, first class, 24 privates, second class; total commissioned, 3 ; total enlisted, 70 ; aggregate, 73.

The President is by law Commander-in-Chief of the Army. To assist him in the execution of the laws, in so far as they relate to the army, in its control, subsistence, and supply, a Secretary of War is appointed by him, through whom he exercises a general supervision. To facilitate this a Department of War has been established, which is sub-divided into the following staff departments or corps:

1. Adjutant-General's Department.
2. Inspector-General's Department.
3. Bureau of Military Justice.
4. Quartermaster's Department.
5. Subsistence Department.
6. Medical Department.
7. Pay Department.
8. Signal Officer.
9. Chief of Staff to the General of the Army.
10. Corps of Engineers.
11. Ordnance Department.

The general staff is the central point of military administration. It comprises all the officers concerned in regulating the details of the service, and furnishing the army with the means necessary for its subsistence, comfort, mobility, and action.

All general orders which emanate from the headquarters of the army, the orders of detail, of instruction, of movement, and all general regulations for the army, are communicated to the troops through the office of the Adjutant-General.

The Adjutant-General is charged with the record of military appointments, promotions, resignations, deaths, and other casualties; with the registry and filling up of commissions, and with their distribution; with the records which relate to the personnel of the army, and to the military history of every officer and soldier; with the duties connected with the recruiting service; the registry of the names of soldiers; their enlistment and descriptive lists, and of deaths, desertions, discharges, etc.; with the preservation of monthly returns of regiments and posts, and the muster-rolls of companies; with receipts and examination of applications for pension, previous to their being sent to the Pension Office, and of inventories of the effects of deceased soldiers.

The annual returns of the militia of the several States and Territories; of the ordnance, arms, accoutrements, and munitions of war appertaining to the same, required by law to be made to the President of the United States, are filed, and the general returns of the militia annually required to be laid before Congress, are also prepared and consolidated in this office.

The Inspector-General's Department is charged with the duty of inspecting and reporting upon the condition of the forts, with their armaments, of the state of discipline of the troops—in short, upon the whole "material and personnel" of the army, and to report whether or not the prescribed rules, regulations, and orders for its government are properly carried into effect.

In the office of the Judge Advocate-General, under whose charge is the Bureau of Military Justice, the proceedings of all courts-martial, courts of inquiry, and military commissions, are received, revised, recorded, and reported upon. It is the duty of the Judge Advocate-General to report at once for the action of the Secretary of War, all fatal irregularities in proceedings, and illegal or unusual sentences. When called upon by the proper authority, he gives an opinion on questions of construction of military law; and through him all communications pertaining to questions of military justice should be addressed.

The Quartermaster-General's Department furnishes to the army its transportation, of whatever nature, quarters, fuel, stationery, etc., and pays for rent of quarters and for all materials to be used in the construction of buildings for its use. To that office are sent all reports and returns of property purchased, issued, worn out in service, lost, sold, destroyed, or remaining on hand, and there are approved all contracts for purchases connected with the above.

The Subsistence Department, as its name implies, has charge of the furnishing of subsistence to troops; all reports and returns necessary to the end that stores may be properly accounted for, are made to this office, and here all contracts for their purchase are approved.

The Medical Department, or Surgeon-General's Office, has charge of the selection of medical offices for detail, and to it all returns and reports in regard to sick and wounded officers and soldiers, and medical stores, are made. With regard to the other bureaus or offices which have been mentioned, their duties are described by their titles.

We may further remark, in brief, that the American army is divided into divisions and departments commanded by generals; that in times of peace it is chiefly employed in occupying the various forts and defences of the country, and in keeping peace with the Indians on the frontiers; that, after forty years of service, the officers of the army may at their own request be retired, receiving *seventy-five* per cent. of their pay; that members of Congress designate the largest proportion of those who are admitted to the West Point Academy, which is the regular school for the education of officers for the army. When, in time of war, it is necessary to have volunteers, they are called for by proclamation of the President, and the State governors immediately answer the call, and send the proportion assigned to them, which are chiefly composed of the militia or State troops; and after the war, these volunteer troops are disbanded and return to the ordinary avocations of life, which fact has been considered by foreigners as one of the marvels of the American Government. The regular army is supplied with soldiers by enlistment, and after entering the service, no man can leave it without the consent of Government, nor without sufficient cause. With regard to the pay of the army, which is always enhanced by long service, we submit the following: general, $13,500; lieutenant-general, $11,000; major-general, $7,500; brigadier-general, $5,500;

colonel, $3,500; lieutenant-colonel, $3,000; major, $2,500; captains, $1,800 and $2,000; regimental adjutant and quartermaster, each $1,800; first lieutenants, $1,500 and $1,600; second lieutenants, $1,400 and $1,500; and chaplains, $1,500. The pay of the common soldier is $13 per month, with rations. There are 25 armories and arsenals in the country, all in command of competent officers, and the Military Departments of the Government number 15, and embrace the whole Union. The amount required for supporting the military establishments during 1872 is about $29,000,000.

As the War Department is the centre of the army, so is the Navy Department the fountain-head of the navy. The duties of this department are distributed through the Secretary's office and eight bureaus, namely: Bureau of Yards and Docks, which has charge of the navy-yards, including the docks, wharves, buildings, and machinery, and also of a Naval Asylum; Office of Navigation, which has charge of the maps, charts, flags, signals, etc., and also of the Naval Academy, Naval Observatory, and Nautical Almanac; Office of Ordnance, which has charge of ordnance and ordnance stores, the manufacture and purchase of cannon, guns, powder, shot, shell, etc.; Office of Construction and Repair, having charge of the construction of vessels of war; Office of Equipment and Recruiting, which has charge of the enlistment of men for the navy, the equipment of vessels, anchors, cables, rigging, sails, coal, etc.; Office of Provisions and Clothing; and Office of Steam Engineering; Office of Medicine and Surgery, the duties of which last two are described by their titles. There is attached to the Navy Department what is called the Marine Corps, whose duties are allied to those of the army, only that they are performed on board ship or at the navy-yards; also a National Observatory, which has earned a world-wide reputation; and also an Hydrographic Office, which, with the Observatory, annually publishes volumes of scientific information of great value.

The largest vessel in the United States navy has a displacement of 5,440 feet, carries 12 guns, and, like the majority in the service, is a screw steamer. Some other ships, however, carry 45 guns. Of those ranking as first-rates there are 5; second-rates, 40; third-rates, 43; fourth-rates, 10; to which may be added the iron-clads, receiving and practice ships, supply vessels and tugs, making in all 179, and carrying in the aggregate 1,390 guns. The officers of the navy, to which we affix their "at sea" salaries, are as follows: 1 admiral, $13,000; 1 vice-admiral, $9,000; 12 rear-admirals, $6,000; 24 commodores, $5,000; 50 captains, $4,500; 89 commanders, $3,500; 164 lieutenant-commanders, $2,800; 201 lieutenants, $2,400; 75 masters, $1,800; 68 ensigns, $1,200; 113 midshipmen, $1,000; 150 in Medical Corps, whose salaries are widely various; 134 in the Pay Corps, with various salaries; and 241 in the Engineer Corps, together with an ample supply of naval constructors, chaplains, professors of mathematics, and civil engineers, whose salaries range from $1,700 to $4,400, and are increased with length of service. The pay of common seamen is $21.50 per month, and while the subordinate grades in the service number 57, their pay ranges from $8 to $56 per month. The academy where young men are fitted for service in the navy is located at Annapolis, and is under rules, in regard to admission, allied to those of the Military Academy at West Point. Of complete Navy Yards there are eight in the United States; five fleets are now doing duty in various quarters of the globe; and within the last year several scientific expeditions have been fitted out, as follows, viz.: one to survey the Isthmus of Tehuantepec and another to survey the Isthmus of Darien, both of which have in view the making of a canal between the Atlantic and Pacific Oceans; and an expedition has also been fitted out for explorations towards the North Pole. Indirectly connected with the navy is a bureau called the Light-House Board, with which, as an active member, has hitherto been connected Admiral Thornton A. Jenkins, but who has recently been assigned to the fleet in the waters of China and Japan. Without going more fully into the subject, for want of space, it only remains for us to add, in conclusion, that the sum of money which will be required to support the American naval establishment during the year 1872 will be about $20,000,000.

14*

# LIFE IN THE LEADING CITIES.

The total number of incorporated cities in the United States is 409, but many of them do not contain more than 2,000 inhabitants. By far the largest proportion of foreigners who come to this country across the Atlantic Ocean, enter the country at the port of New York, which is the largest city in the Western Hemisphere. It was founded by the Dutch, and called by them New Amsterdam. It occupies the greater part of an island called Manhattan, which is $13\frac{1}{2}$ miles long, and contains an area of 22 miles. The cities of Brooklyn and Jersey City, and several other towns, although having each a government of its own, are in reality portions of New York, and their combined population is not far from 1,500,000. According to the last census, the population of New York by itself was 942,292; of whom 523,198 were born in the United States, and 484,109 in the State of New York. Within eight miles of the commercial metropolis, in New Jersey, is a city called Newark, of 100,000 people, but it is so closely identified with the former in its business and social interests as almost to be considered a suburb of New York. During the last fifteen years the number of immigrants arriving there, from various parts of the world, was about 2,341,000, the arrivals for 1870 alone having been

211,190, and it is estimated that about four-fifths of these foreigners found permanent homes in the various States of the interior. The principal street of New York, which runs through its entire length like a backbone, is called Broadway, and for several miles is completely lined with iron and marble buildings, devoted chiefly to business pursuits, and winning for it the reputation of being one of the handsomest and wealthiest streets in the world. But much of this splendor is also found in all its subordinate streets and avenues, where the houses are generally built of brick; and, as a street for private residences, its Fifth Avenue is claimed to be unsurpassed. Projecting, as this city does, into a splendid harbor, where the fortifications are strong and imposing, it is perpetually surrounded with a forest of shipping, which gives the stranger an adequate idea of its very extensive commerce. The value of its real and personal estate has not been definitely settled, but has been estimated at nearly $800,000,000, and the rate of taxation is 2 per cent. per annum. It is supplied with pure water by an aqueduct which cost more than $15,000,000, the water-pipes of which measure some 270 miles. It has 100 miles of sewers, and more than 200 miles of paved streets. Its temples for religious worship are numerous, and many of them very beautiful, the church property of the city reaching in value nearly $15,000,000. Its principal park, known as Central Park, is said to be equal to the best in Europe, and its principal financial street, known as Wall-street, although not more than half a mile in length, has a power which is felt in the remotest corners of the earth. Its hospitals and other benevolent institutions are numerous and liberally conducted in every particular, and the same may be said of its institutions of learning, ranging from first-class colleges to the best of district or common schools. It is abundantly supplied with libraries, many of which are very large, and all of them are conducted on the most liberal principles. Its manufacturing establishments are numberless. Its fire department is noted for its efficiency, and is founded on the voluntary system; and there is a lively military spirit among its young men, and its militia regiments rival veteran regulars in their drill. Its police force is of the first order, and is managed by commissioners. Policemen are appointed during good behavior, and officers rise from the ranks. Patrolmen are paid $800 per annum, sergeants $900, captains $1,200, inspectors $2,000, and a general superintendent $5,000 a year. There are about 700 police stations, 412 miles of streets, and 11 miles of piers in the city. Its newspapers are abundant, and, taken in the aggregate, are probably more influential for good or evil than any similar number on the globe. Its markets for the necessaries of life are fully supplied with everything that can be desired, in the way of meats, flour, fruit, and fish. Its government, although resting upon the most liberal provisions, has for many years been a kind of political arena, in which unworthy men have obtained and exercised the most dangerous powers, and, at the moment of writing these lines, a number of men who were lately at the head of the city government are confined in a common prison for robbing their fellow-citizens to an enormous extent. While it is true that New York is very much of a cosmopolitan city, it has been estimated that two-thirds of its inhabitants are natives of the United States. It is, however, pre-eminently a commercial city, and in several respects is equal to London. The post-office of New York is the most important in the country; and its customs receipts amount to about three-fifths of the total in the United States. The manufactures of the city constitute a leading element of its prosperity and wealth. The most numerous class of workmen are those engaged in making wearing apparel; next to whom come the workmen in iron and metals; then the chemists; workmen in leather, steam machinery, and lumber; navigators; workmen in fibrous substances, glass, and pottery, and the manufacturers of cars and wagons; so on,—to an almost unlimited extent. Nowhere is the habit of eating away from home so general as in New York, owing to the great distance between the dwelling-houses and the places of business; and this habit has made eating-houses, lunch-rooms, refectories, oyster-cellars, and bar-rooms, a prominent feature of the place. Its hotels are quite magnificent, and its boarding-houses as comfortable as any in the world. The eating-houses are found everywhere, and are frequented by the millionaire as well as the vagabond. The city government is vested in a Mayor and Boards of Aldermen and Councilmen, who are annually elected by the people. While it is true that in times of high political excitement it is sometimes afflicted with mobs and riots, the din of business always ceases on the approach of the Sabbath, and that day is observed as a day of rest, of church-going, and of recreation, by its teeming thousands. The spring and autumn are the two great seasons for business; winter, the special season for amusements and all sorts of gayety; while the summer is comparatively sluggish, although, even then, the turmoil of business is far from being dead.

The second largest city in the United States is Philadelphia, which was founded by William Penn in 1682, and contains 674,022 inhabitants, of whom 490,398 were born in the United States, and 428,250 in Pennsylvania. It stands on a plain between the rivers Delaware and Schuylkill, and has several suburban cities, the whole of which form one municipality, containing 120 square miles. The streets of the city proper are laid out in regular order, and the houses are more distinguished for their neatness and comfort than for their richness or extravagance, and in this particular are in keeping with the character of the population. The city is well supplied with parks, one of which, for its collection of trees and scenes of beauty, is considered a successful rival of the great Central Park of New York. Its public buildings are numerous and beautiful; one of them, called Girard College, was built and the institution endowed by one of its citizens alone; but the chief boast of the inhabitants is Independence Hall, which was the meeting-place of Congress during the earlier history of the American Republic. The churches are also numerous, all the religious denominations being well supplied, but this is especially the case in regard to the Quakers, who have hitherto been so numerous and influential as to have given to their city the name of *Quaker City*. The literary and scientific institutions of Philadelphia have always occupied a high position, and the cultured character of its inhabitants has always been manifested by its rich libraries and galleries of art, and by the upright character of its press.

It was here that Benjamin Franklin lived, and worked as a printer, and won his great fame as a philosopher. From the earliest times the central mint of the United States has been established here, and the city has borne an important part in the financial history of the country. Because of its remoteness from the Atlantic Ocean, it may not compete with New York in its foreign commerce, but it carries on an immense trade with the interior country, and is a noted terminus for unnumbered railroads and canals. As a depot for the exportation of coal it is without a rival; and it has always been famous for the extent of its book-publishing business. Within the last few years Philadelphia has greatly increased its manufacturing establishments, until its inhabitants now claim that they can produce everything that may be required for the comfort or convenience of man; indeed, in the variety and extent of its manufactures it is said to be unequalled by any other city in the Union. On this point, we submit one illustration, which is, that it contains the two largest establishments in the world for the manufacture of locomotives, which give employment to about 4,000 hands, and can build one of those wonderful engines in a single day. The capital invested in its manufacturing establishments is estimated at $300,000,000. While the inhabitants of this city are noted for their peaceful disposition and for their love of order, it is also true that it has been the scene of many political or religious disturbances, but which, in these latter days, have been quite unknown. Another of the characteristics of this city is the total absence of tenement houses, and the existence of comfortable homes for the laboring population. As one of her public men informs us, every laborer, who has a family, dwells under a separate roof, which is most frequently his own—in a house lighted by gas, and supplied with an abundance of pure water. As this city is pre-eminently a producing city, so are its native and foreign inhabitants distinguished for their industry, and there is not in the whole land, probably, any other crowded city where among the working classes more genuine comfort and contentment can be found.

The next city on our list is Boston, which contains 250,526 inhabitants, of whom 172,450 were born in the United States, and 127,620 in the State of Massachusetts. If, however, we should add to it the various towns which adjoin it, the population would be nearly double. It was first settled in 1630 by the Puritans, and is the leading city of New England, upon which it has always exerted a paramount influence. It bore a very important part in the history of the American Revolution, and events of great importance have transpired within its limits and in its vicinity. Formerly it was more closely identified with the commerce of the East than any other American city, and at the present time ranks next to New York in the extent of its foreign commerce. The city is chiefly situated on a peninsula, and some of the adjacent parts, with which it is connected by numerous bridges, rise to the height of one hundred and thirty feet above the level of the harbor, which is deep, convenient, and secure. The streets were originally laid out upon no systematic plan, and being accommodated to the unevenness of the surface, many of them are crooked and narrow, but these defects are being annually remedied. Many of the public buildings are handsome, but some of them are more famous for their associations than their imposing appearance. The State House occupies the apex of the city, and presents a commanding view of the sea and surrounding country; and its Faneuil Hall is universally known as the "Cradle of Liberty," because it was here that the orators of the Revolution fired the hearts of the people against England. One of its leading land-marks is the monument of Bunker Hill, where was fought a famous battle. Its wharves and warehouses are on a scale of magnitude surpassed by no other city of the same size. Its churches are numerous, and many of them beautiful, the largest number of them belonging to the Unitarian denomination. It has an extensive park called "Boston Common," which is a delightful resort for the inhabitants during the vernal months. With regard to literary, scientific, and educational institutions, the city is most abundantly supplied. Its schools have a high reputation, and it publishes more than one hundred periodicals. Among its many libraries is one, the largest, which is entirely free to all who may desire to enjoy its advantages; and the fact that the famous Harvard University is located in one of its suburbs, called Cambridge, has greatly tended to give to it its high reputation as a seat of learning. Its benevolent institutions are also numerous and richly endowed, and it has taken a prominent part in providing for the wants and intellectual elevation of the blind and the comforts of the insane. Its infirmaries have always borne a high reputation. The ice-trade is a Boston invention, and is said to have secured for it the important trade which it enjoys with Calcutta, and other portions of the East. On the score of enterprise and culture, the inhabitants of Boston have no superiors, and that circumstance has tended to make them somewhat clannish or exclusive in their manners and conversation, and their modes of doing business; and hence it is that the outside world, especially the cosmopolitan citizens of New York, occasionally indulge in a little ridicule at the expense of the Bostonians. It is a thriving city, and, by means of seven or eight great lines of railway, carries on an important trade in manufactures with the interior country. It is a poor place for idlers and beggars, and yet the most liberal provision is made for the deserving poor. While this city does much to promote the fine arts, it claims a reputation of its own for what it has done in developing the art of music, and it boasts of a church organ which is the largest in the world.

Another of the leading cities of America is Baltimore, which has a population of 267,354, of whom 210,870 were born in the United States, and 187,650 in the State of Maryland. It was founded by the Roman Catholics in 1729; is admirably situated both for foreign and internal trade, having a spacious and secure harbor, and occupying a central position as regards the Atlantic coast of the United States. The site of the city is picturesque, covering a number of eminences; and, although connected with the Northern and Western States by its business ramifications, it has hitherto been considered a representative of the Southern States. It was here that the first gun was fired, by a mob, at the commencement of the late civil war, when a regiment of troops from Massachusetts was assaulted, on their way to Washington. Its proximity to the seat of government, from which it is only 38 miles distant, has added to its importance, and made it popular with the officials of the nation. From the number and prominence of its monuments, it has been called the "Monumental City." The most imposing of these is surmounted by a statue of George Washington, which stands 312 feet above the adjacent harbor; and the city contains a shot-tower which is 250 feet high—the highest in the world. The churches of this city are numerous, and many of them beautiful and imposing; and it boasts of one large park, which is remarkable for the beauty of its scenery, and is a successful rival of those in New York and Boston. The manufacturing facilities of Baltimore are uncommon, and quite equal to its commercial advantages. In its benevolent and educational institutions it is behind none of its sister cities, and its name is associated with many men of culture, connected with literature, science, and the fine arts. It was here that the famous George Peabody first established himself in business, and where he founded one of the largest educational institutions associated with his name.

Among the representative cities of America is New Orleans. It was founded by the French in 1717, and has a population of 191,418. Its site is on the eastern bank of the great Mississippi River, about 100 miles above the mouth of that stream, and as it forms a half circle, has been called the Crescent City. Many parts of it are so low and flat that the waters are kept from overflowing it only by artificial embankments. It possesses unrivalled natural advantages for internal trade, and it is visited by vessels from every quarter of the globe. Every description of craft is employed in transporting to it the rich products of the Mississippi and its many tributaries, whose navigable waters are not less than 15,000 miles in extent, and embrace every variety of climate. Not only is it the receptacle of countless varieties of produce from the interior, but is considered the largest cotton market in the world. The particular spot where all this merchandise is received, and from which it is shipped to foreign ports, is called the levee; it extends along the river for miles, and because of the strange commingling of ships and steamboats and other kinds of vessels, and also on account of its vast proportions and never-ceasing bustle, has been pronounced by travellers one of the wonders of America. It abounds in handsome buildings, and its various public institutions rest on liberal foundations. On account of its low situation and warm climate it is subject to annual visitations from the yellow fever, which is frequently fatal to strangers. Any description of this city would be incomplete without a notice of its cemeteries. Each one is inclosed with a thick brick wall of arched cavities, made just large enough to admit a single coffin, and rising to the height of twelve feet. Within the inclosure are crowded the tombs, which are built wholly above the ground, and are from one to three stories high. This method of sepulture is a necessity, for the earth is so universally saturated with water, that none but paupers are consigned to the earth. The population of the city is exceedingly varied; its chief resident inhabitants are known as Creoles, or the native population; and those who are engaged in mercantile pursuits, and are successful, usually remain there during the winter or business months, spending their summers among the highlands of the interior country. It is also thickly inhabited by colored people, who were once in slavery. It was the scene of quite a famous battle in 1815, between the English and the Americans under Andrew Jackson, who was victorious, and subsequently became President of the United States. The prevailing religion is Roman Catholic, and many churches are modelled upon those of European countries; and notwithstanding the fact that this city is sometimes called the "Wet Grave," and the "City of the Dead," it is celebrated for its continuous round of gayeties, from the beginning of the year to its close.

On leaving New Orleans, if we pass up the Mississippi River about 1,200 miles, we come to the city of St. Louis, which contains 310,864 inhabitants. It was founded by the French fur-traders, and possesses the peculiarity of being located at the geographical centre of the North American Continent; and its advantages as a commercial emporium are probably not surpassed by those of any inland port in the world. The business transacted here by means of steamboats and railroads is enormous; the people are cosmopolitan in their character, and not behind the cities of the eastern States in their industry, liberality, and intellectual culture. And what we say of St. Louis is also true of Cincinnati, on the Ohio, with its 216,239 inhabitants; of Louisville, on the same river, with its 100,753 inhabitants; and of Chicago, on Lake Michigan. With regard to the last named place, we may remark that its rapid growth, in 25 years, from a village to a city of nearly 300,000, is one of the marvels of the age. But, since the first pages of this volume were sent to press, Chicago has met with a calamity by fire, which has been pronounced quite unprecedented. It occurred in October, 1871, and resulted in the total destruction of all the business portions of the city. More than 100 lives were also lost, 80,000 persons, including merchants and mechanics, were thrown out of employment or reduced to beggary in a single night, and the total loss of property was estimated at $200,000,000. It is said to have been the most extensive fire that ever occurred in any country, and the sympathy felt for the sufferers called forth subscriptions of money from every quarter of the globe, amounting in the aggregate to many millions of dollars; and what was still more wonderful was the fact that the regular business of the city was again in successful operation in a very few weeks, although it had to be transacted under many and great disadvantages.

Having elsewhere touched upon the characteristics of Washington, the metropolis of the United States, with its 120,000 inhabitants, we conclude our list of the larger cities with an allusion to San Francisco, which contains about 150,000 inhabitants. The rapidity of its growth can only be compared with that of Chicago; and while the former was chiefly built up by the gold mines of California, the latter owes its prosperity to the agricultural development of the wide and fertile region of which it is the centre. The fact that San Francisco is the largest American seaport on the Pacific Ocean, and that it is at the terminus of the Pacific Railroad, gives it command of the commerce of all the Eastern nations, by which advantages it will probably become a city of vast importance and influence. From the nature of its position, its social characteristics are quite different from those of the Atlantic cities, and it is not behind them in any of those qualities which give power and dignity to a city; yet it stands quite alone in regard to its Chinese population. The high rates of labor in this city generally, and its dependence on importation for all its iron, brass, cotton, hardware, and most of its wool, leather, and hard-wood lumber, prevent the establishment of factories, and all the cutlery, fine tools, and machinery, glass, porcelain, clothing, and shoes are necessarily obtained from abroad at a great expense, thus giving employment to a large amount of shipping.

In our remarks thus far, we have only spoken of those American cities which contain more than 100,000 inhabitants. But there are many smaller cities, which have a world-wide fame on account of their beauty, business characteristics, or historical associations. Among these may be mentioned Charleston, which has about 50,000 inhabitants, is the centre of the rice-producing country of South Carolina, and in whose harbor, at Fort Sumter, was made the first regular assault upon the national forces at the commencement of the late civil war, when the city was a great sufferer; Savannah, the chief seaport of Georgia and the rival of Charleston, having a population of nearly 30,000; Richmond, in Virginia, with more than 50,000 inhabitants, and famous for its beautiful location, its flour and tobacco trade, and for having been the headquarters of the late rebellion; Mobile, in Alabama, with 32,000 inhabitants, possessing characteristics similar to those of New Orleans; Detroit, in Michigan, with nearly 80,000 inhabitants, beautiful for situation, and the commercial gateway to the great lakes of Huron, Michigan, and Superior; Milwaukie, in Wisconsin, with 71,000 inhabitants, the counterpart of Chicago, and its unsuccessful rival; Cleveland, in Ohio, with 93,000 energetic inhabitants; Buffalo, at the eastern end of Lake Erie, with a population of 115,000 souls—near which are the Falls of Niagara; Pittsburg, in Pennsylvania, with a population of 86,000, almost entirely devoted to the coal and iron interests; Albany, in New York, the head of navigation on the Hudson, and famous for its Dutch history, and as being the Capital of the Empire State, with 70,000 people; Rochester and Troy, in the same State, with 63,000 souls; Indianapolis, in Indiana, with 48,000 people, and famous for its surrounding agricultural country; Portland, in Maine, which has 32,000 souls, and one of the best harbors in America; and the cities of Cambridge, in Massachusetts, and New Haven, in Connecticut, where are located two of the leading colleges of the United States.

# FRONTIER LIFE AND DEVELOPMENTS.

The frontiers of America are so extensive, and the pursuits of their inhabitants so various, that an entire volume would not suffice to describe them with minuteness. In taking a bird's-eye view of the domain in question (and a similar view of other subjects is all that has been attempted in the foregoing chapters), we propose to speak of the four following characteristics, viz.: the Indians, the Pioneer Farmers, the Fur-Traders and Trappers, and the Lumbermen.

It is now a settled fact that the Red race, or native Indians of America, are gradually passing away under the march of civilization. According to the most authentic data, the number of Indians who recognize the President as their Great Father is about 300,000. Of these, the Creeks, Cherokees, Choctaws, and Chickasaws, who live on the head-waters of the Arkansas, number some 54,000; and, excepting 4,000 of the Six Nations in New York, 1,000 Cherokees in North Carolina, 600 Penobscots in Maine, and 41,000 of various tribes still holding reservations on the Great Lakes, and the Mississippi and Missouri Rivers, they are the only tribes that have made any satisfactory advances in acquiring the arts and comforts of civilization. It would thus appear that the number of wild Indians who live entirely by the chase, and inhabit the American territories, excluding Alaska, number 200,000 souls. Although nominally obedient to the laws of the United States, these hunting tribes are, in reality, as free to roam as if there were no central government. But with those who are partially civilized the case is quite different. Their wealth has been estimated at $3,300,000, while they support about 70 schools, nearly the same number of teachers or missionaries, and cultivate nearly 1,000 acres of land. The names by which they are known number 150, and their geographical condition is co-extensive with the area of the United States and Territories; and it is a remarkable fact, that of all the races or classes of people who inhabit the United States, the Indians are the only people who are not recognized as citizens by the General Government.

On leaving the hunting-grounds of the Red Men for the haunts of opening civilization, the first thing which attracts attention is the cabin of the pioneer or frontier farmer. Though born and bred in a settled country, this man, who represents a large class, has been tempted by the spirit of enterprise to purchase a few hundred acres of land at the low government price, which he is clearing away as rapidly as possible, and in the midst of which he has fixed his home. It is built of logs, small, and poorly furnished, and, but for the smoke issuing from its rustic chimney, could hardly be distinguished from the stable or barn where he shelters his horses and oxen and cows. Hard work and rough fare are the lot of this poor yeoman, but his mission, as a man, commands the highest respect. He has a growing family about him, and in their welfare are centred all his hopes. Though far removed from schools and churches, and the refinements of life, he plods on year after year, giving his boys the best education he can, thankful that they are approaching man's estate, and cheered with the prospect that, like many of his predecessors in a new country, he will acquire a fortune, and spend his old age in a large frame or brick house, and end his days in peace. Five, ten, or it may be fifteen, miles from this man's cabin is another, built on the same model, and whose owner is a counterpart of himself. Farther on, still another log-cabin comes in view, and so on do they continue to appear, encompassing the entire frontiers of civilization. The ancestors of many of these men were among those who originally fought on the battle-field for the independence of their country, and they themselves, with their brothers and sons, flocked by thousands to its rescue, during the late civil war in America. These men embody the true spirit of the land in which they dwell, and in history they will be long remembered with honor and gratitude, for what they have done, and are doing, to make clear the pathway of empire.

We come now to speak of that class of people, living on the frontiers, known as fur-traders and trappers. The business of collecting and selling furs and peltries was commenced immediately after the first settlement of the country, and for about two hundred years was eminently lucrative, and gave employment to large numbers of enterprising men. Representatives from France and England, as well as the United States, participated in the trade, and several companies of great magnitude and influence were the outgrowth of this trade, viz.: the Hudson's Bay Company, the Northwest Company, and the American Fur Company. Of late years, however, the fur business has greatly declined on the American Continent, but is not yet extinct. The men called traders are those who locate themselves on the borders of the wilderness, and keep for sale ample supplies of all such articles as may be needed by the Indians or trappers, who pay for what they purchase with furs and peltries. The more common articles required are blankets, guns and ammunition, flour and pork, tobacco, knives, as well as trinkets and the baneful fire-water, while the articles for which they are exchanged are buffalo robes, and the skins of the deer, the beaver, and the otter, the sable, the mink, the bear, and the wolf, for all of which there is always a demand in the cities of the Atlantic States. The men known as trappers are either white men or half-breeds (so called, because they are the offspring of French fathers and Indian mothers), and they are the successful rivals of the native Indians in hunting or trapping wild animals. Those who reside in the prairie countries or among the Rocky Mountains chiefly employ the horse in travelling, while those who reside in the densely wooded regions where rivers and lakes abound, employ the bark-canoe in their operations. In the earlier times, when America was yet a wilderness, this latter class of men rendered important service to the English and French nations, by acting as guides and assistants in the exploring expeditions, and they became universally known as *voyageurs*. While there are many American towns and cities which owe their origin to the existence of the fur-trade, the two most noted of these are St. Louis, on the Mississippi River, and Montreal, in Canada, which lies on the river St. Lawrence, but both of these noted cities are rapidly losing their former reputations, and have really become cosmopolitan in their character, as well as cities of great magnitude and importance in the history of commerce.

But by far the most important phase of frontier life in the United States is that connected with the lumbering business. There is no country on the globe which equals America in the extent of its valuable forests, and there is a great and constantly-increasing demand for every variety of lumber, for the building of houses and the countless other things which are made of wood, and indispensable for the comfort of mankind. The manufacture of lumber is of the utmost importance, and is a prominent source of wealth in America, the aggregate value of the trade amounting to more than one hundred millions of dollars, and giving employment to nearly one hundred thousand persons in its various departments. The variety of forest-trees which are cut down and transformed into lumber is very great, but the pine is most abundant, next to which may be mentioned the fir, spruce, and hemlock, all of which are found in the eastern, northern, and northwestern States. The various marketable articles which are manufactured out of these several woods are known as timber, staves, shingles, boards of every thickness, scantling, masts and knees for shipping; and the uses to which these productions are applied are endless, and of vast importance to the people in every sphere of life. In North Carolina they have a peculiar kind of pine, which they not only manufacture into lumber, but from which the inhabitants obtain large quantities of tar, pitch, and turpentine. In Alabama and Mississippi they have still another variety of pine, which is worked into spars and masts by the ship-builders of the country. In Florida, an extensive business is done in preparing the live-oak of that region for use in building the naval vessels of the country,—the Government retaining the monopoly of that valuable product. In many of the western States there is a tree called the black walnut, which is employed to a great extent in the manufacture of elegant furniture, and has competed successfully with the imported wood called mahogany.

With regard to the various classes of people engaged in the lumbering business, throughout the Union, the most numerous are called lumbermen. In all those regions where the white pine and spruce and fir prevail, they form extensive parties, and spend the winter in the dense forests, cutting down trees and dragging the logs to the banks of the streams; and when spring comes, and the streams become full of water, they drive the logs down the rivers, and in immense quantities, all arranged in rafts, deliver them at the saw-mills at the mouths of the streams and on navigable waters, where the logs are turned into all kinds of lumber, and thence shipped by vessels to various parts of the United States as well as to foreign countries. Many of the merchants or companies who employ these lumbermen do business on a scale of great magnitude, and they not only control the various operations in the interior, but are also the owners of the mills where the lumber is made, as well as many of the vessels employed in the carrying-trade. The mills to which we have alluded are generally so located as to be driven by water-power, and as they are very numerous and extensive, they give employment to workmen of many grades, who form a class quite distinct from that of lumbermen. They are for the most part an intelligent and hardy race of men, and fail not, when elections take place, to exert an important influence on the affairs of their own State or those of the General Government.

As we pass into the pine-forests of Carolina, we there find another state of affairs. In that region, the manufacture of lumber is carried on, as already stated, in conjunction with the production of tar, pitch, and turpentine, and by far the largest proportion of the men employed were formerly the colored people called slaves, but now known as freedmen. There, as well as elsewhere, the prevailing business is conducted by organized companies or by men of ample means, who give employment, and a good support, to large numbers of hard-working men. As to those who live in the States bordering on the Gulf of Mexico, especially in Florida, and who prepare the live-oak timber for use at the Navy Yards,—they are mostly men from the north, with northern habits and constitutions, and are exclusively employed by the General Government. They also pursue their arduous labors in the winter-months, and, like the lumbermen of New England, live in tents or cabins, and on the plainest fare. As to the business of spar-cutting in Alabama and Mississippi, it requires so little sagacity, that it is chiefly carried on by those who own the forest-lands; but when we pass on to the northwestern States, where the black walnut prevails, we there find the business of lumbering fully organized, and the durable and rich-looking wood carefully prepared for transportation by steamboats or railroads to the markets on the Atlantic coast. There is also an extensive lumber business done in the Pacific States and Territories, and the "big trees" of California have obtained a world-wide reputation.

# JUDICIAL LIFE.

The Constitution provides that "The judicial power of the United States shall be vested in one Supreme Court, and in such inferior courts as the Congress may from time to time ordain and establish." The Constitution further defines and limits the judicial power as follows: "1. The judicial power shall extend to all cases, in law and equity, arising under this Constitution, the laws of the United States, and treaties made, or which shall be made, under their authority; to all cases affecting ambassadors, other public ministers, and consuls; to all cases of admiralty and maritime jurisdiction; to controversies to which the United States shall be a party; to controversies between two or more States, between a State and citizens of another State, between citizens of different States, between citizens of the same State claiming lands under grants of different States, and between a State or the citizens thereof and foreign states, citizens, or subjects. 2. In all cases affecting ambassadors, other public ministers and consuls, and those in which a State shall be a party, the Supreme Court shall have original jurisdiction. In all the other cases before mentioned, the Supreme Court shall have appellate jurisdiction both as to law and fact, with such exceptions, and under such regulations, as the Congress shall make."

The Supreme Court being established by the Constitution, Congress has from time to time established the following additional "inferior courts" of the United States, viz.: the Circuit Courts, the District Courts, the Court of Claims, the Supreme Court of the District of Columbia, the Territorial Courts, with the Supreme Court, constitute the Judiciary of the United States. The outlines of their powers, jurisdiction, etc., will be briefly presented as follows:

I. The Supreme Court. The original jurisdiction of the Supreme Court is defined in the Constitution, as quoted. Its appellate jurisdiction is also there defined, but is provided to be subject to exceptions and regulation by Congress. This power Congress has exercised in the following instances. Appeals from these Circuit Courts to the Supreme Court, in civil actions, equity cases, and admiralty and prize cases, are restricted to those in which the matter in dispute exceeds the sum or value of two thousand dollars, exclusive of costs. But this restriction does not apply to patent, copyright, or revenue cases; nor does it affect appeals in criminal cases. Congress has also provided that the Supreme Court shall have appellate jurisdiction from judgments or decrees of the highest courts of the several States, in suits where is drawn in question the validity of a treaty or statute of, or an authority exercised under, the United States, and the decision has been against their validity; or where is drawn in question the validity of a statute of, or an authority exercised under, any State, on the ground of their being repugnant to the Constitution, treaties, or laws of the United States, and the decision is in favor of such validity; or where any title, right, privi-

15*

lege, or immunity is claimed under the Constitution, treaties, or laws of the United States, and the decision is against the title, rights, etc. But from the operations of these provisions are excepted cases of persons held in the custody of the military authorities of the United States, charged with military offences, or with having aided or abetted rebellion against the Government.

The Supreme Court sits at Washington, and holds one annual session, commencing on the first Monday in December, with such adjourned or special terms as may be found necessary for the despatch of business. It consists of a Chief-Justice and eight Justices, who, in common with all the United States Judges, hold their offices during good behavior. The salary of the Chief-Justice is eight thousand five hundred dollars; that of each of the Justices eight thousand dollars per annum. Six of the nine constitute a quorum.

II. The Circuit Courts are nine in number; the United States being divided into nine circuits, each comprising three or more districts. Justices of the Supreme Court are allotted by that Court to the several circuits, to assist in holding the Circuit Courts. Each circuit has besides a Circuit Judge with a salary of six thousand dollars; with the same power and jurisdiction as the Justice of the Supreme Court allotted to the circuit. The Circuit Court in each circuit is held by the Justice of the Supreme Court, or by the Circuit Judge of the circuit, or by the District Judge of the district—sitting alone; or by the Justice of the Supreme Court and Circuit Judge sitting together; or (in the absence of either of them) by the other and the district judge. Where two judges hold a

Circuit Court, and differ in opinion, the law provides for a special appeal to the Supreme Court. There are two annual sessions of each Circuit Court, with special sessions for the trial of criminal cases. The jurisdiction of the Circuit Courts is as follows: They have concurrent jurisdiction, with the State Courts, of civil suits at common law and equity, where the matter in dispute exceeds, exclusive of costs, the sum or value of five hundred dollars, and where the United States are plaintiffs or petitioners, or an alien is a party (but not where both parties are aliens); or where the suit is between a citizen of the State in which the suit is brought, and a citizen of another State. They have exclusive jurisdiction of all crimes and offences cognizable under the authority of the United States, except of such as are within the jurisdiction of the District Courts, and of those they have concurrent jurisdiction. They have also original jurisdiction in all patent and copyright cases, and their jurisdiction also extends to all cases arising under the revenue laws. They are also invested with jurisdiction of certain classes of cases removed to them, under special statutes, from the State Courts; including suits between citizens of different States, suits against aliens, and suits and prosecutions against military and other officers of the Government. The Circuit Courts entertain appeals from the District Courts in criminal cases, and in civil cases where the matter in dispute exceeds the sum of fifty dollars.

III. The United States is further divided into districts, for the holding of U. S. District Courts therein. A district usually includes a single State; but the larger States are divided into two or sometimes three districts. For each district there is a District Judge, who holds four regular sessions of the District Court annually. The salaries of the District Judges are different in different parts of the country. The District Courts have original and exclusive jurisdiction of admiralty and maritime cases, of cases of seizures on land and water, under the laws of the United States, and of suits brought for penalties and forfeitures incurred under said laws. They have also jurisdiction, exclusive of the State Courts, of suits against consuls, vice-consuls, etc. They have also concurrent jurisdiction with the Circuit Courts in cases of crimes and offences, not capital, committed under the laws of the United States. Also concurrent jurisdiction with such courts and the State Courts of suits at common law, in which the United States, or any officer thereof, may sue, under the authority of any law of the United States. Also a similar jurisdiction of all suits by aliens, on account of (torts) in violation of the laws of nations or a treaty of the United States.

IV. The Court of Claims sits in the Capitol at Washington, and commences its regular annual session on the same day as the Supreme Court, viz.: the first Monday in December. It consists of a Chief-Justice and four Justices, with a salary of four thousand dollars each. It has jurisdiction of " all claims founded upon any law of Congress, or upon any regulation of an executive department, or upon any contract, express or implied, with the Government of the United States, which may be suggested to it by a petition filed therein, and also all claims which may be referred to said court by either House of Congress;"—also jurisdiction of all counter-claims and demands, on the part of the United States, against any persons making claim against the Government in said court; also jurisdiction of claims to property captured or abandoned during the rebellion; also jurisdiction of the claims of disbursing officers of the United States for relief from responsibility on account of losses of public property by capture or otherwise while in the line of duty; and of some other claims of less general importance. The court is precluded from passing upon claims for supplies taken, injuries done, etc., by United States troops during the rebellion, and from rendering judgment in favor of any claimant who has not been loyal to the United States. Appeals may be taken by the United States to the Supreme Court in all cases where the judgment is adverse to the United States; and by the claimant where the amount in controversy exceeds three thousand dollars. This court is the only court of the U. S. in which the United States can be directly sued as a defendant.

V. The Supreme Court of the District of Columbia consists of a Chief-Justice and three other Justices, and holds its sessions at the City Hall in Washington. The salary of the Chief-Justice is four thousand five hundred dollars, and of each of the other Justices four thousand dollars. This court combines the general powers and jurisdiction of a Circuit Court and a District Court. Any single one of its judges is authorized to hold a District Court. Its jurisdiction extends only to civil proceedings instituted, and crimes committed, in the District of Columbia; and to cases of seizures on land and water made, and penalties and forfeitures incurred, under the laws of the United States within the same limits only. It entertains appeals from the local justices of the peace and police courts; and its final judgments, orders, and decrees are subject to be appealed from to the Supreme Court of the United States.

VI. *Territorial Courts.* When a territorial government is organized by Congress for any Territory, a judiciary is provided, consisting generally of a Supreme Court of three or more judges, District Courts, to be held by the Judges of the Supreme Court separately, Probate Courts, and Justices' Courts. The District Courts are invested with the jurisdiction of the Circuit and District Courts of the United States; and an appeal is given from the District Courts to the Supreme Court. An appeal is also provided from the Supreme Court to the Supreme Court of the United States, in the same manner as from a Circuit Court. When a Territory is admitted into the Union as a State, these courts cease to exist, being supplanted by the State Courts.

# ADDITIONAL NOTES.

AFTER the foregoing chapters on Religious and Educational Life had been printed, we obtained some later official information on those subjects, which we append in this place. In 1870 three States of the Union passed laws compelling the education of all children with sound minds and bodies. The total number of colleges in the country is 368, of which 261 are supported by the different religious denominations. In these institutions there are 2,962 instructors and 49,827 pupils; in 99 of them males and females are instructed, while the balance are confined to males; and besides these, there are 136 institutions for the superior instruction of females alone, in which there are 1,163 teachers and 12,841 pupils. Of medical schools, there are 57; theological schools, 117; law schools, 40; normal schools, 51; and business schools, 84. Connected with these various institutions there are 180 libraries, with 2,355,237 volumes. The benefactions to educational objects by private citizens were quite unparalleled in 1870, amounting in the aggregate to $8,435,990. With regard to the effect of education upon crime, we find that there was one homicide to every 56,000 people, one to every 4,000 in the Pacific States, and one to every 10,000 in the Southern States. At least 80 per cent. of the crime of New England is committed by those who have no education; in all parts of the country, 90 per cent. of the criminals were illiterate; 75 per cent. were foreigners; and from 80 to 90 per cent. connected their career of crime with intemperance. From these figures, the conclusion is inevitable that ignorance breeds crime, and education is the remedy for the crime that prevails.

In further illustration of the preceding article on agriculture, we append the following statement: The total value of farm-products in the United States and Territories, during the year ending June 31, 1870, according to the census, was $2,445,000,000. The largest product was in the State of New York, and the second largest in Illinois.

Now that this little book is finished, the mind of the compiler naturally turns to take a single comprehensive view of the great country which has been briefly described. It is, indeed, one of the wonders of the century and of the world. The extent of its domain and its unbounded resources, the peaceful blending of its many nationalities, the well-nigh unlimited diffusion of intelligence and knowledge, and the free, cosmopolitan character of its people, combine to give it a conspicuous position among the nations. At the very moment when these closing lines are being written, a Diplomatic Embassy from the Tenno of Japan is on the point of visiting the city of Washington, and the fact cannot but have made an impression on their minds, that, after landing on the soil of America, they have been compelled to travel more than three thousand miles before reaching the metropolis. But when the Ambassadors, and the other high officials who accompany them, are informed as to the warm welcome which is in store for them from the Government of the United States, and many of the leading men and corporations throughout the Union, and when they shall have experienced the unbounded hospitality of the American people generally, they will undoubtedly be deeply impressed, and effectually convinced that America and Japan are strongly bound together by the cords of sincere regard and unselfish affection.

www.ingramcontent.com/pod-product-compliance
Lightning Source LLC
Chambersburg PA
CBHW030251240426
43673CB00040B/944